ACLS History E-Book Project

Reprint Series

The ACLS History E-Book Project (www.historyebook.org) collaborates with constituent societies of the American Council of Learned Societies, publishers, librarians and historians to create an electronic collection of works of high quality in the field of history. This volume is produced from digital images created for the Project by the Scholarly Publishing Office and the Digital Library Production Service at the University of Michigan, Ann Arbor. The digital reformatting process results in an electronic version of the text that can be both accessed online and used to create new print copies. This book and hundreds of others are available online in the History E-Book Project through subscription.

Many of the works in the History E-Book Project are available in print and can be ordered either directly from their publishers or as part of this series. For information refer to the online Title Record page for each book. Inquiries regarding this series can be directed to info@hebook.org.

ACLS
HISTORY E-BOOK

I0834478

http://www.historyebook.org

STORIA E LETTERATURA

RACCOLTA DI STUDI E TESTI

79

B. L. ULLMAN

THE ORIGIN AND DEVELOPMENT OF HUMANISTIC SCRIPT

ROMA 1960
EDIZIONI DI STORIA E LETTERATURA
VIA LANCELLOTTI 18

THE ORIGIN AND DEVELOPMENT OF HUMANISTIC SCRIPT

STORIA E LETTERATURA
RACCOLTA DI STUDI E TESTI
79

B. L. ULLMAN

THE ORIGIN AND DEVELOPMENT OF HUMANISTIC SCRIPT

ROMA 1960
EDIZIONI DI STORIA E LETTERATURA
VIA LANCELLOTTI 18

OFFSET REPRINT 1974

EDIZIONI DI STORIA E LETTERATURA
Roma - Via Lancellotti, 18

PREFACE

The lack of a detailed discussion of humanistic script has often been deplored. Thus Paul Lehmann repeats E. Bernheim's complaint that this script has been treated in a stepmotherly fashion, that the question of how, when, and where it arose has not been answered.[1] *Others have pointed out the extreme importance of this neglected form of writing. The style of writing which developed into the type fonts in use today certainly is one of special importance and interest to us. A. Hessel*[2] *contributed little to the story. Stanley Morison's has been the leading treatment in recent years,*[3] *though I must disagree with him in some fundamental respects.*

On a single page of my book[4] *I tried to answer Bernheim's three questions. I developed the theme in an unpublished paper read at the "Convegno Internazionale di Studi sull'« Umanesimo »" at La Mendola in August, 1956. Not even the present fuller treatment pretends to cover the subject completely. The origin is presented in full detail but the later developments are generally restricted: I have dealt only with Florentine scribes who signed and dated their volumes and have left us many examples of their work. There is still much to be done, such as the investigation of the spread of the new Florentine script to other centers and of the various local developments, the identification of unsigned volumes, and the story of the later calligraphers.*

Again, as in 1955, I wish to express my deep appreciation to don Giuseppe De Luca, who by the publication of his magnificent series has done so much for humanistic scholarship.

B. L. Ullman

Chapel Hill, N. C., February 1958

1 *Bayer. Akad. d. Wiss., Phil.-hist. K .*, 1918, Abh. 8.

2 "Die Entstehung der Renaissanceschriften," *Arch. für Urkundenforschung*, XIII (1936), p. 1.

3 "Early Humanistic Script and the First Roman Type," *The Library*, XXIV (1943), p. 1.

4 *Studies in the Italian Renaissance* (Rome, 1955), p. 313.

Chapter I

BACKGROUND AND INSPIRATION — COLUCCIO SALUTATI

The ancient Roman Empire had its various book hands — square capitals, rustic capitals, uncials, half-uncials, as well as the cursive scripts used for ordinary writing. These were used throughout its domain. When the Empire broke up two opposing tendencies became apparent in many aspects of life: not only did the several parts of the former Empire develop many individual characteristics, as might be expected, but they also continued some of their old practices. So in writing: uncial and half-uncial remained in use, but at the same time new book hands began to develop out of cursive. Under half-uncial influence a simple script was developed in France at the end of the eighth century just at the time when Charlemagne was forming his empire, and it spread rapidly throughout the lands under the Emperor's rule. This Carolingian script reached its finest flower in the ninth century, then gradually decayed. By the thirteenth century its transformation into Gothic was complete. The characteristics of Gothic are lateral compression, angularity, and what I have called fusion, the overlapping of rounded letters, as in *do*.[1] In a more cursive form it became the *bastarda*. To these peculiarities of Gothic may be added the great increase of abbreviations. How much the newly founded universities of Europe, with their stationers and "pieces" (*pecie*) of books which they rented out for copying, with their impoverished students who needed inexpensive books rapidly produced, contributed to these developments is a matter not yet investigated, so far as I know.

[1] This is not the same as the peculiarity of Beneventan script called union by Lowe, for in Beneventan the letters do not overlap but are tangential (E. A. Lowe, *The Beneventan Script* [Oxford, 1914], pp. 140, 149).

The development of Gothic indicated above applies particularly to France, Germany, and England. In Italy matters did not go so far. While the Carolingian script was degenerating elsewhere, in Italy it remained relatively pure and graceful. The large round hand of twelfth-century Italian manuscripts stands out among the more crabbed scripts developing elsewhere.[2] It is true that Gothic script swept over Italy, but generally speaking it did not become so extreme as across the Alps. Furthermore, there was a very definite restraining force at an important and influential university center. It was at the University of Bologna that the new interest in Justinian brought about the production of numerous handsome large codices of that author and then of other authors, in a script appropriately called *rotunda*, Gothic though it was.[3] A modification of this remained as the finest of the formal book hands of northern Italy in the fourteenth century.[4] Bologna's university also made no small contribution to incipient Italian humanism, being attended by Petrarch, Coluccio Salutati, and other early humanists. The humanists of the fourteenth century, men who read more, perhaps, than their predecessors, preferred manuscripts in large, clear writing, in *littera antiqua*, i.e., in the Carolingian script of the ninth to twelfth centuries, particularly, perhaps, the large twelfth-century Italian script already mentioned. Petrarch, Boccaccio, Salutati, and many others wrote in a legible Gothic script, a less formal variety of the *rotunda*, not compressed or angular but preserving the important Gothic element of fusion. I am here referring to their book hands, not to their cursive notarial scripts.[5]

It is important for the development of our theme to recall here what Petrarch and Coluccio have to say about contemporary handwriting. Petrarch writes to Boccaccio that a copy of his (Petrarch's) epistles is being made, not in the spreading luxuriant lettering, fashionable at a time when scribes are painters, that pleases but tires the eyes, as if it were invented for anything else

[2] See Fig. 1.

[3] See Fig. 2.

[4] See Fig. 3 for the work of a professional scribe employed by Coluccio Salutati.

[5] See Figs. 4–6 for the formal writing of Petrarch, Boccaccio, and Coluccio Salutati.

than reading, but in a trim, clear hand, appealing to the eye.[6] He quotes Priscian's etymology of *litera* "quasi legitera," i.e., legible. He adds that orthography and grammar will not be neglected. The former especially was in the scribe's province, as we shall have occasion to see. Elsewhere Petrarch well describes the minuteness, compression, and excessive abbreviations in contemporary manuscripts, which are hard on the eyes.[7] The letters in abbreviations, he says, seem to ride "piggyback". There are other passages in which Petrarch complains of the scarcity of satisfactory copyists.[8] On the other hand, he praises a manuscript of Augustine given him by Boccaccio: "Huic tali amicitie tue dono . . . et libri decor et vetustioris litere maiestas et omnis sobrius accedit ornatus" (*Fam.* XVIII, 3, 9; 1355). This manuscript, still in existence (Paris, B. N. lat. 1989), was, it is significant to note, written in the eleventh century.

Petrarch was sixty-two when in 1366 he criticized current handwriting as hard on the eyes. Coluccio was almost the same age (sixty-one) when in 1392 he wished to obtain a Cicero "in littera grossa" for his failing eyesight.[9] In 1395 he asked his French

6 *Epist. fam.* XXIII, 19, 8 (1366): "Non vaga quidem ac luxurianti litera — qualis est scriptorum seu verius pictorum nostri temporis, longe oculos mulcens, prope autem afficiens ac fatigans, quasi ad aliud quam ad legendum sit inventa, et non, ut grammaticorum princeps ait, litera "quasi legitera" dicta sit — sed alia quadam castigata et clara seque ultro oculis ingerente, in qua nichil orthographum, nichil omnino grammatice artis omissum dicas." Cf. *Fam.* XIII, 4, 28 (1352): "Si oculos tuos artificiosis literarum tractibus assuetos scriptura incultior [*of Petrarch*] offendit...".

7 *Sen.* VI, 5, dealing with the completion of his *De vita solitaria* in 1366: "Hoc... opus, breve licet, fidus tandem vix explicuit sacerdos quidam, litera non tam anxie exculta quam nostre atque omni etati, nisi fallor, idonea. Adolescentia enim cunctis suis in actibus improvida et insulsa miratrix inanium, contemptrix utilium, perexiguis atque compressis visumque frustrantibus literulis gloriari solita est, acervans omnia et coartans atque hinc spatio, hinc literarum super literas velut equitantium aggestione confundens, que scriptor ipse brevi post tempore rediens vix legat, emptor vero non tam librum quam libro cecitatem emat."

8 Cf. *Sen.* V, 1; X, 1.

9 *Epist.*, ed. F. Novati, II (1893), p. 386. Boniface (born 680) was between 62 and 66 years old when he wrote that because of his failing eyesight he could not clearly make out tiny, joined letters and asked that a manuscript to be copied for him be written in "discretis et absolutis litteris" (*Epist.* 63). Were complaints such as these responsible for the development of Carolingian script a generation

friend Jean de Montreuil for a copy of Abelard in "antiqua littera", as no other script was more pleasing to his eyes.[10] The next year he wrote the same Jean that he wanted copies of Augustine and Quintilian in the best lettering, as like Italian script as possible.[11] He seems to mean a script more like the plain Gothic he himself used than the cramped French book hand, not to mention the *bastarda*. About the same time he wrote concerning a copy of Augustine that he had seen which was in rather large script and which he would like to obtain because he was now an old man.[12] He went on to say that he would like to turn his fading eyesight away from the reading of his own copy, tiring because of the small letters, to the more pleasant task of reading a copy in a larger script.[13] We do not know whether he received this manuscript; if it exists, it has not been identified.[14] But the manuscript which Coluccio complained about is still available, and the writing is truly tiny: the body of each letter is about one millimeter high. In a writing space of 244 millimeters we find 59 lines, that is, each line, including spacing, is only some four millimeters high.[15]

Why so much attention to the complaints of two aging men of the fourteenth century? Because they explain what happened. It may at first sight seem strange that it was the clear script of fourteenth-century humanists like Petrarch and Coluccio rather than the crabbed Gothic of France, Germany, and England that was the first to be reformed. It is not always the institution or

later, just as the complaints of Petrarch and Coluccio, voiced when they were about the same age as Boniface, led to the humanistic reform?

10 *Epist.* III (1896), p. 76. This must mean twelfth-century Carolingian script, for Abelard died in 1142.

11 *Epist.* III, p. 147: "in optima littera et quanto magis fieri poterit italice similis."

12 *Epist.* III, p. 163: "qui liber, cum scriptus sit littera satis grossa, me iam senem illexit ut illum habere desiderem."

13 "Te deprecor et obtestor ut me voti mei compotem facias, ita quod beneficio tuo possim a lectione libri quem habeo parvitate litterarum michi plurimum tediosa ad gratiorem legendi laborem, quod prestabunt ampliores littere, iam caligantes oculos applicare."

14 I cannot accept Novati's suggestion (III, p. 163, n. 1) that it is Fies. 12-13 of the Laurentian Library. There is no sign of ownership by Coluccio. The marginal notes are not his.

15 Vat. Ottob. lat. 349. See Fig. 7.

individual most in need of reforming that actually gets reformed first. At any rate, it would seem that the difficulties of Coluccio in particular had something to do with the reform, as we shall see. Eyeglasses had been invented, it is true, but they were neither widely used nor very satisfactory. So we may say that presbyopia started the reform of handwriting. Thanks to the improvement of eyeglasses in modern times, we determine our need for them and their strength by the ability to read the telephone book. In 1400 it was easier to change handwriting than to change glasses.

But that is not the whole story. In the universities of the thirteenth and fourteenth centuries the students' texts were copied from *exemplaria* of the same period. In other words, most of the books read by students and masters were written in the familiar Gothic script. And the reading in the monasteries and elsewhere was chiefly of books composed and copied in the same period, from Thomas Aquinas and the other schoolmen to the cyclopaedia of Vincent of Beauvais and the dictionaries of Uguccione and Balbi. The literature of earlier periods, classical and mediaeval, was relatively less read, and few manuscripts of the preceding centuries were used. To be sure, not all Gothic script was hard to read. Of the twenty-nine manuscripts reproduced by Destrez (on thirty-six plates), few are difficult to read except for the excessive abbreviations.[16] The Bologna codices, as was to be expected, are particularly legible and have fewer abbreviations. But many of them are unusually fine copies, as indicated by the illumination.

The humanists, on the other hand, were not satisfied with the current product. They wanted older and better texts of the authors they knew and they searched tirelessly for works unknown to their contemporaries. They read more and their eyes suffered in consequence.

The hypothesis just suggested seems to be confirmed by the remains of the libraries of the two humanists who did not like some of the current handwriting, Petrarch and Coluccio. Nolhac listed thirty-eight extant manuscripts of Petrarch's library. After subtracting the six that contain Petrarch's own works, we find that eight of the thirty-two were written in the tenth to twelfth centuries (three of the tenth, two of the eleventh, three of the

[16] Jean Destrez, *La Pecia* (Paris, 1935), *Album de planches.*

twelfth).[17] Fourteen more manuscripts owned by Petrarch have been found since then, chiefly by Mlle Pellegrin and Billanovich.[18] Eight of these were written in the tenth to twelfth centuries. Of the total of forty-six, one-third belong to these centuries.

Well over a hundred manuscripts of Coluccio's library are known to me.[19] About one-third are of the ninth to twelfth centuries, most of them of the end of that period. Of course we cannot be sure that this large proportion held true for the complete collections of Petrarch and Coluccio, but it may serve to add a bit of confirmation to the view just expressed that both scholars attempted to obtain early manuscripts. In any event, it is clear that Coluccio became quite familiar with the more graceful and generally more legible script of the Carolingian period. And it is precisely with Coluccio that, in my belief, humanistic script begins.

The argument for this novel view runs as follows. A manuscript of Apuleius and the letters of Pliny in the Laurentian Library (Marc. 284) once belonged to Coluccio, in my opinion. The evidence for this is the use of "Carte LXXVIIII" at the top of fol. 1, not now legible under sunlight but visible under ultraviolet rays. This is a type of entry which is found in most of the manuscripts owned by Coluccio. There are marginal notes in it which seem to me to be in his hand. Furthermore, many of Coluccio's manuscripts passed to the S. Marco collection, and so a manuscript in that collection (which is now divided between the Nazionale and Laurenziana of Florence) has a much greater chance of having belonged to Coluccio than other manuscripts do.

17 Pierre de Nolhac, *Pétrarque et l'Humanisme*, I (Paris, 1907), pp. 113 ff.

18 E. Pellegrin, "Nouveaux manuscrits annotés par Pétrarque à la Bibliothèque Nationale de Paris," *Scriptorium*, V (1951), p. 265; E. Pellegrin and G. Billanovich, "Un manuscrit de Ciceron annoté par Pétrarque au British Museum," *Scriptorium*, VIII (1954), p. 115; G. Billanovich, "Petrarch and the Textual Tradition of Livy," *Journal of the Warburg and Courtauld Institutes*, XIV (1951), p. 137; "Un nuovo codice della Biblioteca del Petrarca: il San Paolo," *Rendiconti dell'Accademia di Archeologia Lettere e Belle Arti di Napoli*, XXVI (1951), p. 253; "Un amico e un libro del Petrarca," *Miscellanea in memoria di Luigi Ferrari* (1952), p. 99; "Uno Suetonio della Biblioteca del Petrarca," *Studi petrarcheschi*, VI (1954), p. 1; L. Minio-Paluello, "Il 'Fedone' latino con note autografe del Petrarca," *Accademia Nazionale dei Lincei*, ser. VIII, IV (1949), p. 107.

19 The list will be published in a book on which I am at work.

Now this manuscript of Apuleius and Pliny as originally copied in the tenth century ends on fol. 77r at *Ep.* V, 6, as do other manuscripts of its class. Another hand added V, 7 and part of V, 8, ending on fol. 77v at the word *curiosi*, which is in the middle of a sentence and of a line in the manuscript. Obviously that is all the material that the scribe had available.[20] It has always been assumed that these epistles were added from a Verona manuscript after that manuscript was discovered by Guarino in 1419. But it seems to me that these added epistles are in the hand of Coluccio, who died in 1406. Other humanists knew of the Verona manuscript before 1419, including two Arretines, one of whom long lived in Florence, and a Veronese. So there is no objection to supposing that a Florentine too received a copy of part of it.

I have stated my belief that this added material in the Florence manuscript is in the hand of Coluccio. But for many years the manuscript perplexed me. The writing looked like Coluccio's both in its general appearance and in the shapes of some of the letters. Yet, on the other hand, there were letter forms that belonged to humanistic writing, such as the minuscule *d* and the long *s* at the end of a word. Finally I solved the problem by concluding that Coluccio was experimenting with a new script. I was helped to this decision by the fact that some of his marginal notes in this manuscript also show humanistic traits.

An examination of Coluccio's marginal notes is revealing.[21] First on fol. 74v (Fig. 9) we have a nest of notes written in Coluccio's usual Gothic script as found in many of his other manuscripts. The final *s* is always round. There is no hint of any change. Next a comparison of fols. 1r and 6v (Figs. 10-11) is fruitful. Compare *Aristippus* in Fig. 10 with *Aristoteles* in Fig. 11. They are obviously written by the same man, but the former has the round Gothic *s* in final position, the latter has the straight Carolingian (and humanistic) *s*. The same variation is seen on fol. 5r (Fig. 12) in *Promptis* and *Coraulares*. The *s* of the former is a variant of the round *s*, often found along with the other form in Gothic writing in general and in Coluccio's in particular. The two words were written at the same time, in ink of identical color.

20 See Fig. 8.

21 See Figs. 9-12.

The two forms of round final *s* occur together in Figs. 9 and 10.

Let us return to the two epistles of Pliny added by Coluccio on fol. 77r and 77v of this manuscript and analyze the script. On these two pages thirty-five examples of the Gothic uncial *d* occur and twenty-one of the straight *d*, which humanistic writing reintroduced from Carolingian. No attempt is made to differentiate the use of the two forms according to preceding or following letters. Round *s* in its two forms is found at the end of words fifteen times, seven in the smaller form, eight in the slightly lengthened version. Straight *s* occurs twenty-three times in final position — the regular usage in early humanistic script. Note (Fig. 8) that in the first line of the second added epistle *suades* occurs twice, first with Gothic *d* and *s*, then with humanistic *d* and *s*. Another humanistic innovation was the ouster of the Tironian symbol for *et* shaped like the figure 7 and the restoration of the ligature & (our ampersand). Three of the former and four of the latter occur. Also the restoration of the *ae* ligature in two forms (one in a form familiar today, the other with a subscript *a* similar to a cedilla) drove out the simple *e*. On this folio five examples of the simple *e* and five of the ligature occur. Then again, Gothic fusion of round letters is on its way out. There are still good examples of this practice but there are more examples of union, in which the two letters touch each other but do not overlap. This I consider a transitional method, on the way toward complete separation. Of the latter, I find only one example, in *culpe* (line 21 of the page in Fig. 8). This is immediately followed by a good example of fusion, in *posteritatis*.[22]

What led Coluccio to make these changes in his usual writing style? No doubt he was influenced by some of the early manuscripts he owned. Some of these changes show his attempts to adapt himself in part to their script. It was a very common practice of Coluccio's to write his name in the short last line of a text. He frequently adjusted the size of his script to that of

[22] Comparison of the script of fol. 77 with that of the notes on fols. 1-76 is rewarding. Cf. e.g., the *g* of *ego* in line 8 with those in Fig. 9. Some of the marginal notes elsewhere in the manuscript are by a different hand. Fol. 78r contains some *probationes pennae* in humanistic script. It would be unprofitable to speculate whether they have a bearing on our problem.

the manuscript; sometimes he wrote his name smaller, sometimes larger than usual.[23] On one occasion he wrote his name in Greek letters (Kolykios), apparently because a long Greek quotation was to follow but was not filled in (Laur. Marc. 328, fol. 79v; Macrobius *Sat.* V, 19, 25 after *scribit*). He also trimmed his name at times so that it would not extend out into the margin. In keeping with this practice he wrote "Liber Colucii pieri" on fol. 271v of Laur. 16, 31, "liber Colucii p." on fol. 279v, and "liber Colucii" on fol. 63. In Laur. Marc. 668, fol. 111v, he squeezed in "Coluci(us)," abbreviated, at the end of the line; on 95v he took a whole line to write "Colucii Pieri Liber" in large letters to match those of the *explicit*. Similarly in other manuscripts. In Vat. lat. 3972, a manuscript written in the notarial, or cursive, script of the time, he added "Liber Colucii pieri" at the end of the text (fol. 164r) in a cursive hand to match the text; similarly on fol. 91r.[24] These variations in the writing of his name show a willingness to adapt his writing to circumstances. Unfortunately the formulas he used in his ownership notes do not contain the key letters *d* and final *s*.

As to the marginal notes in his many manuscripts, I am unwilling at this time to commit myself on any except those in the Apuleius-Pliny manuscript previously discussed. The difficulty is that the identification of his hand depends on conformity with his customary Gothic practice. Humanistic characteristics are evident in the notes of many of his manuscripts but they may indicate that they are not in his handwriting rather than that he was experimenting. At least in no manuscript do we find as good a case as in the Pliny codex.

We now leave the Coluccio who experimented for the Coluccio who inspired and encouraged.

23 Smaller, e.g., in Vat. lat. 2056, fol. 94v; larger and with heavier shading in Florence, Naz. Magl. XIV. 49, fol. 83r.

24 He used cursive script also in British Museum Harl. 2655, fol. 50r, and Laur. Fies. 176, fol. 217r, but that is because these were among his earliest accessions, made when cursive was still his usual style. The manuscripts themselves are not in cursive.

Chapter II

THE INVENTOR — POGGIO BRACCIOLINI

In the preceding chapter I attempted to prove that Coluccio Salutati owned the Laurentian manuscript Marc. 284, added the epistles of Pliny on fol. 77, with their experimental admixture of Gothic and humanistic characteristics, and wrote marginal notes that reveal a similar admixture. In this way he made a tentative first step towards the invention (perhaps we should say the development) of humanistic script. While I am myself completely convinced of the correctness of these conclusions, I can understand a skeptical attitude. On the next and more important step, there can, I believe, be no room for skepticism. What the Pliny manuscript was to our first chapter another manuscript will be to this. It is a Laurentian manuscript (Strozzi 96) that contains one of Coluccio's own treatises, *De verecundia*, and one of his letters. It was carefully and thoroughly corrected by the author himself in his typical Gothic hand.[1] It must therefore have been copied before 1406, when Coluccio died. Now this manuscript is written in a well developed humanistic hand. What is more, it is quite certain, in my opinion, that this is the writing of Poggio Bracciolini.[2] It is not only one of the earliest approximately

[1] Fig. 13 shows fol. 22v of this manuscript with a long correction by Coluccio in the third line from the bottom. Note the uncial *d*. The same facsimile in my *Studies in the Italian Renaissance* (Rome, 1955), p. 313. Fig. 14 reveals corrections by Coluccio in the tenth line and in the next to the last. The difference in the appearance of the two pages is caused by their being made at different times and by a slight difference in size. The letter (or short treatise) contained in the manuscript is in Novati, *Epistolario di Coluccio Salutati*, III (Rome, 1896), p. 239.

[2] There is an erasure after the date on fol. 38v. There are traces of two adjoining long letters which might conceivably be *gg* of *Poggius*. Another erasure is on fol. 27v.

datable examples of humanistic script, written at the very latest in the early part of 1406, since Coluccio died on May 4 of that year, but actually the very first.[3]

Before analyzing in detail the script of Strozz. 96 and comparing it with Coluccio's experiment on the one hand and Poggio's known writing on the other, let us consider the circumstances under which Strozz. 96 was copied and try to narrow down its date.

Poggio, born in 1380, received his early education in Arezzo.[4] He began his advanced studies at Bologna, he tells us, but seems not to have stayed there long, probably because of lack of funds. The civil law course took eight years, the notarial course only two. That fact apparently caused the impoverished young man to abandon law at Bologna and to choose notarial studies, this time at Florence. For in the late 1390's he went to Florence, carrying with him all his wealth, which consisted of five lone soldi. He may have found some sort of employment for a time. Walser assigns to this period his occupation as a scribe and tutor, of which we know from the contemporary biographer Vespasiano da Bisticci. But I believe that this activity belonged to a later period, partly because scribal activity would come more naturally after his notarial studies than before and partly because, as we shall see, Vespasiano's statement fits in so well with a somewhat later period of Poggio's career. Perhaps he began the notarial course at the Florentine Studio soon after his arrival. At any rate, he finished the course by 1402, for in that year he was accredited as a notary.[5] Probably, therefore, Poggio began his studies in 1400 or possibly 1399. He became acquainted with Coluccio, perhaps through Giovanni Malpaghini or one of the other professors at the Studio, possibly even before he began his studies.

In a letter dated October 18, without indication of the year,

[3] As we shall see, the earliest dated manuscript in Poggio's hand is of the year 1408. We shall also see that assignment of another manuscript that he copied to an earlier year is erroneous.

[4] For the details of Poggio's life see Ernst Walser, *Poggius Florentinus* (Leipzig, 1914). Of his studies at Bologna, Poggio merely says: "Cum essem Bononiae discendi gratia." Walser is probably right in assuming that he was studying law.

[5] An official document furnishes this information (Walser, *op. cit.*, p. 327; cf. p. 11, n. 2).

Coluccio urged Pietro Turchi to help Guccio Bracciolini, the father of "ser Poggii mei".[6] Since the title "ser" indicates that Poggio was already an official notary, the letter was written in 1402, as Walser observed, not in 1401, as dated by Novati.[7] In a postscript to this letter Coluccio remarked that, in order that Turchi might be more inclined to do this service, he asked Poggio to copy this letter (except for the signature); in this way Turchi could get some notion from the character of the handwriting (*littere forma*) of the man whose father he was going to help.[8] Obviously the handwriting was unusual and attracted attention; it could have been nothing else but the new humanistic script, perhaps unveiled to public view for the first time in this letter to the chancellor of Carlo Malatesta, ruler of Rimini.

Possibly even while he was still a student, certainly after he finished his studies, Poggio worked for Coluccio. This is indicated by the letter just mentioned and by the copying of the Strozzianus. He continued copying and doing other work for Coluccio even after leaving Florence, as we shall see in a moment.[9] It is to this period in Florence (1402-03) that I would refer Vespasiano's remark that Poggio was a fine copyist of *lettera antica* (the *antiqua littera*, or Carolingian, that Coluccio mentioned) and in his youth copied for money; in this way he met his needs for books and other things.[10]

[6] *Epist.* III, p. 555.

[7] Walser, *op. cit.*, p. 11, n. 2.

[8] "Quoque magis moveare, iussi ser Poggio, qui patrem tibi recommendat, quod hanc epistolam preter nomen meum exemplet, ut littere forma percipias aliquid coniecture cuius hominis patri sis serviturus." Walser, *op. cit.*, p. 11, quite incorrectly interprets *exemplet* as "composed" (*verfasste*). Whether Turchi was so impressed that he came to the rescue of Poggio's father, we do not know. At any rate he did not imitate the new script, for a book he copied at Rimini in 1408 (Vat. lat. 238) is written in formal Gothic.

[9] Novati suggested that a scribe mentioned in a letter of Coluccio which, with considerable hesitation, he assigned to 1401, might be Poggio (III, pp. 501, 505), but Sabbadini demonstrated that the letter was written in 1392 or 1393. At that time Poggio was twelve or thirteen years old (R. Sabbadini, *Giovanni da Ravenna* [Como, 1924], p. 247).

[10] "Fu bellissimo iscrittore di lettera antica, e nella sua gioventù iscrisse a prezzo: e con quello mezzo sovveniva a' sua bisogni, di libri e d'altre cose" (Vespasiano da Bisticci, *Vite di uomini illustri del secolo XV* [Milan, 1951], p. 291). It is not without significance that Poggio began paying taxes in Florence in this very year 1402 (*Epist.*, ed. T. de Tonellis, I [Florence, 1832], p. 158).

Perhaps Berlin, Ham. lat. 166 (to be discussed below), copied by him in 1408, was commissioned and suitably rewarded by Cosimo de' Medici. The book was in Cosimo's hands before 1425, as will be seen later.

In November or December of 1403 Poggio went to Rome, where he eventually became papal secretary. On December 23 of that year Coluccio answered Poggio's report of his safe arrival in the eternal city. As a postscript he added that he was waiting impatiently for the copy being made by Poggio of a manuscript of Cicero belonging to Iacopo Angeli da Scarperia. Angeli, another disciple of Coluccio, had been in Rome for three years. As will be shown below, the copy made by Poggio has not been identified. It is my belief that Strozz. 96 was copied in 1402 or the early part of 1403, before Poggio left Florence for Rome.

Let us now analyze the script of Strozz. 96 and compare it with Coluccio's experiment in the Pliny manuscript. The uncial *d* has been eliminated entirely. Round *s* is used only at the end of a line, written above when it is necessary to save space. The *et* ligature is always used. For the most part round letters stand apart, though there are many cases of union, or touching. Fusion, however, is rare. In the matter of the *ae* diphthong the treatment varies, as in Coluccio. The simple *e* is retained in some words. When Poggio writes the diphthong he does it in two ways, one similar to our modern printed form, the other with a subscript *a*, like a cedilla, though the latter is less common. This form is useful when a scribe in copying a manuscript that has the simple *e* fails to make the necessary change at once. In these respects Poggio resembles Coluccio in the Pliny manuscript. Both are consistent in writing the diphthong in case endings. In over two hundred case endings Poggio fails to write the diphthong only three times. On the other hand he once wrongly writes *fixae* for the adverb. He regularly writes the diphthong in *haec* and *quae*, but in the one instance of *hec* Coluccio omits it. Both write the diphthong in *aequus* (Poggio has four examples). An interesting situation is revealed in the spelling of *quaero* and its compounds in Strozz. 96. On fols. 1-12 only the simple *e* is used (eight times). Thereafter only the diphthong occurs (ten times). Evidently the change is deliberate, on Poggio's own initiative or perhaps on Coluccio's suggestion. Other peculiarities in the matter of the diphthong in this manuscript are worth noting. *Prae* as preposition or prefix is always written *pre* (forty-four times). The adjective *foedus* and its derivatives are always spelled with the simple *e* (four times). *Aetas* and its derivatives have the form *etas* in the first part (three times), but *aetas* occurs on fol. 33. *Grecus* is the regular form (nine times). *Coeteri* is always so written (six times) but in three cases the *o* is expunged. Poggio had difficulty in distinguishing forms of *capio* and *coepi*. He mistakenly wrote *accoeptus* twice, *suscoepi* twice, *decoeptio* once, *incoepi* twice, but either he or Coluccio expunged the *o* in every case. *Coepi* was written correctly three times, but in one of these examples the *o* was expunged. These details will be of interest when we come to discuss other manuscripts copied by Poggio.

Another feature of the Strozzianus is of great interest, the spelling of *mihi* and *nihil*. All his life Coluccio retained the mediaeval forms *michi* and *nichil*. In 1406, in what may have been his last letter, he wrote to none other than Poggio himself, then in Rome, to protest against the latter's spelling of *mii* and *niil*.[11] I think he actually meant *mihi* and *nihil*, but since the *h* was silent, he wanted to bring out the contrast in pronunciation between *mi(h)i* and *michi* (*miki*). As Novati says, it is to Poggio that we owe the restoration of the ancient spelling, as a result of Poggio's stubbornness — in Coluccio's words Poggio was *dure cervicis*. Poggio, never one to use mild language, bluntly described the mediaeval spelling as a sin and a sacrilege (*nefas et sacrilegium*). Now in the Strozzianus the score is 37 to 5 in favor of *michi* and *nichil*. Once *michi* is followed immediately by *nihil*. It seems to me that Poggio was trying, probably under instruction from Coluccio, to write in the latter's manner but that he slid unconsciously into his own spelling occasionally. In manuscripts that Poggio copied later he almost invariably wrote *mihi* and *nihil*.

The treatment of *mihi* and *nihil* in the Strozzianus has some kinship with the spelling of *auctor* and its compounds. The evidence is overwhelming that Coluccio preferred the spelling *autor*. Many examples are found in his autograph notes in various manuscripts. In the Strozzianus we discover twenty instances of *autor* and three of *auctor*, but nineteen of the twenty examples of *autor* were correct-

11 *Epist.* IV, pp. 162-163 and note.

ed to *auctor* either by the scribe himself, i.e., by Poggio, or by Coluccio. My explanation is that Poggio regularly kept the spelling *autor* of Coluccio's autograph copy, except that three times he unwittingly substituted his own spelling *auctor*. Then he seems to have convinced his chief that the spelling *autor* was incorrect. As a result Poggio went back to his manuscript and corrected to *auctor*, overlooking one example in the process.[12] In the books he copied later Poggio always spelled *auctor*.

Somewhat similar is the case of *otium* and its derivatives. Coluccio's spelling was *ocium*, as we can see in some of his autographs. That is what Poggio wrote in five instances in Strozz. 96 but all but one were corrected to *otium*. Again we cannot say on whose initiative this was done, but we know that Poggio's spelling in other manuscripts was *otium*. Coluccio spelled the name of Sallust with one *l*. Poggio so spelled it on fol. 22 but later another *l* was added.

In preparing their parchment for writing, scribes ruled not only horizontally to keep the lines straight but also vertically, on both left and right, so that all lines might begin and end at the same point, but for the most part they were not very successful as far as the right margins were concerned. In our earliest Latin manuscripts abbreviations and ligatures were employed at the ends of lines in order to achieve a relatively straight right margin. One device to fill out a short line was to write an *i* (or we may call it the first stroke of an *m*, *n*, etc.) and then to delete it lightly. Poggio seems to have taken this matter of even margins more seriously than most scribes. One may well raise the question whether he and particularly his imitators did not set the stage for the "justification" of the line introduced by the first printers and followed ever since. This convention is so fixed in our minds that it has hampered the production of books by photographing typewritten pages and has led to great expense to develop typewriting machines that can produce an even margin. Be that as it may, it is interesting to trace Poggio's practice, beginning with Strozz. 96. Here he used the cancelled *i* a number of times. He also wrote a cancelled *o* five times where the space was too large for an *i*. I do

12 In most cases it is not possible to tell who made the corrections but some can be positively attributed to Poggio, e.g. one on fol. 14r.

not recall seeing an *o* used in this way in earlier manuscripts. An expunged *u* (fol. 14r) was perhaps intended to serve the same purpose, as the next word does not begin with a *u*. Large forms of letters also occur, such as a round *s* lying on its back, a usage by no means original with Poggio.

But the most interesting device in Poggio's bag of tricks was word division. He and some of his followers broke all the rules in the interest of justifying the line. Of course, earlier scribes were not always careful to observe the rules and Poggio's *comp-onat* (fol. 18r) is not without precedent. But examples like *cla-udum* (fol. 25v) and *a-dhibebantur* (fol. 4v) probably are to be found very rarely before his time.[13] We shall see little more of this in Poggio's later work, but his imitators went much farther.

It is time to turn to Poggio's manuscripts to trace the development of some of his writing practices.[14]

1. Strozzianus 96 (parchment) has been discussed. Written in 1402 or 1403.

2. Berlin, Hamilton lat. 166 (parchment) is the earliest dated and signed product of Poggio's formal book hand. It contains Cicero's letters to Atticus and carries the subscription: "Scripsit Poggius anno domini MCCCCVIII a mundi vero creatione VI mil. et DCVII".[15] It seems to have been in the possession of Cosimo de' Medici, perhaps transcribed for him; probably it is the

[13] I may be mistaken in this. I have seen thousands of manuscripts, but as I was not concerned with this phenomenon I may have overlooked some examples. One manuscript examined since beginning this study (British Museum Add. 11979), a Valerius Maximus dated 1392, has many queer divisions, e.g., *iu-ssus*, *sa-ucio*, *m-ortis*, *m-aximo*, *m-acchinationibus*, *oppr-essis*. In Fig. 3 *qu-od* is so divided. In Munich, lat. 560 Hartmann Schedel (fifteenth century) added a title in which he divides *Ge-rmanicum*.

[14] I gave a list of Poggio's books, both those copied by him and those he owned, in *Studies*, etc., p. 315, but the present list has three additions to those he copied.

[15] See Fig. 15. Facsimile of fol. 14r in H. Sjögren, *Commentationes Tullianae* (Uppsala, 1910), of part of fol. 40r in P. Schmiedeberg, *De Asconi codicibus et de Ciceronis scholiis Sangallensibus* (Breslau diss., 1905), and of fol. 162r in Stanley Morison, "Early Humanistic Script and the First Roman Type", *The Library*, XXIV (1943), Fig. 11. The manuscript is at the moment in the Westdeutsche Bibliothek, Marburg. I have not seen it but have a complete microfilm.

manuscript in "lettera antica" listed in the catalogue of Cosimo's library made in 1418.[16]

We cannot attempt to solve here the complicated question of the relations of the manuscripts of this work. Schmidt suggested that Poggio made his copy from Coluccio's manuscript (Laur. 49, 18), a reasonable suggestion.[17] But Sjögren denied this on the basis of internal evidence, and maintained that the two manuscripts were independent.[18] Sabbadini backed up Schmidt, and Annelise Modrze in a detailed discussion completely confirmed Schmidt.[19] Coluccio got his copy from Pavia, taken either from Petrarch's manuscript or from its exemplar, once in Verona; both of these manuscripts may have been in Pavia at that time.[20]

There are some differences in script between the Berlin codex and the Strozzianus, differences produced by the five or six years'

[16] In Epist. II, 22 (ed. Tonelli, I, p. 149), written in 1425, Poggio wrote: "Praeterea opus est mihi epistolis Ciceronis ad Atticum manu mea scriptis, quas habet Cosmus noster". It is reasonable to suppose that the Berlin autograph is the one mentioned. For the catalogue of 1418 see F. Pintor, *La libreria di Cosimo de' Medici nel 1418* (Florence, 1902).

[17] O. E. Schmidt, "Die handschriftliche Ueberlieferung der Briefe Ciceros", *Abh. phil.-hist. Cl. sächs. Ges. Wiss.*, IV (1887), p. 355.

[18] H. Sjögren, *op. cit.*, p. 25, and his edition, I (Uppsala, 1916), p. XVI.

[19] R. Sabbadini, *Storia e critica di testi latini* (Catania, 1914), pp. 74, 80; Annelise Modrze, in *Zentralblatt für Bibliothekswesen*, 51 (1934), p. 499. Sabbadini thought that the Berlin manuscript was copied either at Florence or Lucca, probably the latter. Walser, *op. cit.*, p. 27, n. 4, seemed to attribute to Sabbadini, *Le scoperte dei codici latini e greci ne' secoli XIV e XV* (Florence, 1905), p. 73, the view that the Berlin manuscript was copied from the Pavia codex discovered by Bartolomeo Capra in 1409. Sabbadini did not mention the Berlin manuscript at this point. What Walser perhaps meant was that Poggio in 1408 copied the Pavia manuscript which Capra came upon the next year. But Modrze's discussion made this view impossible.

[20] The 1426 catalogue of the Pavia library (E. Pellegrin, *La Bibliothèque des Visconti et des Sforza ducs de Milan, au XVe siècle* [Paris, 1955]) lists a manuscript of Cicero's letters to Atticus (No. 610) which may have been either the Verona archetype or Petrarch's copy of it. Two other manuscripts in the catalogue (Nos. 622 and 857) between them contained the same text, but No. 857, containing the first part, was "in carta et littera notarina" and could therefore not have been the one that Capra discovered, as this was "ex vetustissima littera" (Sabbadini, *Storia*, p. 76). By a misprint Pellegrin omits "et littera", found in the first edition of this list by G. D'Adda, *Indagini storiche... sulla Libreria Visconteo-Sforzesca del Castello di Pavia*, I (Milan, 1879), but gives it correctly on p. 22.

interval, such as another kind of *g*, which, however, disappears in some later examples, but the general appearance is the same. There is some uncertainty at the beginning about some letters: the *ct* ligature is occasionally omitted; at other times, it has an experimental flatness at the top instead of the rounded form used later in this and other manuscripts. On fols. 58 and 59 Poggio reverts to the round final *s* of Gothic three times and once even to the round *r*.

The treatment of diphthongs is similar in the two manuscripts, but there are interesting differences. As in the Strozzianus, *pre*, *Grecus*, *fedus*, *etas* are the regular spellings in the Berlin codex: *pre* occurs 706 times, *prae* four; *Grecus* sixty times, *Graecus* never; *fedus* (adj.) eleven times, *foedus* never; *etas* twenty-four times, *aetas* seven. The endings of nouns and adjectives almost invariably show the diphthong. In the Strozzianus there are only three examples of simple *e* in endings as against two hundred or more cases of *ae*. It seems reasonable to suppose that the three exceptions were due to a *lapsus mentis* while copying an exemplar in which the simple *e* was probably used throughout. The Berlin manuscript starts out with eight examples of *e* to none of *ae* on the first leaf, but the diphthong rapidly overtakes the monophthong. In the entire manuscript the diphthong appears in the ending 1294 times, the single vowel 192 times. Besides, in many of these cases *e* is used in proper names about which Poggio was uncertain. Yet Poggio is becoming more indifferent to the diphthong, and this tendency increases.

About *ceteri* there no longer is uncertainty; it is always so written (137 times). *Cepi* (for *coepi*) occurs forty-nine times, *caepi* twice. In the first fifty leaves *sepe* outnumbers *saepe* 31 to 8, but the final score is only 61 to 42. *Quaero* is so spelled 147 times while *quero* is found twenty-six times. *Queso* is the spelling sixty-four times, *quaeso* once. *Aequus* occurs only eighteen times as against thirty-three for *equus*. Here again Poggio shown less interest in the diphthong than he did in the Strozzianus. In still another respect Poggio was a backslider: in the Strozzianus he always writes the diphthong in *quae*, but in the Berolinensis we find many examples of *que*: to be exact, 591 of *quae*, 221 of *que*. He is more consistent in spelling *haec* (371 times) as against *hec* (thirteen times).

The treatment of the word *Caesar* is particularly interesting. Only two instances of the monophthong are found. But more than this, *Caesar* is the only word in which the diphthong is frequently written as two separate letters: sixty-two cases (besides nine in capitals) as against 321 of the ligature.

The new spelling is regularly used: *auctor*, *otium* (one exception), *mihi*, *nihil* (one exception). *Salustius* occurs once but is corrected. Word division is normal, but *con-icio* occurs once. No special characters, such as the deleted *i*, are found at the ends of lines. Thus little attention is paid to justifying the margins. Accent marks appear occasionally in the adverbs *eó*, *illó*, *pené*, *uná*, *quó*, *palám*, and in *consequére* (fut.) and *ruére*. It will be of interest to watch these phenomena in later manuscripts copied by Poggio.

The Strozzianus has an admixture of minuscules and uncials in its capitals. The Berolinensis, like all later manuscripts, is more strict. But the capitals will be discussed at the end of this chapter. At this point I wish to mention merely the usage in the Berolinensis and later manuscripts in the writing of *ii* in capitals. The second *i* is taller than the first.[21]

3. Laur. 67, 15 (parchment) was copied between December 1, 1408, and the end of January, 1409, as the reference in the subscription to the Pope's stay at Siena shows: "Hunc librum scripsit Poggius Florentiae summo cum studio ac diligentia diebus XII Romano pontifice [Gregorio XII] residente iterum Senis cum sua curia. Valeas qui legis".[22] The name of Gregory XII was added in the margin by Poggio in Gothic script. Contained in the manuscript is Eusebius' Chronicle (*De temporibus*) in the translation of Jerome, with the continuation by Prosper. If it were not for the subscription the attribution to Poggio might be and probably would have been questioned. The writing is smaller, more crowded, and less rounded than usual. This is probably to be explained by the desire to compress this long text into the seventy-six large leaves on which it is written and by the haste (twelve days, as Poggio boasts) with

21 An example may be seen in Morison, Fig. 11.

22 See Fig. 16. Photographs of part of a page and of subscription in Walser, *op. cit.*, Plate IV; latter also in Morison, *op. cit.*, Fig. 17. The book is No. 29 in the inventory of Poggio's library (Walser, p. 420). Used by Mommsen in his edition of Prosper (*Mon. Germ. Hist.*, *Auct. Ant.* 9, p. 368); one of over sixty fifteenth-century codices listed by him. Some of these (especially the four copied by Antonio di Mario) may have been transcribed from Poggio's manuscript or its exemplar.

which it was transcribed. The manuscript measures 315 by 221 mm. and has thirty-nine lines to a page. An indication of haste is the frequent failure to tie *ct* in a ligature, a failure that I have not noticed in any other examples of Poggio's book hand except for a few at the beginning of the Berlin manuscript (No. 2). Another sign of haste is the almost complete absence of the *ae* ligature after the first few pages.[23] On fol. 1 the diphthong is usually written except that in accordance with his custom Poggio writes *pre* (three times) and *Grecus* (four times). But on ten or so scattered pages thereafter only the simple *e* is found except in the word *Caesar* (thirteen times as against twice for *Cesar*). Fusion is generally used whenever possible, even in *ba*. The minuscule *a* is always used, though in all other manuscripts, earlier and later, Poggio employs the uncial *a* except in his "manus velox" (to be mentioned later) and occasionally in his Gothic marginal notes. Coluccio mixed the two in his experiment in the Pliny manuscript. All in all, this manuscript is the least typical of Poggio's formal hand. As for capitals, the second *i* of *ii* is taller, as in the Berlin manuscript.

In this manuscript one finds for the first time among Poggio's manuscripts an accent mark over the preposition *a* to prevent confusion, though it is rare.

In word division the Eusebius manuscript is not very striking. I can report only that it has *a-utem* and *resta-uratis* (fol. 1v) and that it wavers in the division of *ct*: sometimes the division comes before the *c*, sometimes after it. An elongated round *s* on its side is used at times to fill the line.

4. Vat. lat. 3245 (parchment) was copied in the papacy of John XXIII (1410–15), as we know from a letter of presentation by Poggio's son Iacopo to Bernardo Bembo (fol. 70v): "Quereretur haud iniuria Poggius pater se patriis privari laribus et a filio pientissimo destitui, nisi facile perciperet se in amplissimam rem publicam, nobilissimam familiam a prestantissimo equite Bernardo Bembo cooptari. Quod cum equo animo ferat, suscipe eum ut te dignum est. Hospes erit non ingratus, presertim cum phylosophiam et leges a Cicerone editas a se vero Iohannis XXIII pontificis tempore

[23] Not every page of this and the following manuscripts has been checked for the use of the diphthong; a random sampling was taken, usually covering every tenth folio.

scriptas afferat. Vale. Tuus Iacobus Poggius Florentinus". Actually the date of writing must have been before 1415, for in October of 1414 Poggio was already on his way to the Council of Constance. The manuscript has Cicero's *Academica* I, 2 (*Lucullus*) and *De legibus*.[24] Poggio's ownership note is not found in the manuscript, but perhaps it once appeared on a leaf now lost. How would Iacopo know that his father copied the manuscript during the papacy of John XXIII except from an entry similar to those in Laur. 67, 15 (No. 3 above) and Laur. 50, 31 (No. 6 below)? Walser (p. 419) is probably right in identifying the manuscript with item 13 in the Poggio inventory: "De legibus accademicorum... manu Poggi". It will be pointed out below that in other cases statements in the inventory that manuscripts were "manu Poggi" were based on Poggio's own entries in these manuscripts.

The *g* in this manuscript is of the flaring type found in the Eusebius. *Pre* and *Grecus* with their compounds follow earlier practice: *pre* occurs 122 times, *prae* not at all; *Grecus* appears 31 times, *Graecus* nowhere. *Aetas*, on the other hand, varies: the diphthong and the simple *e* occur seven times each. But the greatest surprise is in the reduction in the number of examples of *ae*, both in endings and elsewhere. Whether the diphthong is written or not is a matter of caprice, it seems. The score is 321 to 38 in favor of *que*. Even so most of the examples of *quae* are in clusters: three each on fols. 1r and 38r, eight on fol. 7r, four on fol. 42r. A few other examples must suffice: *hec* 104 times, *haec* 18; *quero* 58, *quaero* 34; *sepe* 24, *saepe* 5; *equus* 10, *aequus* 2. *Fedus* (adjective) and *ceteri* are always so written. There is a definite lowering in the number of diphthongs written, a process which continues in Poggio's copies. Not that the diphthong ever disappears entirely, but Poggio seems to have come to the conclusion that it was not worth the effort to make the extra stroke. Occasionally he would have qualms and would become more faithful in writing the diphthong. I noted no accent marks over *a*, etc., but a more careful examination than I had the time to make might reveal some. The spellings *quur*, *quom*,

24 See Fig. 17. Reproduction of part of fol. 63r in Pierre de Nolhac, *La bibliothèque de Fulvio Orsini* (Paris, 1887), Pl. II. In Poggio's inventory No. 13 (Walser, *op. cit.*, p. 419). Fulvio Orsini, who owned the manuscript, says that it was copied by Poggio; this statement he, of course, based on Iacopo's letter.

quoius, *quoi*, and *quui* make an appearance, perhaps because they were in the exemplar. Fusion and union are frequent. Unusual word division at the ends of lines does not occur. A new procedure appears in the avoidance of hyphenation at the botton of a page. On fol. 51r, where the last word, *vicissitudines*, was too long, Poggio wrote the last syllable below the three preceding letters to avoid putting it on the next page. In later manuscripts Poggio soon abandoned his new principle, but some of his imitators followed it.

5. Laur. 48, 22 (parchment), containing Cicero's Philippics and Catilinarians, was probably written in the last two months of 1425.[25] At the end of the Philippics (fol. 37r) the subscription reads: "Explicit. Poggius scripsit". After the Catilinarians (fol. 121r) we read: "Finis libri. Scripsit Poggius Romae". On the flyleaf, a table of contents written by Poggio: "In hoc volumine continentur Philippicae Ciceronis XIIII, item in Catilinam orationes IIII". There has been difference of opinion about the date. Novati thought it might be the Cicero that Poggio was copying in Rome in 1403 and that it was corrected by Coluccio.[26] But the distinguished scholar was completely wrong on this last point, as he not infrequently was in matters of handwriting. Besides, Coluccio mentioned merely a Cicero, without indicating its contents. Rather, this manuscript is the copy of the exemplar Poggio requested September 1, 1425, writing from Rome (*Epist.* I, p. 161), and received October 20 (*Epist.* I, p. 165). On June 5, 1428, Poggio wrote that he was correcting his copy from an old manuscript just found (*Epist.* I, p. 216). Clark furnished the decisive argument by showing that the notes in the margin were entered by Poggio, not Coluccio, from a manuscript of the ninth century now in the St. Peter's collection of the Vatican (Basil. S. Petri H. 25).[27] This was, of course, the old manuscript to which Poggio alluded. Another argument against the 1403 date is that the complete text offered

25 See Fig. 18; the same plate in my *Studies*, etc., p. 312. In Poggio inventory No. 4 (Walser, *op. cit.*, p. 418).

26 *Epist.* III, p. 656. See my *Studies*, etc., p. 236, and Walser, *op. cit.*, p. 105, n. 1. The references to Poggio's letters are to *Poggii Epistolae*, ed. T. de Tonellis, 3 vols. (Florence, 1832-61).

27 A. C. Clark, *The Vetus Cluniacensis* (Anecdota Oxoniensia, Classical Series X [1905]), p. LXII, and the second edition of the Philippics, etc., in the Oxford Classical Texts (Oxford, 1917), p. X.

by Poggio's copy was not discovered that early. In 1430 Aurispa asked Traversari for the recently discovered complete Philippics: "Antonianas Ciceronis perfectas ut nuper inventae sunt".[28] I cannot conceive that Aurispa would use *nuper* of a period twenty-seven years earlier when dealing with the discovery of a manuscript, or that he would have waited that long before trying to obtain a copy. Apparently he wanted a copy of Poggio's manuscript or of Niccoli's (Laur., Marc. 268). The old manuscript used by Poggio in 1428 (now in the St. Peter's collection in the Vatican) cannot be meant, for it lacks about half of Oration XI, half of XII, the last four-fifths of XIII, and all of XIV. As the manuscript was found by Cardinal Orsini in 1426 and left by him to St. Peter's, it was presumably incomplete when he discovered it in Germany. It is high time that the view that Angeli discovered the complete Philippics in 1403, for which there is not a shred of evidence, and that Poggio copied them in that year, which likewise lacks substance, be abandoned.

The letter *g* in this manuscript returns in part to the form found in the Strozzianus, Poggio's earliest known book in his formal style. *Caesar* is always spelled with the diphthong (ninety-one examples in the scattered pages examined). Otherwise the diphthong is used on these pages only in *caesus* (four times), presumably because of the supposed etymology of *Caesar*, and once each in three other words. Poggio occasionally employs a *v* for a *u* without distinction: *civis*, *ciuis*. Fusion occurs but union is more common. Nothing exceptional is found in word division except *persu-asi* (fol. 15v), and *dece-ptum*, etc., but attention may be drawn, in view of later developments, to the unwillingness to separate ligatured *ct* at the end of a line. This reluctance produces *flucti-bus*, with *ti* projecting into the margin, and *lect'* (for *lectus*), with *t'* in the margin. An accent mark was noted on the adverb *pené* to distinguish it from the noun *p(o)en(a)e*. Other accent marks (really marks indicating length) were found on *abutére*, *patére*, *impendére*. No such accents occur in the Strozzianus; this may be another argument against the date 1403 for Laur. 48, 22. The last word of a page is not allowed to run over to the following page,

[28] R. Sabbadini, *Carteggio di Giovanni Aurispa* (Rome, 1931), p. 69.

but the word often extends into the margin. This principle was first observed by Poggio in No. 4 (1410–14).

Fig. 18 reveals a characteristic feature of Poggio's writing style and that of his imitators. In long marginal additions or notes, he is apt to depart from his humanistic writing and to return, at least in part, to the Gothic of such men as Coluccio. In this reproduction one sees the uncial *d* of Gothic alongside the minuscule *d* of humanistic script, the round lengthened final *s*, and an earlier *g*. This script is not used in margins in the Strozzianus but is found in the Berlin Cicero, the Eusebius (in the subscription, shown in Morison's Fig. 17), and in all of his later manuscripts. It is a mixture of his "manus velox" (to be mentioned later), which is itself a formalized Gothic, and the new humanistic style, varying in the proportions of each style. Several of these writing practices fit a later date rather than an early one.

6. Laur. 50, 31 (parchment), containing Cicero, *De oratore. Paradoxa*, *Brutus*, *Orator*, has the subscription "Scripsit Poggius secretarius domini Martini Papae V" on fol. 93v, "Liber Poggii" on fol. 100v, and "Scripsit Poggius Martini Papae V secretarius. Valeas qui legis" on fol. 166r. On the flyleaf, a table of contents by Poggio: "In hoc volumine continentur De oratore libri III, Paradoxa, Brutus, Orator".[29] Poggio became secretary to Martin V in May of 1423. Martin died in February of 1431. But we can date the copying of the Cicero manuscript more closely. On May 15, 1423, Poggio asked Niccoli for parchment and for the text of the three rhetorical works, saying that he will either copy them or have them copied.[30] He received first the *De oratore*, was copying it himself April 14, 1425, had almost finished copying it May 12, and had completed it by June 14, 1425. Just when he finished the other works is not so clear. In the letter of April 14 he comments that next he plans to copy *Orator* and *Brutus* and asks Niccoli to send either his own copy or that of Nicola de' Medici. On May 12 he repeats that he has not yet received these two works,

29 See Fig. 19. Facsimile of part of fol. 93v in Morison, *op. cit.*, Fig. 12, and of last page in V. Federici, *La scrittura delle cancellerie* (Rome, 1934), Pl. LXXXII, 1. In inventory of Poggio's library No. 5 (Walser, *op. cit.*, p. 418).

30 These details, based on Poggio's letters, in Walser, *op. cit.*, p. 104, n. 2. The letters referred to are in *Epist.* I, pp. 88, 148, 149, 153, 155.

commenting that surely Niccoli can "dig up" (*eruere*) a copy in so large a city as Florence, with its great abundance of books. Nor had he received them on June 14 or June 23. As there is no further mention of the matter, we may assume that he obtained the two works and finished his copy of them in the last half of 1425. Whether the manuscript of the *De oratore* that Niccoli sent was his own copy we cannot tell, for the manuscript that has passed as his (Laur. 50, 46) must be rejected, as will be brought out in Chapter III. The *Brutus* and *Orator* in Poggio's manuscript are said to have been copied from Florence, Naz. Conv. Soppr. I. I. 14.[31] This manuscript was copied by Niccoli, as we shall see in the same chapter. So Niccoli must have sent his own copy, not that of Nicola de' Medici.

There are several resemblances to the preceding manuscript (Laur. 48, 22), written in the same year. The *g* is the same, *v* is occasionally used for *u*, marginalia show the same final *s*. The diphthong *ae* is scarce. On twenty-four scattered pages *Caesar* is always so spelled (nine times); there are only five other instances of the diphthong on these pages, three of them in the words *aetas*. But *etas* also occurs three times. Fusion is fairly frequent. In word division the situation is about as in the preceding manuscript: in *actuose*, *tu* projects into the margin to avoid splitting *ct*. There is some inconsistency: *conscrip-sisse* but *scri-ptor*. Accent marks are used on the adverbs *pené* and *eó*. Only on two verso pages (38v, 85v) are the last words hyphenated, never on a recto page.

Berlin, Ham. 166; Laur. 48, 22; 50, 31; and 67, 15 are the only manuscripts in Poggio's book hand known to me in which Poggio indicates that he was the scribe. Vat. lat. 3245 is vouched for by Poggio's son Iacopo, probably on the basis of a now missing leaf. The first came into the hands of Cosimo de' Medici and therefore does not appear in the inventory of Poggio's library made after his death. The inventory labels Laur. 50, 31 and 67, 15 as "manu Poggii". This attribution is obviously based on the subscriptions, not on independent knowledge. Therefore the absence of such an attribution in other items is no proof that they were not

31 F. Heerdegen in his edition of the *Orator* (Leipzig, 1884) argued on internal evidence that Laur. 50, 31 was copied from Conv. Soppr. I. I. 14, and J. E. Sandys accepted this view in his edition (Cambridge, 1885), p. LXXXVII.

copied by Poggio. This explanation is intended to clear the way for claiming as products of his hand other existing manuscripts listed in the inventory. Yet it must be admitted that without a signature positive proof cannot be furnished.

7. Florence, Riccardiana 499 (parchment), containing Cicero's Verrines, was copied by Poggio in 1425 or possibly early in 1426.[32] At the end in the same ink as the text: "Liber Poggii secretarii Papae". Let it not be thought that the absence of "Poggius scripsit" shows that Poggio did not do the copying. As seen above, Laur. 50, 31 has only "Liber Poggii" after one of the works in that manuscript and a fuller subscription after two others. If my suggestion of a missing leaf with Poggio's name in Vat. lat. 3245 is inacceptable, we have another unsigned Poggian autograph. The writing of Ricc. 499 is, I believe, that of Poggio, as Bandini saw [33] but Walser did not. As for the date, the secretaryship no doubt refers to that under Martin V (1423-1431). The information furnished by Poggio's letters confirms this. On June 23, 1425, Poggio asks Niccoli for parchment for the Verrines but says nothing about borrowing a text. On February 9, 1426, he returns the exemplar to Niccoli.[34] Apparently a letter in which he requested that exemplar is lost.

To get a better picture of the situation it would be well to look at a few other letters in which Cicero's orations and other works are mentioned. On May 15, 1423 (*Epist.* I, p. 89), Poggio asks Niccoli to forward a letter to Francesco Barbaro in which he requests the return of his manuscript of Cicero's orations. On September 11 (*Epist.* I, p. 93) he informs Niccoli that he has again written Barbaro. On November 13 (*Epist.* I, p. 95) he tells Guarino that he has written Barbaro twice in six months without receiving

[32] See Fig. 20. Poggio inventory No. 3 (Walser, *op. cit.*, p. 418). The title in the manuscript reads: "M. Tullii Ciceronis accusationum liber primus incipit". The inventory has: "Liber accusationum qui vocatur verrinae", etc.

[33] A. M. Bandini, *Catalogus Codicum Latinorum Bibliothecae Mediceae Laurentianae*, II (Florence, 1775), p. 518 (on 56, 31) in listing some of Poggio's transcriptions: "Codex continens libros septem in Verrem apud amplissimum March. Subdecanum Riccardium". The absence of "Poggius scripsit" was used by H. Ebeling as an argument that Laur. 49, 24 was not copied by Poggio (*Philologus*, XLV [1886], p. 369).

[34] Walser, *op. cit.*, p. 104, n. 3; *Epist.* I, pp. 155, 175.

a reply and asks Guarino to intervene and persuade Barbaro to send back the manuscript, which was "mea manu conscripta". On November 6 (*Epist.* I, p. 100) he writes Niccoli to send his (Poggio's) paper copy of Cicero's speeches and the Cluny manuscript, for Barbaro has done him wrong by withholding his (Poggio's) copy; he also wants Niccoli to write to Barbaro, for Niccoli had lent the book to Barbaro in the first place. It is to be inferred, therefore, that the manuscript in Barbaro's hands included the five Cluny orations (*Pro Milone*, *Pro Cluentio*, *Pro Murena*, *Pro Sex. Roscio*, *Pro Caelio*). The original Cluniacensis is listed in Poggio's inventory as No. 73: "orationes tulii V antique". The paper manuscript, presumably a hastily made copy in "manus velox", or Gothic script, may have included the eight speeches discovered by Poggio in France and Germany: *Pro Caecina*, *De lege agraria III*, *Pro Rabirio Postumo*, *Pro Rabirio perduellionis reo*, *Pro Roscio comoedo*, *In Pisonem*. This manuscript turns out to be Vat. lat. 11458 (on which see below). Walser suggests that the copy made contained the thirty-one speeches listed in inventory No. 8, but for this there is no proof. At any rate, I am certain that the Verrines were not involved, for Poggio carefully distinguished Philippics and Verrines from "orationes". His meaning is further clarified by the phrase "orationum particularium" in a letter of August 25, 1425 (*Epist.* I, p. 160). This must mean single orations as contrasted with series such as Philippics and Verrines, which are long enough for separate volumes. Again, in the letter of February 9, 1426, he says that he is returning the Verrines but retaining the "orationes".

An earlier reference to the copying of the Verrines can be detected, I believe, in a letter of May 12, 1425 (*Epist.* I, p. 150). After asking Niccoli to send him various texts, among which the Verrines are not included, he requests Niccoli to send him twenty quaternions of parchment in folio ("mensurae folii") as soon as possible, for he hopes to have a copyist. On June 14 (*Epist.* I, p. 153), after referring to this letter, he says that later he requested a larger size because he plans to have his scribe copy Cicero's orations (apart from the Verrines, I take it), and the number of these is too large for the originally requested quaternions (this "later" letter, written between May 12 and June 14, is not preserved). Poggio goes on to say that he managed to obtain fourteen quaternions in Rome and wants Niccoli to supply twenty more. The Cluny speeches are again demanded, but specifically without parchment. In the letter of June 23 alluded to above, he writes: "Membranas quas cupiebam ad mensuram folii volo pro Verrinis transcribendis uno volumine", the Tusculans and *De finibus* in another volume, letters to Atticus in a third. The question now is whether the size of the parchment is adequate and he desires Niccoli to take that question under consideration. He has, he adds, a satisfactory scribe available who can complete many books. On August 18 and September 1 and 8 (*Epist.* I, pp. 159, 161, 162) he is still waiting for parchment for the Verrines and Philippics. On October 20 (*Epist.* I, p. 165) he receives some parchment and a text of the Philippics, but the parchment is insufficient for the Verrines. On November 3 (*Epist.* I, p. 167) he indicates that Niccoli has purchased more parchment. This was received soon after, for on December 15 (*Epist.* I, p. 171) he writes that the second lot of parchment is of a larger size than the first, and the smaller size is intended for the Verrines. The rest of the parchment for these orations he will find in Rome.

Twenty quaternions would be just right for the Verrines; Ricc. 499 contains 165 fols., five leaves over twenty quaternions. It is, however, written on sixteen quinternions and part of a quaternion. My suggestion is that while the scribe was copying other orations, including the five in the Cluniacensis, and several other works as well, Poggio copied the Verrines in Ricc. 499 in December, 1425, or January, 1426. Between May 12 and November 3 of 1425 Poggio asks for texts or is having copies made of *Orator* and *Brutus*, Verrines, "orations" (always carefully distinguished from Verrines and including a larger number), letters to Atticus, Lucretius, Tusculans, *De finibus*, Philippics, Spartianus, Justinus, Seneca's prose works, unnamed histories. All this was more than enough to keep a scribe busy, especially when he was idle a large part of the time, as Poggio repeatedly notes, because of the failure to receive manuscripts and parchment. There are no requests between November 3 and December 15, and it is to be inferred that manuscripts flowed in copiously and kept the scribe more than busy and so Poggio came to his rescue. The fact that Poggio's ownership note, which a scribe was not apt to have entered for him, was written in ink of the same color as the text is an additional reason for claimimg the Riccardiana manuscript as an autograph.

The diphthong *ae* occurs oftener in the Riccardiana volume than in the manuscripts immediately preceding it but still is not as common as the simple *e*. At least twice the diphthong (in the cedilla form) is wrongly used: *aeadem*, *calamitatae*. This may suggest that Poggio did not do the copying; yet even he could make mistakes and there are many similar errors in other books that he copied. As in other of his manuscripts, *v* is sometimes used for *u*. A new characteristic is that the second *i* of *ii* is often taller even in minuscule, in imitation of Poggio's usage in majuscule. The marginalia are in Poggio's Gothic script. Accented *a* occurs. Unusual word division is found in *mi-tteret*. Hyphenation is not avoided in the final word of a page.

8. Vat. lat. 2208 (parchment), containing Seneca's Epistles, had at the end (now erased but visible under ultraviolet rays): "Liber Poggii." [35] Only the style of writing of the manuscript enables one to attribute it to Poggio's hand. On February 9, 1426, Poggio requests Niccoli to send him a copy of Seneca, saying that he had asked for one before. He recalls that Coluccio had had a copy and wants Niccoli to find out whether Bruni now has it. On March 20 he writes Bruni about it, saying he has a French scribe who will copy it. He renews the request in an undated letter, probably written in April or May. A letter of Bruni probably written in April or early May of 1426 [36] seems to be an answer to a letter of Poggio's on the same theme now lost, for it alludes to matters not mentioned in the published letters of Poggio. Bruni reports that Cosimo has promised to send "that book" (i.e., the Seneca) in a few days. Poggio again asks Bruni on September 27 to send it, as he needs it to correct works already copied and to transcribe others. On October 23 he urges Niccoli to remind Bruni to send the Seneca. He now makes clear that the letters of Seneca are already copied and that he has an unemended copy of other works. Bruni's copy is therefore needed to correct these manuscripts. The request is repeated briefly in another letter to Bruni misdated "VII Kal. Octobris" (Septem-

[35] See Fig. 21. Poggio inventory No. 19. I owe my acquaintance with this manuscript to Profs. Campana and Weinstock.

[36] *Epist.*, ed. L. Mehus (Florence, 1741), IV, 23 (I, p. 141).

ber 25); perhaps it should be October 26. On January 17, 1427, Poggio writes Bruni: "Libellus tuus iam transcriptus est," and the context, by a comparison of pages 197 and 204, shows that Seneca is meant. On October 21, 1427, he acknowledges receipt of a Seneca from Niccoli.[37] Probably therefore the Vatican manuscript was copied in the spring of 1426. Laur. Edili 161 is a manuscript of Seneca's Epistles which belonged to Coluccio. The Vatican manuscript is not a copy of it, but may have been corrected from it, since some of the changes in Poggio's manuscript agree with Coluccio's text.

On flyleaf 2v the entry "Celsus emit" was apparently written in the fifteenth century. It may be that this Celsus was a member of the Celsi family of Ravenna and Venice.

Perhaps the most remarkable feature of the script of this codex is the experiment on fol. 144r of using a slanting script (Fig. 21, ten lines from the bottom). After writing less than two lines Poggio wisely abandoned the experiment. Was he influenced to try it by Niccoli's example (to be discussed in Chapter III)? In any event, Poggio appears not to have tried this style again. It certainly had no effect on the future development of script.

The *g* continues the type mentioned in the preceding manuscripts. Occasional use of *v* is to be seen. The abbreviation for *ur* has the shape of a horizontal figure 8, a form kept in later manuscripts. The diphthong *ae* has all but disappeared. Out of several hundred cases on seventy-five pages only two have it. Even *Caesar* is spelled *Cesar* every one of the six times it occurs, though in one case *Caesar* is written in the marginal index. In word division at the end of the line nothing very striking can be reported. Hyphenation of the last word of a page is generally avoided. An expunged *o* occurs at the end of a line, but as the next word begins with an *o*, Poggio may merely have meant to avoid a hyphen after a single letter. An unusual feature is the writing of *despectus* as *desp^{c}-tus* (Fig. 21). The adverb *illó* is accented.

9. The dating of the rest of Poggio's transcriptions is less certain than that of the manuscripts described thus far. The collection of Ciceronian works in Florence, Ricc. 504 (parchment),

[37] *Epist.* I, pp. 175, 176, 178, 192, 195, 197, 204, 213. Walser (p. 106, n. 3) is incomplete.

is one of them, though I am not entirely certain that the script is Poggio's rather than that of one of his scribes.[38] It has a table of contents in Poggio's usual capital letters on fol. 1v (flyleaf): "In hoc volumine continentur opere M. Tullii Ciceronis, videlicet de finibus bonorum et malorum libri V, de amicitia qui inscribitur Lelius liber I, de senectute qui inscribitur Cato Maior liber I, Topicorum liber I, Partitiones rhetoricae, Somnium Scipionis, fragmentum Academicorum. Liber Poggii." On fol. 139r (end) is the note "Liber Poggii." This manuscript has been correctly identified by Walser as No. 1 in the inventory, which reads: "Opere tuliane: de finibus bonorum et malorum. de amicitia. de senectute. Topicorum liber. Partitiones rectorice. somnium scipionis. framentum academicorum." [39] This is not the manuscript of the *De finibus* which Poggio was having copied by a scribe when he wrote about one on November 3, 1425 (*Epist.* I, p. 169), which manuscript Walser rightly identifies with inventory No. 12, containing only that treatise. It seems plausible, however, that our manuscript was written soon after, in 1426 or 1427. As Walser remarks, Poggio was concerned about building up his library on his return to Rome from Britain in 1423.[40] Four of the eight manuscripts we have discussed were copied in 1425-26 and three of these consisted of works of Cicero. It seems that his special project in that period was to round out his Ciceronian corpus, the foundation of any proper library, especially since he was responsible for discovering new members of that corpus. So I would tentatively assign our present manuscript to that period.

It is possible that the exemplar of the *De finibus* was a manuscript of Coluccio's (Florence, Archivio di Stato, Carte Strozziane, Serie 3, N. 46), as many of the marginalia are identical, but the matter needs further investigation.

An examination of five pages reveals no example of *ae* except one (*quae*) in a title in capitals on fol. 2r. The *ur* abbreviation in the shape of a horizontal figure 8 is found, as in Vat. lat. 2208. The ligatured *st* and *ct* are not as tall as in others of Poggio's manuscripts, except that the short *st* occurs also in Vat. lat. 2208.

[38] See Fig. 22.
[39] Walser, *op. cit.*, p. 418.
[40] Walser, *op. cit.*, p. 84.

10. Laur. 49, 24 (parchment), containing Cicero's letters to Atticus, should belong to the same period as the preceding. Walser's report on the ownership mark is incomplete and misleading. Originally it was "Liber Poggii secretarii apostolici," written in capitals in exactly the same ink as the text. The next owner erased the last three words, obviously with the intention of substituting his own name, but before doing so he changed his mind, perhaps thinking it would be interesting to keep the name of the great Poggio. So he carefully traced the erased letters and added some words so that the whole now reads: "Liber Poggii secretarii apostolici olim fuit sed nunc domini Baenedicti Martinozi aequitis aurati est in presens." The last five words are in erasure and the original writing cannot be made out. A Nicolaus de Martinotiis bought a manuscript of Aeschylus (now Laur. 91 sup. 5) in 1430. Perhaps he was a member of the same family. Schmidt and Walser deny that Poggio was the copyist,[41] but the writing seems to me typical and the use of ink of the same color in the ownership signature and in the text is a significant confirmation. Walser appears to base his idea of Poggio's book hand on the atypical Eusebius.

We must stop to try to untangle the complicated story of Poggio's manuscripts of Cicero's letters to Atticus. In a letter to Niccoli written "in vigilia Paschae" (April 7), 1425 (*Epist.* I, p. 145), he complains that he has not received a reply to an earlier letter (not now known) in which, in behalf of Antonio Loschi, he asked for Cicero's letters.[42] Since Poggio almost always says *Epistolae ad Atticum* when he means that collection, he here is presumably referring to the *Epistolae ad familiares.* Loschi is not again mentioned in connection with Cicero's letters. Just a week later, April 14 (*Epist.* I, p. 149), Poggio tells Niccoli that he has need of the copy of Cicero's *Epistolae ad Atticum* written in his own hand, now in the possession of Cosimo de' Medici. This must be the manuscript now in Berlin, copied in 1408, which was dis-

[41] See Fig. 23. For details see O. E. Schmidt, *op. cit.*, p. 359; Walser, *op. cit.*, p. 105, n. 3. A facsimile of fol. 4r in W. Arndt and M. Tangl, *Schrifttafeln zur Erlernung der lateinischen Palaeographie*, ed. 4 (Berlin, 1904), Pl. 30A.

[42] It is a curious fact that Loschi had a hand in obtaining copies of both collections for Coluccio Salutati over thirty years earlier (see my *Studies*, etc., pp. 243-244). Perhaps Loschi wanted a copy of the text as corrected by Niccoli.

cussed above. Poggio goes on to say that he wants to correct a copy being made by a scribe "satis mendose propter exemplar," full of mistakes because the exemplar is faulty or hard to read. This copy may well have been written on paper, though Walser's statement that it was obviously (*offenbar*) on paper cannot be substantiated. If it was a paper manuscript, then it must be the manuscript described in the inventory as No. 6: "Epistole ad acticum in papiro" and is, I believe, to be identified with Vat. Ottob. lat. 2035, to be mentioned below. On May 12 (*Epist.* I, p. 150) Poggio repeats his request to Niccoli for Cosimo's copy of *Epistolae ad Atticum.*

On June 23, 1425 (*Epist.* I, p. 155), Poggio asks Niccoli for parchment to copy *Epistolae ad Atticum.* This is obviously (and here the word "obviously" is justified) for a different copy, for he now requests parchment for a manuscript whose transcription has not yet begun, whereas in the letters of April 14 and May 12 the copying is under way: "scriptor illas scripsit satis mendose propter exemplar," "liber transcribitur sed nimium mendose." On July 7 (*Epist.* I, p. 157) Poggio complains about Niccoli's failure to send various codices, including the letters of Cicero, "quamquam et ipse quoque [Cosmus] addubitare videtur de epistolis Ciceronis." The allusion to Cosimo shows that the *Epistolae ad Atticum* are meant.

What then of Laur. 49, 24, which we seem to have forgotten in the preceding discussion? It appears to me that the parchment which Poggio asked for on June 23, 1425, was intended for this manuscript, which, as I see it, was copied by Poggio in the latter half of that year. Internal evidence will have to be sought to determine its relation to the Berlin manuscript and to Vat. Ottob. lat. 2035. There is one other reference to *Epistolae ad Atticum.* On January 6, 1430 (Florentine style; actually 1431), Poggio writes that he has dismissed a copyist who transcribed a decade of Livy and the letters to Atticus. This is presumably still another, i.e., a third, manuscript.

When we examine the script of Laur. 49, 24, we find the *g* resembles that of Vat. lat. 2208. The *ur* abbreviation is in the form of a horizontal figure 8, as was indicated above for other manuscripts written about 1425-26. An examination of a large number of pages reveals only two examples of *ae*, and these in *Caesar* (once when written in capitals); on the other hand there are 138 occurrences of *Cesar*. But in marginal notes the spelling *Caesar* is regular. For the most part words are divided at the end of a line before ligatured *ct*, as in earlier manuscripts, but a glance through some sixty pages brought to light seven examples (twelve per cent) of division between *c* and *t*, with the ligaturing stroke attached to the *c*.[43] This absurd practice, in which the connecting stroke is left dangling pathetically, was continued by Poggio and other scribes, as we shall see. The first example known to me dates from 1410 in a manuscript copied by Giovanni Aretino (see Chapter V). Hyphenation in the last word of a page is frequent. The adverbs *eó* and *ádhuc* have accents.

11-13. Vat. lat. 1843, 1849, 1852 (parchment), containing the first, third, and fourth decades of Livy, belong together as a set.[44] The writing space is identical in all three: 243 by 166 mm., and the width is divided by vertical ruling into 6-154-6 mm. The first volume ends with *explicit* and ownership mark in capitals (fol. 196v): "T. Livii ab urbe condita liber decimus explicit lege feliciter liber Aurispae secretarii apostolici." But the name Aurispa is in erasure; the original name must have been Poggio's, though we cannot now make it out even with ultraviolet rays. The words of the *explicit* (except for *Aurispae*) are in the same ink as the text. The second volume ends (fol. 182r): "T. Livii Patavini historici preclarissimi liber XXX explicit belli Punici secundi lege feliciter. Liber Poggii." All this is written in the same red ink. In the third volume there is no *explicit* but at the end (fol. 147r) we find: "Liber Poggii secretarii" in ink that differs from that of the text.

As early as April 14, 1425 (*Epist.* I, p. 148), Poggio urges Niccoli to finish up the matter of the decade of Livy, i.e., to send it to him. Evidently this is not the first request. We hear nothing further until September 27, 1427 (*Epist.* I, p. 212), when Poggio asks Niccoli to send Tacitus and also parchment for the use of Paulus de Marganis, who wishes to copy the third decade

43 An example is shown on the facsimile in Arndt-Tangl, *loc. cit.* For one in another manuscript see Fig. 24.

44 See Figs. 24-25. Facsimile of 1843, fol. 63r, in my *Studies*, etc., p. 312; additional details on pp. 308-313.

(Books XXI-XXX); then Poggio's copyist will transcribe it.[45] He adds: "Send me my book," which ought to refer to a Livy. Could this be the decade of April 14, 1425? On October 21 (*Epist.* I, p. 214) he acknowledges receipt of the Tacitus and repeats his request for parchment, "item pro Titi Livii Decadibus, prout olim scripsi." On December 6, 1427, he thanks Niccoli for the parchment but the sheets are too large; he does not want to put two decades in one volume.[46] On June 5, 1428 (*Epist.* I, p. 217), he returns Tacitus and a decade of Livy to Niccoli. This would seem to be the third decade, as Tacitus and the third decade are coupled in the preceding letter. On October 30, 1428 (*Epist.* I, p. 223), he thanks Niccoli for books and parchment received. He adds that his scribe has reached the end of the ninth book of the first decade. On November 27 (*Epist.* I, p. 264) he praises Niccoli for his diligence in regard to the fourth decade, which is being copied. It does not make any difference, he says, whether it is emended before or after it is copied. In other words, he could emend the exemplar or the copy of it. He has, he adds, two tolerable exemplars as well as some faulty ones. From a letter of July 15, 1429 (*Epist.* I, p. 285), we learn that Niccoli has received Livy's decades from Poggio, who wants them illuminated and bound in separate volumes. The first and fourth decades, copied by the same scribe, are larger and should, he says, be trimmed to the size of the third decade. On January 6, 1431 (*Epist.* I, p. 340; dated 1430, but this is no doubt Florentine style), he says that his scribe copied during the year (1430) the third decade so that all might be by the same hand. Obviously this refers to the volumes mentioned in the preceding letter.

All this would seem to concern only one set, together with an extra copy of the third decade. This last was copied first (letters of April 14, 1425, September 27, 1427, June 5, 1428). Beginning with October 21, 1427, he has the idea of copying the rest and so requests parchment "pro decadibus" (note the plural). On October 30, 1428, a scribe is finishing the first decade, on November 27 he is copying the fourth. Before July 15, 1429, the three volumes are in Niccoli's hands for binding. On January 6, 1431, Poggio decides to have the

[45] See my *Studies*, p. 310.

[46] A. Wilmanns, *Zentralblatt für Bibliothekswesen*, 30 (1913), p. 305.

third decade recopied to make a matching set. The three manuscripts with which this discussion began, Vat. lat. 1843, 1849, 1852, should be those manuscripts, especially perhaps since they are illuminated, just as Poggio wished his set to be. Yet it seems to me that the handwriting is that of Poggio, not that of a scribe closely imitating his style. He perhaps wrote them in 1425-26, when, as he himself says, "momordit me tarantula et dum fervor adest" (*Epist.* I, p. 149; April 14, 1425) and "vereor ne hic ardor transcribendi qui nunc adest liquefiat" (*Epist.* I, p. 150; May 12, 1425). On June 14, 1425 (*Epist.* I, p. 154), he tells Niccoli he wants to abandon his siesta in favor of copying manuscripts. One has to read all the letters of this period to realize the extent of his plans for copying and secondarily for having a scribe assist him. Gradually more and more of the copying seems to have been done by scribes as the fever dies down. As early as September 27, 1427 (*Epist.* I, p. 213), he says that he has not yet finished copying Niccoli's Varro because he has become rather negligent in copying. On July 15, 1429 (*Epist.* I, p. 285), he writes that he will from now on abandon the work of copying manuscripts, except for one book (Pliny) that he wants in his collection, if he can find a scribe. The thought is repeated on September 3, 1430 (*Epist.* I, p. 321). After this year there is no further mention of copying, except of his own compositions, and manuscripts are rarely referred to, except those of newly found works.

Only one volume of Livy appears in the inventory of Poggio's library (No. 37, p. 421 Walser): "ti. tulius ab urbe condita in pergamena". The three volume set made by a scribe was probably sold as a whole. Of the autograph copies, the first volume (1843) was sold to Aurispa; the second (1849) does not have the words "ab urbe condita" in the *incipit*, which the inventory includes. Therefore the third (1852) is probably the one mentioned in the inventory.

The *ur* abbreviation in the form of a horizontal figure 8 occurs in these three manuscripts as in other of the later manuscripts. The *g* is similar to those in the recently discussed manuscripts. The second of two *i*'s is taller in the capitals of Poggio's signature in Vat. 1849 (see Fig. 25), as in earlier manuscripts. Copious sampling failed to reveal any use of *ae* in the first writing except for *aeris* on fol. 182r of Vat. 1849 (see Fig. 25). On fol. 2r of Vat. 1843 *colonia deducta* was corrected to *coloniae deductae* (*ae* in ligature), but that was the easiest way to correct. In the margin, but not in the text, we find the spelling *Caesar*, not to correct but to call attention to the name. Thus on fol. 17v the text has *Cesare*, the margin has *Caesar augustus*. The spelling *extimplo* seems to be the regular one.

The dangling connecting stroke of the *ct* ligature occurs when a word is divided between *c* and *t* at the end of a line. I have noted eighteen examples in Vat. 1843, eleven in Vat. 1849, one in Vat. 1852. Two curious examples are found on fols. 140v and 150v of Vat. 1843: *auc-ctoribus* (see Fig. 24) and *dic-ctatore*, where Poggio forgot that he had already written the *c* with its useless appendage. Unusual word divisions are *fui-sse* in Vat. 1843, *hu-ic* and *promis-ssorum* (*sic*) in Vat. 1852. Vat. 1843 has marginalia written by Poggio in a pre-humanistic style, as do his other transcriptions. Accents have been noted on *é* and the adverbs *eó* and *uná* in Vat. 1843 and on *á* in Vat. 1849.

In commenting on a letter of Coluccio, Novati expressed the opinion that some of the additions in Laur. Fies. 12 and 13 (Augustine) were made by Poggio.[47] This is possible, though no certainty can be reached. One objection is that *ct* is sometimes written without ligature, but this occurs also in Laur. 67, 15 (No. 3 above). Novati's further suggestion that Coluccio annotated these two volumes is to be rejected, as the script of the notes is definitely not Coluccio's.

Though not pertinent to the present study, I add here manuscripts and documents in Poggio's less formal hand, which has been labelled *manus velox*, and which retains a Gothic character. Actually, it was the Gothic script with which he had grown up and which was more natural for him. The script in the margins of his books is intermediate between it and his book hand, as has been noted.

Madrid, Bibl. Nac. X, 81, paper. Contains Sigebert, Asconius, Valerius Flaccus. Copied 1416. "Poggius Florentinus". Fig. 27; facsimile of fol. 43r in Schmiedeberg, *op. cit.*, p. 58, Plate I. This facsimile and a photograph always show *e* for *ae* except in *Caesar* and *caedes*, and in these words the letters are separate, not ligatured. The volume is alluded to in *Epist.* I, p. 29 (December 15, 1416). Not seen by me.

Rome, Vat. lat. 11458, paper. Contains Cicero, *Rab. Post.*, *Rab. perd.*, *Rosc. com.*, Valerius Probus, *Not. iuris*; Victorinus, excerpts; Cicero, *Caec.*, *De or.* (fragment), *Leg. agr.* I-III, *Pis.*, selections from

[47] *Epist.* III, p. 656; Fig. 26.

Cael., *Flacc.*, *Font.* Copied 1417. Discovery announced by A. Campana in *Nel cinquantesimo di "Studi e Testi"*, 1900–1950 (Vatican, 1950), p. 79. This very valuable manuscript will be published by him.[48]

Other examples of Poggio's script are in the Archivio of Florence, e.g., Arch. Mediceo A. P. F. VI. p. 717. Also in the Vatican: Karl August Fink, "Poggio-Autographen kurialer Herkunft", in *Miscellanea archivistica Angelo Mercati* (*Studi e Testi*, 165, 1952), p. 129, with facsimiles.

For the sake of completeness I list manuscripts owned by Poggio.[49]

1. Florence, Laur. 37, 11, parchment, *s.* XIV. Seneca, *Trag.* "Liber Poggii". Inventory No. 22. On September 29, 1425 (*Epist.* I, p. 164), Poggio acknowledges a letter of Niccoli which indicated that the latter had come upon a copy of the Tragedies, which Poggio had long desired. On October 20 (*Epist.* I, p. 165) he reveals that the book has arrived but that the price is too high; perhaps he will turn it over to a more prosperous friend (cf. also *Epist.* I, p. 166; November 3, 1425). It may be that he kept the volume after all, and that it is to be identified as Laur, 37, 11.

2. Laur. 45, 16, parchment, *s.* XV. Xenophon, *Cyropaedia*, translated by Poggio. Written in an awkward humanistic script. The *explicit* reads: "Xenophontis historia a Poggio Florentino in Latinum traducta explicit per me Iohannem Pontremulensem 1447 Kalendis Aprilis". "Liber Poggii secretarii". Inventory No. 92. Copied soon after the completion of the translation. An addition on fol. 2 may have been made by Poggio.

3. Laur. 47, 19, parchment, *s.* XV. Poggio, *In avaritiam*, *De nobilitate*, *De infelicitate principum*, *An seni sit uxor ducenda*, *Contra hypocritas*. Copied by a scribe trained in Poggio's script, but the last treatise is in a cursive hand. "Liber Poggii secretarii apostolici". Possibly corrected by Poggio (in the Gothic style he used in margins). Inventory No. 85. The first part was probably copied soon after

48 A probable copy of this book is Florence, Laur. Conv. Soppr. 13, alluded to by Bandini (II, p. 517) as a copy made by Poggio, which it is not. It preserves the subscription of the Vatican manuscript, telling of the discovery of the orations by Poggio.

49 Included are manuscripts which passed through his hands even if he did not retain them to the end of his life. The list is a corrected form of that given in my *Studies*, p. 316, where there are further details on some points.

1440, when *De infelicitate principum* was published. *Contra hypocritas* was published in 1449.

4. Laur. 53, 27, parchment, *s.* XV. Columella. Copied by a scribe trained in Poggio's script. "Liber Poggii", to which a different hand added "quem vendidit Iohanni Cosme de Medicis". Perhaps corrected by Poggio (in his Gothic style). Poggio discovered a Columella in 1417. The sale to Giovanni di Cosimo (1424–63) perhaps was made in the late 1430's or early 1440's. Poggio married in 1436, his childrem came along in 1438, 1440, 1441, 1442, 1448, 1450. In 1437 he sold a manuscript of Jerome's letters to Leonello D'Este for one hundred ducats, a price he had previously been offered and declined (*Epist.* II, p. 122).

5. Laur. 63, 26, parchment, *s.* XV. Valerius Maximus. Copied by a scribe well trained in Poggio's script; it is hard to believe he was the stupid scribe who was copying Valerius in 1427, but so it seems.[50] "Liber Poggii secretarii summi pontificis", to which was added, probably by the same hand but in different ink, "quem vendidit Iohanni Cosme". For the probable time of sale see preceding item.

6. Laur. 79, 10, parchment, *s.* XV. Aristotle, *Ethics*, translated by Leonardo Bruni. "Finit bonis avibus anno domini 1427 mense Septembris die XV hora nona per...". The name was erased, but by ultraviolet rays one can make it out as "Alexium". "Liber Poggii secretarii apostolici". Inventory No. 67. The translation was completed over ten years before this manuscript was copied.

7. Florence, Naz. Conv. Soppr. I. V. 42, parchment, *s.* XIII-XIV. Thomas Aquinas, on Aristotle's Physics. "Liber Poggii". Inventory No. 72. In 1420, while in London, Poggio devoted himself to Aristotle with the help of Thomas Aquinas, but he does not specifically mention the Physics (*Epist.* I, p. 39). The manuscript passed to Giorgio Antonio Vespucci, who gave it to S. Marco, Florence.

8. Vatican, lat. 1629, parchment, *s.* XV. Plautus (twenty plays). Copied by a scribe trained in Poggio's script. "Liber Poggii secretarii apostolici". To this was added: "nunc vero a me Iohanne Atrebatensi episcopo emptus est michique traditus per dominum Baptistam et Iohannem Iacobum liberos ipsius Pogii acceptis ab me ducatis largis viginti quinque die XXVIII Ianuarii MCCCCLIX presentibus I.

50 Wilmanns, *loc. cit.*; cf. Walser, *op. cit.*, p. 110.

Laison scutifero et Petro Feure de Falon". The bishop of Arras is Jean Jouffroy. Inventory No. 24. The complete Plautus was brought to Rome in 1429 by Nicholas of Cues but Poggio was denied the opportunity of having it copied until 1431. In January of that year, when Poggio had not yet had access to it, he dismissed the better of two scribes (*Epist.* I, p. 340). Presumably the other copied the Plautus. L. Delaruelle, *Guillaume Budé* (Paris, 1907), p. 8, wrongly inferred from the colophon that Poggio copied the manuscript.

9. Vatican, lat. 1873, parchment, *s.* X. Ammianus Marcellinus. Presented by Poggio to Cardinal Colonna. Walser, p. 56, n. 4. No indication of Poggio's or Colonna's possession.

10. Vatican, Ottob. lat. 2035, paper, *s.* XV. Cicero, *Epist. Brut.*, *Q. Fr.*, *Oct.*, *Att.* Notes, Greek additions, titles, and initials by Poggio but no ownership mark. I owe my knowledge of the manuscript to Prof. A. Campana. Inventory No. 6; see above p. 44.

11. Vatican, Urb. lat. 436, parchment, *s.* XV. Aemilius Probus (= Cornelius Nepos), *De excellentibus ducibus.* Copied by a scribe trained in the script of Poggio. "Liber Poggii". Perhaps some marginal notes by Poggio. Inventory No. 44.

12. Rome, Biblioteca Nazionale, Vitt. Em. 205, parchment, *s.* XV. Poggio, *De praestantia Caesaris et Scipionis.* This was later bound with a paper manuscript containing other works of Poggio. "Liber Poggi secretar", but this ownership claim was not written by Poggio. The manuscript may have been copied when the work was composed in 1435.

13. Madrid, Bibl. Nac. M, 31, paper, *s.* XV. Manilius, Statius, *Silvae.* At one time this manuscript was bound with Madrid, X, 81, mentioned above, but without Sigebert, as an old table of contents in M, 31 shows. Copied 1417. Inventory No. 59.

14. Phillipps 12278, parchment, *s.* XV; later in Catalogue 81 of William H. Robinson Ltd., 16 Pall Mall, London, now sold to a private collector. Cicero, *De officiis.* Copied by a scribe trained in Poggio's script. Black Florentine binding of fifteenth century. Cannot be proved to have been Poggio's but the binding fits the inventory description (No. 10).

Some manuscripts which have been attributed to Poggio's hand are now lost or must be rejected. The lost (or unidentified) manuscripts include three listed in the inventory of Poggio's library: 2. Cicero, "de natura deorum, de divinatione,... manu Poggii"; 11.

"de offitiis... manu Poggi"; 47. "Quintilianus in papirio... manu Poggi".[51] It was in the Medici library in 1495: E. Piccolomini in *Arch. Stor. Ital.*, Ser III, XX (1874), p. 60, No. 435. Bandini (on Laur. 46, 7) reports that N. Gédoyn in his translation of Quintilian (1718) stated that Poggio's copy (No. 47 of the inventory?) was in the collection of the Earl of Sunderland. I have found no trace of this. A manuscript of Quintilian in the Vatican (Urb. lat. 327, parchment) has the subscription "Scripsit Poggius Florentinus hunc librum Constantie... Hec verba ex originali Poggi sumpta". This manuscript was written by a scribe well trained in the Poggian style, even to the extent of employing the dangling *c* ligature at the end of a line with the *t* at the beginning of the following line, but of course the last sentence in the subscription makes it impossible to credit Poggio with the copying.

Two manuscripts owned by Poggio's son Battista are known to me. Walser's suggestion that one of them, Laur. 35, 21, Lucan, is inventory No. 53 must be rejected, as the manuscript seems to have passed directly from Giorgio Antonio Vespucci to Battista. The other, Vat. lat. 1943, Biondo's *Roma Instaurata*, is credited to Poggio Bracciolini in the card catalogue in the Vatican Library, but there is no indication that Battista obtained it from his father.

Vat. lat. 3330 and 3331, Livy, dated 1455 and 1453, were credited to Poggio's hand by Fulvio Orsini. Nolhac and others accepted this attribution, which is quite inadmissible, as I have shown in my *Studies*.

British Museum, Add. 8799 contains Poggio's *De varietate fortunae*, etc. A note on fol. 1 by Luigi Rigoli, librarian of the Riccardiana in Florence, asserts that the manuscript was copied by Poggio, as shown by its similarity to Poggio autographs in the Riccardiana.[52] The statement is certainly incorrect, as the script is a sloping humanistic cursive with no resemblance to Poggio's hand. A chronicle in this book contains as its last entry a reference to 1461 and the manuscript was probably written in the next year; Poggio died in 1459.

Munich, Staatsbibliothek, lat. 69 has the following subscription

[51] We now know that this copy passed to Poggio's son Iacopo (N. Rubinstein in *Italia medioevale e umanistica*, I [1958], p. 398).

[52] Listed in the Guilford sale (Evans, Dec. 8, 1830), No. 221.

by the scribe (fol. 204r): "Liber Poggii secretarii apostolici explicit" The manuscript was therefore copied from that owned by Poggio, now lost.[53] This sort of thing was very common; see the Quintilian just mentioned (Urb. lat. 327) and note 48.

Bandini (II, p. 503) stated that Gabriel Riccardius had an Asconius transcribed by Poggio. No such copy exists in the Riccardiana today. The only Asconius is 757, which certainly was not Poggio's.

We have surveyed Poggio's writing over a period of some twenty-five years. The changes are not great but some of them are surprising. Starting out as a diphthong writer, he returned to the older practice of using the simple *e*, resorting to the diphthong only occasionally. In another matter too he reverted to Gothic practice, in employing fusion to a greater extent after his early inclination to avoid it. To the spellings *mihi* and *nihil* he held fast throughout. In letter forms he was quite consistent. There was some variation in the shape of the *g*, a new shape was given to the *ur* abbreviation about 1426 (Vat. lat. 2208), the *v* was introduced in 1425 (Laur. 48, 22), the taller second *i* in a pair is met in minuscule as early as 1408 (Berlin, Ham. 166). The employment of Gothic writing in the marginal notes and additions also is seen that early in the same manuscript and is maintained throughout. Word division at the end of lines is fairly regular in the whole period. As we have noted, pains were taken in most manuscripts to avoid splitting the *ct* ligature, but in the latest group of manuscripts we encounter the split *ct* with the connecting stroke suspended helplessly over the *c*. Some of these practices, especially the last two, were preserved by Poggio's imitators, as we shall see in later chapters. In Laur. 67, 15, written in December of 1408 or January of 1409 (No. 3 above) and in Laur. 50, 31 (No. 6 above) Poggio used the phrase "Valeas qui legis" in the colophon. This phrase probably originated with him; it was employed by some of his imitators, as we shall see. In Berlin, Ham. 166 (No. 2 above) the phrase "Lege feliciter" occurs. This too had wide currency, but it is not clear whether it started with Poggio. Vat. Urb. lat. 327, the Quintilian whose scribe copied Poggio's name,

53 The comment of Marx in his edition of Celsus, p. LII, that the subscription is rather an attempt to lure purchasers than a statement of fact, is more cynical than correct. The scribe simply copied what he found in his exemplar.

preserves this phrase, so that we can be sure that Poggio used it in his now lost Quintilian.

The long gap of eleven or more years between 1414 (or earlier) and 1425 for which we have no formal copies by Poggio is easily explained. From 1414 to 1418 he was in Constance or, using Constance as a base, on one of his four voyages of discovery— not to to find a passage to India or a strange continent but to seek manuscripts of unknown works of ancient Roman writers. What copying he did was in *manus velox*. The next four years (1418-1422) Poggio spent in England. In 1423 he returned to Rome and almost immediately started to build his library. He depended largely on Niccoli in Florence for both parchment and the texts to be copied, but Niccoli was very slow. Thus on May 15, 1423, Poggio asked for parchment and the texts of Cicero's *De oratore*, *Orator*, and *Brutus*, but at first he got only the *De oratore*, and that only after repeated requests, so that he did not complete his copy until June, 1425. This copy is Laur. 50, 31, discussed above, the first book he copied, apparently, after his return from England. The other two treatises were added later.

Where did Poggio, with the help of Coluccio, get the idea for his new script? Obviously in manuscripts of the eleventh and twelfth centuries. But what particular manuscript or manuscripts? That question cannot be answered precisely. We can, however, observe that Poggio had access to a large number of books of those centuries, at least thirty or forty and probably many more, in the library of his master Coluccio, as was indicated in Chapter I. Coluccio himself may have been influenced to some extent in his experiment by the script of the manuscript at the end of which he tried it, Marc. 284 (Figs. 8-12). But this is surely not the prototype of Poggio's script. In fact, I do not believe that Poggio had any specific prototype. His script is probably a combination of characteristics found in various manuscripts. Among the books owned by Coluccio perhaps the one closest to Poggio's handwriting is a Solinus in the British Museum (Eg. 818; see Fig. 28). Yet the similarity is not very great. For one thing, the London manuscript lacks the proper shading. In this respect other manuscripts are closer.

Thus far we have been concerned with the origin of Poggio's minuscules. His majuscules are an entirely different matter. With one exception, all his manuscripts reveal capitals based on inscriptions rather than on manuscripts. The one exception is the Strozzianus.

Here we find A in the rustic capital style without cross stroke, uncial E alongside capital E, uncial H, manuscript forms of G and V, even a minuscule *s*. But in the main the letters are respectable capitals, perhaps already influenced by ancient inscriptions. Certainly beginning with the Berlin manuscript of 1408 Poggio developed a majuscule script very closely based on inscriptions. It may be seen in *incipits*, *explicits*, titles, ownership notes, and tables of contents. Poggio had opportunity to see ancient inscriptions at Florence and Fiesole, and of course at Rome he was surrounded by the ancient monuments. When he left Florence he was already interested in inscriptions through the influence of Coluccio. This we can infer from the letter of Coluccio written in December, 1403, already mentioned, in answer to Poggio's report of his arrival in Rome. In it the Florentine chancellor thanked his former disciple for his promptness (*tam celeriter*) in sending copies of some ancient inscriptions. The phrase *tam celeriter* shows that Poggio on his departure from Florence was asked by Coluccio to do this. Poggio's continued interest in ancient inscriptions is well known. In 1429 he published a small collection of inscriptions in his *Sylloge*, a pioneer effort which has been called his most important work.[54] He was not the first to gather inscriptions, indeed in part he himself used an earlier collection, but his book was the seed from which later collections grew, down to the great *Corpus Inscriptionum Latinarum*. Most of the inscriptions were from Rome. Since many of them still exist we can get some notion of the style of lettering that influenced him. For the most part they were imperial and other formal inscriptions, such as those on the arches of Titus, Septimius Severus, and Constantine and on the obelisk now at St. Peter's. On such monuments he found his flaring R and the M with the outside strokes slanting left and right. The QV of Vat. 2208, with the tail passing beyond the V, is very much like that on the Arch of Titus (*C. I. L.* VI, 945; Huebner 245)[55] and the Column of Trajan (*C. I. L.* VI, 960; Huebner 265). The I *longa* Poggio took as early as 1408 (No. 2) from inscriptions, but he used it only in the second of two *i*'s, as it appears on St. Peter's obelisk (*C. I. L.* VI, 882; Huebner 78), IVLII, and on the Arch of the Argentarii (*C. I. L.* VI, 1035; Hueb-

[54] Walser, *op. cit.*, p. 145.

[55] Aemilius Huebner, *Exempla Scripturae Epigraphicae Latinae* (Berlin, 1885).

ner 467), PII. The latter is particularly close to Poggio's usage, as the second I is only slightly taller than the first. In this same inscription, as in others in the *Sylloge*, horizontal lines are used above numerals, and that is Poggio's regular practice (Figs. 17, 25). His use of dots between all words in titles, etc., was of course in direct imitation of the inscriptions. Sometimes he centers the dots but more often he puts them at the bottom of the line of writing.

There is one capital letter, however, that Poggio seems to have preserved in a form not drawn from inscriptions: G. In his usual form of this letter the tail is long and descends well below the line, sometimes curling toward the left. The curl is so decided in the Berlin manuscript of 1408 that the letter resembles an S. But in the Strozzianus of 1402 there is no such curl and the letter turns inward, like the numeral 6. However, in his ownership mark in Vat. Urb. lat. 436 Poggio wrote an inscriptional G and, more important, it is found several times in No. 2, written in 1408. The lower curve of S often projects to the right, beginning with the Strozzianus, and this is a non-inscriptional trait. Nonetheless, it is to Poggio that we owe the introduction into the humanistic script he invented of square capitals based on inscriptions. It happens that the same thing took place in the early stages of Carolingian script. It is possible that Poggio recognized this fact, but he went directly to the inscriptions rather than to the Carolingian imitations. It may, however, be that by mere chance both Carolingian and its humanistic counterpart took their majuscules from inscriptions. Or this parallel development may not be due entirely to chance but partly to the unconscious recognition in both periods that the square capitals of the inscriptions were the most suitable majuscule companions of the minuscule script then in use. In any event, it was an important decision that Poggio made between 1403 and 1408 to imitate the lettering on ancient monuments in his majuscule script. It was then, not at the end of the century, that this momentous step was taken.[56]

[56] James Wardrop in *Signature*, New Series, 2 (1946), p. 6, attributes the development to "that antiquarian interest in the lapidary vestiges of Roman culture which set Felice Feliciano and Mantegna a-burrowing in the Campagna", stating that "from the fruits of such expeditions dates the first significant change in Italian calligraphic practice. Thenceforward, scribes began to assimilate the conventions of Classical Roman capitals, first to the majuscules and later... to

All of Poggio's copies in humanistic script are on parchment; the two in the Gothic *manus velox* are on paper. The paper copies were meant to be for temporary use; the finely written parchment codices were intended not only for Poggio but for posterity as well (*Epist.* I, p. 265; 1429). Much the same situation holds for those which scribes copied for him. Apart from Madrid M, 31, which may be said to be in *manus velox* like its Poggian companion X, 81, only Ottob. lat. 2035 is on paper. Perhaps a study of the connection of this manuscript of Cicero's letters to Atticus with Laur. 49, 24 and other manuscripts might supply a reason.

So much for Poggio the inventor of a new system of handwriting. We proceed to consider a rival system, that of Niccolò Niccoli.

the minuscules of the humanistic script". We may grant that at the end of the fifteenth century a new wave of interest in inscriptions and their script set in, but surely Poggio cannot be ignored as the one who started the movement.

CHAPTER III

A RIVAL SYSTEM — NICCOLÒ NICCOLI

In his stimulating and valuable monograph on "Early Humanistic Script and the First Roman Type" Stanley Morison suggested Niccolò Niccoli as the possible inventor of the new script but he did not press the point.[1] As Niccoli was older than Poggio this thought is a natural one. But the date we have given to Poggio's copying of the *De verecundia* (1402-03) and that of the Berlin Cicero (1408) precede anything that has been attributed to Niccoli. Besides, as Morison says, Niccoli was not a professional scribe. Niccoli's script is not, even at its most formal, the kind that ultimately produced the early printed fonts.

Niccoli is a man of some mystery. Like his close friend Poggio, who was his junior by sixteen years, he came under the influence of Coluccio Salutati. Since they both lived in Florence, we have no letters addressed to him by Coluccio. Furthermore, Coluccio's references to him in letters to others are few and brief. We have many letters of Poggio, Bruni, and Ambrogio Traversari to Niccoli but none of his replies. In fact, the only letter of his known to me is the one to Cosimo which will be quoted in a later chapter. He wrote only one short book, as we shall see, and that is not extant.[2] We know him from the remarks of his contemporaries and from his library, which he left to S. Marco in Florence, now divided between the Laurentian library and the Nazionale Centrale

1 *The Library*, XXIV (1943). Before him G. Voigt had suggested that Niccoli perhaps was the inventor, Poggio in any case the master (*Die Wiederbelebung des classischen Alterthums*, ed. 3, I [Berlin, 1893], p. 398).

2 The *Commentarium* can hardly be called a book or even a treatise. It is a mere list of classical authors and northern monasteries where manuscripts of their works could be found, together with a list of lost and found works; R. Robinson, "The Inventory of Niccolò Niccoli", *Classical Philology*, XVI (1921), p. 251. Besides, it is practically a copy of a list made up by Poggio (N. Rubinstein in *Italia medioevale e umanistica*, I [1958], p. 383).

of Florence. The S. Marco librarians carefully noted on the flyleaves of many books that these came from the legacy of Niccolò Niccoli. It is surprising that no one has published a list of these books. [3]

Niccoli's handwriting too is somewhat of a mystery because he did not sign his name to any of the manuscripts that he copied. The reason is that, unlike Poggio, he did not copy manuscripts to be sold or to be kept for posterity. This is indicated too by the fact that he invariably wrote on paper in spite of having available in Florence the best parchment in Italy, as we know from Poggio's numerous requests to him for writing material.

The script of Niccoli in the manuscripts generally attributed to him is not of a formal humanistic type such as that practiced by Poggio and his imitators. Rather it is a humanistic cursive, with a sprinkling of Gothic. It is in fact the kind of hand that led to the italic type fonts, just as the script of his friend Poggio was the prototype of the roman type fonts. To be sure, Vespasiano da Bisticci says: "Le [copie] scriveva di sua mano o di lettera corsiva o formata, che dell'una lettera e dell'altra era bellissimo scrittore; come si vede in Sancto Marco di più libri che vi sono di sua mano, dell'una lettera e dell'altra." [4] He immediately proceeds to say that Niccoli had succeeded in obtaining Tertullian, Ammianus, and Cicero's *Orator* and *Brutus*. It may be mere chance that Niccoli's copies of these are written in his cursive style. However, until someone can make a convincing identification of a formal ("formata") script of Niccoli, I, at least, shall remain skeptical about Vespasiano's statement.

If Niccoli did not sign his copies how can we identify them and determine their dates? The question is not easily answered. For some manuscripts we have fifteenth-century statements that Niccoli copied them. We know from various letters that Niccoli transcribed certain works, and this information leads us to examine copies of those works once in Niccoli's collection. Comparison

[3] In a footnote C. Wotke lists a few such books, mostly Greek, in the Laurentian library as if they included most of those left; the number is far greater (Wotke in *Wiener Studien*, XI [1889], p. 301, n. 5).

[4] Vespasiano da Bisticci, *Vite di uomini illustri del secolo XV*, ed. P. D'Ancona and E. Aeschlimann (Milan, 1951), p. 435.

of handwriting leads to further identification. I shall list in chronological order, as far as possible, those which I accept as Niccoli's handiwork, then those which I reject, after which I shall deal with the script and its bearing on the identification.

1. Florence, Nazionale Conv. Soppr. I. I. 14 (S. Marco 261). Fig. 29. Cicero, *Orator, Brutus.* From the collection of Niccolò Niccoli, presented to S. Marco. Until Landriani discovered a complete manuscript of Cicero's rhetorical works in the cathedral library of Lodi in 1421 only mutilated manuscripts of the *De oratore* and *Orator* were circulated in Italy, and the *Brutus* was entirely unknown. Thus Niccoli's copies must have been written in or after 1421. We can, however, date his *Orator* more closely. We saw in the preceding chapter that Poggio asked for the text of the three works in May, 1423. He did not receive the *De oratore* until April, 1425, and the other works somewhat later. On the other hand, Giovanni Aurispa wrote Ambrogio Traversari on February 11, 1424, that Niccoli was having the *Brutus* copied for him.[5] On August 27, 1424, he wrote that while he was still in Constantinople (i.e., in 1423) Niccoli informed him that he was having *De oratore* copied for him; this, added Aurispa, had not yet been received. Traversari replied on September 1 that he was surprised that Niccoli had not yet sent *De oratore*, *Orator*, and *Brutus.* On September 13 Aurispa again asked Traversari to urge Niccoli to send Cicero's works, and on October 26 he repeated his request for *Orator* and *Brutus.* Finally on December 1 he reported the arrival of *Orator* and *Brutus* and awaited the copying of *De oratore.* Let us see if these bits of information can be put together into a meaningful picture.

Just when and how a copy of the Lodi *De oratore* became available to Niccoli we do not know. Vespasiano da Bisticci tells us that *Orator* and *Brutus* were brought to Niccoli from Milan in 1423. Since Naz. Conv. Soppr. I. I. 14, which contains these works, once belonged to Niccoli, Sabbadini assumed that it was

[5] These and the following references to Aurispa's letters are from R. Sabbadini, *Carteggio di Giovanni Aurispa* (Rome, 1931), pp. 8, 15, 18, 19, 20. Aurispa seems to have sold the *Orator* and *Brutus* manuscript, for in 1430 he asks for another (p. 67).

the manuscript brought from Milan.[6] But by comparison with other manuscripts I conclude that the script is that of Niccoli and that the Milan manuscript was merely loaned to Niccoli so that he could make a copy. If Sabbadini is right in saying that Laur. 50, 18, which is dated October 1, 1423, is a copy of the Niccoli codex, then the transcription of the latter took place earlier in the same year.

Niccoli sent his transcriptions of the three works to Poggio as a loan so that the latter could copy them, but to Aurispa he presented copies. Why did Poggio receive the *De oratore* before the other two and why did Aurispa receive his copies in the reverse order? Niccoli perhaps did not carry out his promise of 1423 to Aurispa about the *De oratore* because his manuscript was being used for the production of copies for others. In April and May of 1425, Poggio had it. After its return Niccoli presumably had the copy made for Aurispa, though we do not really know that the latter received it.

Up to October 1 of 1423 the *Brutus* and *Orator* were not available to Poggio because Laur. 50, 18 was being copied for Cosimo de' Medici. The next year they were being copied for Aurispa. We may well conjecture that Niccoli had many demands for the loan of his books and for copies of them. Poggio's importunities tell only one side of the story; unfortunately we do not have Niccoli's letters. Kroymann calls five existing manuscripts of Tertullian direct copies of Niccoli's manuscript and Clark says that six of our Ammianus manuscripts were copied directly from Niccoli's; Hosius finds eight manuscripts most closely related to their source, Niccoli's Lucretius.[7] Vespasiano's remark that when Niccoli died it was discovered that two hundred of his

[6] Vespasiano, *loc. cit.* Two leaves of a ninth-century *Brutus* were recently found in Cremona, and the fortunate discoverer, Isabella Pettenazzi, suggests that the leaves once formed part of the Lodi manuscript (*Boll. Stor. Cremonese*, XX [1955-57], p. 83). This seems reasonable enough, especially since we know that a certain Cosimo of Cremona copied the Lodi manuscript for Barzizza, but Dr. Mainardi, to whose kindness I owe my knowledge of Signorina Pettenazzi's article, writes me that there are indications to the contrary. The matter awaits further investigation. R. Sabbadini, *Storia e critica di testi latini* (Catania, 1914), p. 432.

[7] See notes 10, 12, and 15.

manuscripts were out on loan may be exaggerated but fundamentally it has a truthful ring about it.[8]

2. Nazionale Conv. Soppr. I. V. 43 (S. Marco 335). Fig. 30; Morison, Figs. 8 (fol. 1r), 16 (fol. 245r). Ammianus. A fifteenth-century librarian of S. Marco wrote on the flyleaf: "Ex hereditate doctissimi Niccolai Niccoli Florentini cuius manu est scriptus." This testimony is the best we have for assigning any manuscript to Niccoli's hand. On November 6, 1423, Poggio remarked to Niccoli (*Epist.* I, p. 97) that he was glad to hear that Niccoli had finished copying Ammianus. This establishes the date of the manuscript as 1423 if we admit that Niccoli was the copyist.[9] It was copied directly from the ninth-century manuscript found by Poggio at Fulda in 1417, now in the Vatican (lat. 1873), which fact confirms the ascription to Niccoli.[10] In a letter of 1448 (*Epist.* II, p. 375) Poggio stated that the Fulda manuscript was in the possession of Cardinal Colonna, and the paper copy made by Niccoli was in the library of Cosimo de' Medici. Both parts of this statement, that Niccoli's copy was on paper and that it was in Cosimo's library, confirm the identification of the S. Marco manuscript as the Niccoli transcript, for Cosimo placed Niccoli's manuscripts in the monastery of S. Marco.[11]

3. Nazionale Conv. Soppr. I. VI. 11 (S. Marco 529). Fig. 31. Tertullian. A fifteenth-century librarian of S. Marco wrote on the flyleaf: "Ex hereditate Nicolai de Nicolis viri doctissimi Florentini cuius etiam manu scriptus." The copy was made from one transcribed in Germany in 1426 for Cardinal Giordano Orsini. The Cardinal's manuscript is now Naz. Conv. Soppr. I. VI. 10. Thus Niccoli's transcription was made in 1426 or soon after.[12]

[8] *Op. cit.* p. 437.

[9] Not between 1410-15 as Morison concludes from the handwriting (*op. cit.*, p. 9). Similarly his dating of No. 4 is incorrect.

[10] C. U. Clark, *The Text Tradition of Ammianus Marcellinus* (New Haven, 1904), pp. 60-61, 67; his edition (Berlin, 1910), p. V; R. Sabbadini, *Le scoperte dei codici latini e greci ne' secoli XIV e XV*, II (Florence, 1914), p. 192.

[11] Mehus' statement in the preface to Ambrosius Traversarius, *Latinae Epistolae*, p. XXXVII, that Niccoli copied the manuscript for Cosimo, must have been based on Poggio's letter.

[12] R. Sabbadini, *Scoperte*, II, pp. 255-256; E. Kroymann in *Akad. d. Wiss., Wien, Sitzber.* 138, III (1898), p. 15.

4. Florence, Laur. 73, 7. Fig. 32. Celsus. Note on flyleaf signed by Baccius Baldinus: "Hic Celsi liber exaratus est manu Nicolai Niccoli, viri diligentis et eruditi, qui abundavit copia antiquorum exemplariorum, cuiusque scripturae Angelus Politianus magnam fidem habere solitus erat; itaque ipsius testimonium saepe citat. Quod tibi, lector, cognitum esse volui, ne forte, cum tu non satis vetustum librum videres, subito contemneres neque ipsi aliquid auctoritatis habendum putares." This Baldinus was not the engraver (ca. 1436–1487) but the librarian of the Laurentian at the end of the sixteenth century.

Sabbadini believed that Panormita brought an old manuscript of Celsus found in Siena to Florence in 1427, that from this Niccoli made his copy, and that Antonio di Mario also made his (Laur. 73, 5) in the same year from the same source.[13] But Marx was skeptical about Panormita's bringing the manuscript to Florence. He thought Niccoli went to Siena to copy it; in support of this view he cited a letter of Poggio dated October 21, 1427 (*Epist.* I, p. 214), in which Poggio said that he had heard that Niccoli had gone to Siena for some reason or other.[14] Marx also maintained that Antonio's copy (Laur. 73, 5) was based on Niccoli's, not directly on the old Siena manuscript. One slight difficulty suggests itself: Antonio finished his copy July 8, 1427, in Florence. That would mean that Niccoli's copy was made in Siena not later than July 1. It would seem odd that Poggio did not hear of this trip until four months or more later. In any case, Sabbadini and Marx agree that Niccoli's transcription was made in 1427.

5. Laur. 35, 30. Fig. 33; Morison, Figs. 9 (fol. 99r), 15 (fol. 164r); Leonard-Smith Lucretius Plate VIII (fol. 135v). Lucretius. Mehus' attribution of this manuscript to Niccoli has met general acceptance.[15] Poggio found an old Lucretius in Germany in 1417. A letter of his to Francesco Barbaro first published in full by A. C. Clark reveals that he did not obtain the old manu-

[13] R. Sabbadini, *Storia*, pp. 297-298, 310-313.

[14] F. Marx in his edition of Celsus (*Corpus Medicorum Latinorum*, I [Leipzig, 1915]), pp. XL ff.

[15] Mehus, *op. cit.*, p. L; Sabbadini, *Scoperte*, II, p. 233, n. 1. For Niccoli's manuscript and its descendants see C. Hosius in *Rheinisches Museum*, 69 (1914), p. 109.

script itself or even copy it himself: [16] "Lucretius mihi nondum redditus est, cum sit scriptus. Locus est satis longinquus neque unde aliqui veniant. Itaque exspectabo quoad aliqui accedant qui illum deferant. Sin autem nulli venient, non praeponam publica privatis." This means that a copy had been made by a local scribe in the monastery or town where the old manuscript lay but had not been delivered to Poggio in Constance because of communication difficulties. Should it not arrive soon he would give up his public duties and go after it. Clark dates the letter between January and May of 1418. Niccoli's copy was therefore made from the transcript that Poggio obtained.[17] When it was made cannot be precisely determined. On April 14, 1425 (*Epist.* I, p. 148), Poggio asks Niccoli to send him the Lucretius, which will be transcribed in fifteen days and then returned. The request is renewed on May 12 (*Epist.* I, p. 150) and on June 14 (*Epist.* I, p. 154), but on the latter date he extends the time limit to a month. Poggio tries again on September 14, 1426 (*Epist.* I, p. 187). On May 17, 1427 (*Epist.* I, p. 208) Poggio writes Niccoli that Bartolomeo da Montepulciano, his old companion during his manuscript hunts, was trying to get him (Poggio) a Lucretius, but must proceed with caution, "barbari enim sunt et suspiciosi." Obviously Bartolomeo was trying to get hold of the old German manuscript of which Poggio had received only a copy. Just before the sentence quoted and just after it Poggio talks about other German manuscripts. Perhaps Niccoli was not satisfied with the condition of the text in the copy he had from Poggio and wanted the original. On December 13, 1429 (*Epist.* I, p. 295), Poggio expostulates with Niccoli for having kept his Lucretius twelve years — which is about right — and two weeks later he raises the figure to fourteen — which is exaggerated. He adds plaintively in both letters that he would like to read his Lucretius, which he never had been able to finish. That is the last we hear of Lucretius. Possibly Niccoli held off making his own copy until he was satisfied with the text and for that reason did not return Poggio's manuscript. A paper copy is mentioned in Poggio's

16 *Classical Review*, XIII (1899), p. 125.

17 Cf. Max Lehnerdt, *Lucretius in der Renaissance* (1904).

inventory (No. 63). This could have been the one made for Poggio in Germany.

In Laur. 35, 30 short summaries precede every book of Lucretius. These presumably originated with Niccoli.

6. Nazionale Conv. Soppr. I. IV. 26 (S. Marco 329). Fig. 34. Aulus Gellius. On July 8, 1431, Traversari wrote to Niccoli (VIII, 2) that he was awaiting with interest the last fourteen books of Gellius, which Niccoli had copied and emended, and would be glad to insert the Greek words as Niccoli requested. Sabbadini naturally assumed that the last fourteen books would be VI-VII, IX-XX (VIII is missing in all manuscripts).[18] Now our early manuscripts are divided into two groups, one containing Books I-VII, the other IX-XX. Sabbadini concluded that Niccoli's manuscript was a complete one, mutilated at the beginning. Not knowing, however, that Niccoli's manuscript still exists, he was unaware of its contents. It contains Books IX-XX, like other manuscripts of the second group, but they are numbered X-XXIII, which would seem to give fourteen books. This is because not only IX, but also XV and XXII are skipped in the numbering — or rather Niccoli's XXI has XXII in the *explicit*. After independently identifying the script as Niccoli's, I found that Hertz in Vol. II of his *editio maior* of 1885 (p. LXIV) stated that the manuscript was in Niccoli's hand, basing this view on Mehus.[19] A flyleaf containing the S. Marco ownership note and probably a statement that it came from Niccoli, perhaps even that it was in his hand (as in other manuscripts), has, it seems, been lost. The last pages, containing the preface, were added by a later hand, as Hertz recognized.

7. Nazionale Conv. Soppr. I. I. 12 (S. Marco 228). Fig. 35. Plautus, last twelve plays. During the Middle Ages in general and among the early humanists only the first eight plays of Plautus were known. In the 1420's Nicholas of Cues discovered at Cologne a manuscript containing, besides the first four, the last twelve, new to the humanists. This manuscript is now Vat. lat. 3870 of the tenth or eleventh century. Poggio mentions Nicholas' various

[18] R. Sabbadini, *Scoperte*, I, p. 92.

[19] Mehus, *op. cit.*, p. XLIII, does not give the S. Marco number, but Hertz identified the manuscript from his description.

discoveries from 1427 on (*Epist.* I, p. 208, etc.), but the Plautus is not alluded to until February 26, 1429 (*Epist.* I, p. 268; dated 1428 but presumably in Florentine style). Poggio lists the plays as given to him by Nicholas in a letter. Nicholas brought the manuscript itself to Rome in December, 1429 (*Epist.* I, p. 304), and gave it to Cardinal Orsini, who refused to let anyone see it for some time (*Epist.* I, pp. 320, 338). The manuscript finally reached Florence in June of 1431 and Niccoli made his copy of the last twelve plays after September of 1431 or early in 1432, for in that year it was restored to Orsini.[20] The S. Marco flyleaf, presumably indicating that the manuscript was the gift of Niccoli, is missing.

8. Nazionale Conv. Soppr. I. VI. 6 (S. Marco 574). Fig. 36. John Chrysostom, commentary on Paul's Epistles to Titus, Timothy, and Philemon, three letters to Olympias, in the translation of Ambrogio Traversari. From Niccoli's collection. Mehus (p. XXXII) says that the monk Michael perhaps wrote the first work and (without "perhaps") the first six sermons of the second (fols. 1-65v). I do not know on what he bases the identification of the first scribe, but in my opinion the same man copied fols. 1-65v. I agree with Mehus that Niccoli wrote sermons VII-XIII, including the *explicit* of XIII and the *incipit* of XIV, on fols. 65v-88v. The third hand, attributed to the translator Ambrogio by Mehus, copied sermons XIV-XVIII (fols. 92v-102r) and wrote at the end: "Absolvi II Kalendas Novembris in nostro monasterio Fontis Boni anno domini 1432." This is the monastery of Camaldoli in the former castle of Fontebuono, and presumably that is why Mehus credited Traversari with the copying of this portion. A fourth hand wrote the letters to Olympias (fols. 103r-115r). He also copied the commentary on Second Timothy and Philemon (fols. 119r-155r) but at a different time and with different ink. On fol. 148v he wrote: "Explicit... feliciter 18 Iulii 1429." As the entire manuscript came to St. Mark's from Niccoli's library, it is obvious that it was written for Niccoli. I have no simple explanation of the two dates in the manuscript but I judge that Niccoli wrote his

20 Sabbadini, *Storia*, p. 329. In *Ottanta lettere inedite del Panormita* (Catania, 1910), p. 135, Sabbadini observes that Niccoli was away from Florence when the manuscript arrived and that he did not return until September.

part in 1432. Traversari made the translation between 1429 and the last half of 1432.[21]

Vespasiano da Bisticci relates that one day Ambrogio translated Chrysostom on the Epistles of Paul in the presence of Cosimo and Niccoli, and that the latter wrote down what Ambrogio translated in a cursive hand, of which he was a very swift writer. Still he could not keep up with Ambrogio and often had to tell him to slow down. These translations in Niccoli's hand, says Vespasiano, are still in S. Marco.[22] If our manuscript is the one Vespasiano meant, his tale cannot be accurate.

9. Nazionale Conv. Soppr. I. X. 44 (S. Marco 346). Fig. 37. Plutarch, Lives of Alexander and Caesar translated by Guarino, of Aristides and Cato translated by Francesco Barbaro. From Niccoli's collection. Only the lives translated by Guarino were copied by Niccoli, another scribe did the rest. But in view of the fact that the book was left to S. Marco by Niccoli, the second scribe must have copied for Niccoli. Since Guarino finished his translation of the Caesar in 1415, Niccoli may have made his copy as early as that year.[23] Barbaro's translations were completed in 1417, the earliest possible year therefore of the transcription of Aristides and Cato.[24] But of course the book may have been copied much later. Mehus was correct in assigning the copying of the first two lives in this manuscript to Niccoli.[25]

All nine of these manuscripts were written by the same man, I am quite sure. Certain of his highly individual characteristics will be discussed in a moment and can be studied in the illustrations. But is the writer to be identified as Niccoli? At first a skeptic, I have come to the conclusion that he was the scribe. No one bit of evidence is absolutely convincing, but the cumulative effect is formidable. In the first place Nos. 1, 2, 3, 8, 9 were in the possession of Niccoli as attested by the statements on the flyleaves written by librarians of S. Marco. Nos. 6 and 7 are

21 A. Dini-Traversari, *Ambrogio Traversari e i suoi tempi* (Florence, 1912), p. 132, based on Mehus, *op. cit.*

22 *Op. cit.*, p. 244.

23 R. Sabbadini, *Epistolario di Guarino Veronese*, III (Venice, 1919), p. 324. But a copy exists with the date 1414 (see Chapter V).

24 *Ibid.*, p. 61, based on Traversari, *Epist.* VI, 16.

25 *Op. cit.*, p. XLIX.

also from S. Marco but the flyleaves which would have contained the reference to Niccoli as the donor are missing. Nos. 4 and 5, in the Laurentian library, were presumably retained by Cosimo de' Medici, to whom Niccoli's library was given by the collector's executors and who placed most of them in S. Marco. Nos. 2 and 3 were copied by Niccoli according to a fifteenth-century librarian of S. Marco, and this is the best evidence we have for any of the manuscripts. The excellent scholar Mehus identified the script of all nine manuscripts as Niccoli's, but he had no other information than we have, that about Nos. 2 and 3 and the identity of the script of the rest with that of these manuscripts.[26]

Confirming evidence is furnished by contemporary letters which indicate that Niccoli had a copy of Cicero, *Orator* and *Brutus* (contained in No. 1), that he copied Ammianus (on paper) and Gellius (Nos. 2, 6), and that he had access to and presumably transcribed copies of Tertullian, Celsus, Lucretius, and Plautus (Nos. 3, 4, 5, 7). Kroymann gives evidence to show that No. 3 (Tertullian) is a direct copy of the manuscript brought from Germany in 1426 (now Naz. Conv. Soppr. I. VI. 10).[27] It is quite possible that other transcriptions of Niccoli may be found in the S. Marco collections of the Laurenziana and the Nazionale Centrale of Florence, but it is a wild exaggeration to say, as J. A. Symonds did, that he "transcribed nearly the whole of the codices that formed the nucleus of the Library of the Mark." [28]

Eight of the nine manuscripts can be dated between 1423 and 1432. It is disappointing that no earlier specimens have been identified. Perhaps they exist but are disguised under a different style of writing.

The most striking characteristics of Niccoli's writing are his *g*, final *s*, *ct* and *et* ligatures. The lower part of the *g* is large and often irregular, *ct* has a sweeping connecting stroke, *et* is tall. Other peculiarities are in *e* and *x*, especially the combination of

26 As Mehus does not give the library numbers it took some time to locate some of the manuscripts. Nos. 7, 8, and 9 have not, so far as I know, been identified by modern scholars since Mehus' day. Of the nine, Morison mentions only three (Nos. 2, 4, 5).

27 *Loc. cit.* (see note 12).

28 *Renaissance in Italy, The Revival of Learning*, Chapter III.

these two. Sometimes *r* sinks below the line. Ascenders tend to turn to the right at the top or to have small loops. In fact, almost every letter has some individual touch, as may be seen from the reproductions.

Another test can be applied: the diphthong test. First, however, a brief history of the diphthong question among the early humanists must be presented. Investigation of orthographical matters was thoroughly under way in Salutati's day, though only a beginning was made of writing the diphthongs, as we saw in Chapter I. Guarino was the first to write a treatise on diphthongs, probably in 1415.[29] In the introduction he says he will give what he remembers from Latin and what little of Greek he learned from Chrysoloras: "Decrevi quod una tumultuaria lucubratione potuero ad te diphthongos colligere quae Latinae lectionis memoria suppeditarit aut si quid paululum Grecae ex doctissimo ac in primis humanissimo praeceptore meo Manuele Chrisolora degustavi." Then he presents a list of words that should be written with *ae* or *oe*, both Latin words and those transliterated from Greek.[30] The allusion to Chrysoloras is significant and important: it reveals that the Greek scholar who came to Florence in 1396 largely through Coluccio's efforts, and who enlightened the Florentine chancellor on some points of Greek orthography, was in part, perhaps in large part, responsible for the concern with diphthongs, certainly in the case of Guarino, probably also in that of Niccoli. In his *Erotemata*, an elementary Greek grammar probably written soon after his arrival in Florence,[31] Chrysoloras carefully distinguishes the diphthongs from the monophthongs. Gasparino Barzizza, who deals with diphthongs in his *Orthographia* of 1418,[32] perhaps was influenced by Guarino's treatise, as Sabbadini inferred from Barzizza's remark: "Nec sum in eo occupatus ut artem aliquam

29 That is the date suggested by Sabbadini, *La scuola e gli studi di Guarino Guarini veronese* (Catania, 1896), p. 48.

30 The treatise was printed several times. I used the edition of 1485 (Venice, Bernardinus de Benaliis; Hain 8115), in which this work follows *Regulae grammaticales*, and also a manuscript in the Marucelliana of Florence (C 376), copied by P. Cennini. *Quod* is used in the sense of *quoad*; the edition of 1478 has *quantum*.

31 G. Cammelli, *Manuele Crisolora* (Florence, 1941), p. 83.

32 Sabbadini, *Scuola*, p. 48.

de diphthongis tradere velim, quae enucleata sit ac diffinita; nam id accuratissime a nonnullis ex nostris hominibus factum esse video." [33]

A number of Niccoli's contemporaries alluded to his concern with diphthongs. In 1413 Guarino attacked Niccoli in a diatribe containing these words: "Proxime venit in manus ab eo editum in lucem opusculum quod ille ad erudiendos compilavit adulescentes; inscribitur autem orthographia... Tot in ea contra artis praecepta describuntur vocabula ut correptas natura syllabas diphthongis annotare non pudeat." [34] In 1420 Lorenzo di Marco Benvenuti published a diatribe against Niccoli in the course of which he said: "ut sciolus videaris inter puerorum greges et buccinatorum choros diphtongos repperis et antiquas, ut ais, litteras consectaris." [35] In 1424 Leonardo Bruni launched an invective in which he wrote: "O praeclare consumptum sexagesimum annum, siquidem nondum puerilibus ludis exivit, sed diphtongos etiam nunc digammaque meditatur." [36] Giuseppe Brippi wrote verses in which he referred to the same preoccupation of Niccoli: "efficit ipse Scribere diphthongos." [37] And in the *Paradiso degli Alberti* Niccoli's highest ambition is "una bella lettera antica, la quale non stima bella e buona, se ella non è di forma antica et bene dittongata." [38] The dramatic date of the Paradiso is 1389 but the actual date is probably later.[39] The single manuscript, which I have examined, is of the fifteenth century.

There is then quite a bit of evidence from 1413 to about 1426 that Niccoli was concerned with diphthongs, though, of course,

33 *Ibid.*

34 R. Sabbadini, *Epistolario di Guarino Veronese*, I (Venice, 1915), p. 38. Sabbadini denied "risolutamente" that Niccoli wrote an *Orthographia* (*Guarino*, III, p. 25). G. Zippel's attempts to find a copy were futile (*Niccolò Niccoli* [Florence, 1890], p. 47). I checked his suggestions as to possible manuscripts of this work and found them incorrect.

35 G. Zippel in *Giornale storico della letteratura italiana*, XXIV (1894), p. 172.

36 Wotke in *Wiener Studien*, XI (1889), p. 298; somewhat differently in G. Zippel, *Niccolò Niccoli*, p. 85.

37 Mehus, *op. cit.*, p. LXXXI.

38 Ed. A. Wesselofsky, I, 2 (Bologna, 1867), p. 327.

39 That was my view even before seeing H. Baron, *Humanistic and Political Literature in Florence and Venice* (Cambridge, 1955), p. 34, who makes a good case for 1426 or soon afterwards as the date of composition.

some of the writers may merely have echoed what others said and wrote.

Let us now see how the nine manuscripts attributed to Niccoli in the preceding discussion meet the diphthong test. No. 1 (*Orator, Brutus*) on eight scattered pages has *ae* every time, and also where it does not belong: *schaemata* and *plaeraeque*. *Plaereque, alienae*, and *Scevola* were corrected to *Plaeraeque, aliaenae*, and *Scaevola*. Elsewhere I noted *Nevius* corrected to *Naevius*. *Ceteri* is so spelled (three times). *Paene* was corrected to *pene*, which seems less strange when we note that such is the spelling in later manuscripts. On other pages of this manuscript I noted two other corrections of this word from *paene* and *poene* to *pene* and one original spelling of *pene*.

No. 2 (Ammianus) has *ae* or *oe* on ten pages except for *Megera*. *Ethio* was corrected with a cedilla. The enthusiasm for diphthongs caused some errors: *moetu* (the *o* was later expunged), *agilitatae, aepulis*. The cedilla is used at the end of a line in abbreviated *quae* to save space, in *Aethio* presumably as a correction, and one other time. The adverb *paene* is spelled *pene* (twice).

No. 3 (Tertullian) on twenty pages follows the same general pattern. *Paene* is again spelled *pene* in the one instance found. Even *interpraetari* and *estotae* have the diphthong. In a few cases the prefix *pre* is so written. Niccoli seems to have had trouble with *saeculum*. It is so spelled four times, *seculum* four times, and *seculum* with a cedilla once. *Ceteri* is so written.

No. 4 (Celsus) on ten pages has only *ae*, even in *caeteri* (twice), *inaedia, Aeretria* and *caeleriter*.

No. 5 (Lucretius) on twenty-one pages regularly reveals *ae*, even in *aegestas* and *Eaecus*. Exceptions are *leta, letificos, fetus, Dedala, leva*. *Aeger* occurs three times, *eger* once; *foedus* once, *fedus* once. On seventy-five pages *prae* as preposition or prefix is written fifty times, *pre* thirteen times. It looks as if the writing of *e* for *ae* was due to oversight in copying from a manuscript that had only *e*.

On twenty-two pages No. 6 (Gellius) regularly has *ae*, even in *castitatae* (ablative), *huiuscae, compraecationes*, and *praetium* (twice). Exceptions are *tedium* (once), *e* once in an ending, once in *istec*, once in the prefix *pre*. *Ceteri* is the regular spelling (three times), as is *Lacedemon* (twice).

No. 7 (Plautus) is much the same. Here too *istec* is found (four times as against *istaec* once) on thirty-two pages. Other spellings are *caena* (four times), *aedepol* (twenty-one times). *Etas* occurs once but *aetas* ten times; *illec* and *illaec* once each. Other spellings are *ceteri* (twice), *Menechmus* (twice), *pene*, *hedus* (twice), *mechus*, *palestra*, *Dedalis*.

No. 8 (Chryostom) reveals nothing unusual on eleven pages. *Ceteri* appears seven times, *seculum* eight, *scena* three.

On twenty pages No. 9 (Plutarch) has the usual preponderance of *ae*. *Ceteri* is found eight times, *caeteri* four. *Coepisset* is used twice for *cepisset*; *letus* for *laetus* three times. *Prelio* occurs four times, *proelio* once. Single examples include *aedidisse*, *saeveritate*, *praessum* (for *pressum*), *levam*.

Accent marks appear in one or another of these nine manuscripts as follows: *á*, *é*, *ó*; the adverbs *eó*, *illó*, *uná*; *éadem* (nom.), *stabiliréque*, *impendére*.

When a word is divided at the end of a line between *c* and *t* no ligature is used. Generally the word is so divided as to put the ligatured *ct* at the beginning of the next line. No ligature joins capital CT.

Unusual word division is confined to *a-u*, so often found in Poggio: *la-udes*, *ca-usa*, *a-udio*, *a-utem*, *ha-ud*, etc.

No. 5 (Lucretius) ends with the words "lege feliciter amen", the first two of which are often found in humanistic manuscripts from Poggio on. No. 1 (*Orator*, *Brutus*) has "lege feliciter" in the *incipit* of the *Brutus*.

All nine manuscripts were written on paper in a cursive hand. Niccoli made no pretense of producing beautiful manuscripts either for himself or for such collectors as Cosimo de' Medici. He was anxious to present a good text, copied from an old manuscript and emended by himself. His copies served as exemplars for many fine manuscripts, but he himself strove only for legibility. He has no fine illuminated initials, he makes no particular effort to justify his pages, he does not avoid dividing the last word of a page.

The watermarks are of slight help. I have dated Nos. 1 and 2 to 1423. They are the only ones that have a large N for a watermark and the same style of basilisk.[40] The bow and the horn

[40] C. M. Briquet, *Les Filigranes*, ed. 2, 4 vols. (Leipzig, 1923). For the N see No. 8426, etc.; for the basilisk, No. 781, etc.

are found in No. 2 (1423) and No. 8 ("1423 or shortly before"). No. 8 also seems to have a basilisk but apparently of a different style. No. 4 (1427) too has a bow and perhaps a basilisk like that in No. 8. The very common mountain is found in six of the manuscripts but it occurs alone in No. 3 ("1426 or soon after") and No. 7 ("1431 or 1432"). Apart from this No. 9 has an entirely different set of watermarks from the others, which may indicate an early date.

Besides the manuscripts listed others have been claimed for Niccoli. The most important is Cicero's *De oratore* (Florence, Laur. 50, 46). Bandini is responsible for this identification.[41] The chances are against Niccoli even possessing this manuscript, for it does not contain his name as owner but that of the abbot of Settimo, near Florence.

Two different scribes, neither of them Niccoli, copied the codex. The first wrote fols. 3–52 (the end of a gathering) on parchment; the second copied fols. 53–191 on paper. The second scribe also served as corrector of the first part and added a summary of *De oratore* on fols. 1-2. Bandini identified only the second scribe as Niccoli; Morison believes that Niccoli copied the entire manuscript.[42] The two scripts are quite different from each other and neither has the characteristic letter forms of the nine manuscripts attributed to Niccoli. The second scribe (who as corrector of the first, would be more likely than his predecessor to be Niccoli) has a *g* more like Poggio's than Niccoli's. He uses uncial as well as minuscule *d*. His round *s* is really round. The *ct* ligature is not usual, yet *c* often has the dangling ligature stroke when a word is divided between *c* and *t*; this was used by the first scribe too (see Fig. 6 in Morison). This peculiarity never appears in the nine Niccoli manuscripts. The *i* is dotted, not stroked. The *et* ligature is quite different, etc., etc. The first scribe bears even less resemblance to Niccoli.

Though the spellings *mihi* and *nihil* are the more common in both parts, the second scribe corrected to *michi* twice on the first two folios of the text.

[41] A. M. Bandini, *Catalogus codicum latinorum Bibliothecae Mediceae Laurentianae*, II (Florence, 1775), p. 524.

[42] *Op. cit.*, pp. 8–9 and Figs. 6–7.

Both parts of the manuscript fail miserably in the diphthong test. On about one hundred pages the first scribe wrote *e* forty-five times, *e* with cedilla fourteen times, *ae* four times. On some thirty pages the second scribe wrote *e* 124 times, *e* with cedilla eleven times, *ae* once — a very strange situation if either scribe were Niccoli, famous for his use of the diphthong.

In connection with No. 1 the history of the text of the *De oratore* was presented. No complete text was known to the humanists until Landriani found a manuscript in 1421. Now since the Laurentian manuscript has the complete text, it could not have been copied before that date — not in 1405-15 as Morison supposed. Actually it probably belongs to a time well beyond 1421.

Another pretender is Laur. 52, 8, an epitome of Boccaccio's *Genealogia deorum*. Bandini again is the responsible (or should we say 'irresponsible'?) identifier. Just how irresponsible he was is revealed by this amazing situation: Bandini states that the epitomator was Domizio Calderini, though his name does not appear in the manuscript. A comparison of the *incipit* with that in Laur. 53, 34 shows that the same work is involved, and in 53, 34 it is in fact attributed to Calderini.[43] Now Calderini was born about 1444 and Niccoli died in 1437! How Niccoli could have copied the manuscript some thirty or more years after his own death is not immediately apparent — or did Calderini compose the work ten or more years before his own birth? No confusion of two persons by the same name is involved. Bandini thoughtlessly made the identification on the basic of handwriting and in so doing victimized Morison, who dated the copying between 1400 and 1410 (see his Fig. 10).[44] If this script is Niccoli's then hundreds, even thousands of other manuscripts in a sloping humanistic hand were copied by him.

Avena made the suggestion that Laur. Strozz. 141 (Petrarch, *Buc.*, *Epist. Metr.*) was written by Niccoli because we know that he went to Padua to copy Petrarch's works, and this is the only

43 A. Hortis, *Studi sulle opere latine del Boccaccio* (Trieste, 1879), p. 220.

44 In a very valuable article, "What Is the Origin of the Scrittura Umanistica?" *La Bibliofilia*, LIII (1951), p. 9, David Thomas anticipated me in pointing out Bandini's absurdity.

manuscript directly derived from the autograph (Vat. lat. 3358).[45] But the script is entirely unlike Niccoli's. There is no indication that he even owned the volume.

Bandini and others have sought to identify as Niccoli's the handwriting of marginal notes in various manuscripts. In only two cases can this view be accepted; in the rest we must reject it or at best say that it cannot be accepted on the basis of comparison with the script described as Niccoli's in the preceding pages. One exception is Laur. Marc 268, a thirteenth-century manuscript of Cicero's Philippics once owned by Niccoli.[46] Fig. 38 shows a marginal note on fol. 7r, whose script is clearly that found in the nine manuscripts previously discussed.

Bandini thought that Laur. 49, 7, containing Cicero's letters *Ad familiares*, was copied by Petrarch and annotated by Niccoli. No one takes the former suggestion seriously today, but it is certain that Niccoli added at least the note in the right margin and the word *gessisse* at the bottom of fol. 9v (Fig. 39).

Laur. 49, 18, the copy of Cicero's letters to Atticus which belonged to Coluccio Salutati, is said to have notes that Niccoli added.[47] Schmidt and Sjögren disagree as to the extent of his annotation. There is good reason to doubt that Niccoli owned or annotated this manuscript. On fol. 225v, after Salutati's ownership note, we find: "Donatus Acciaiolus emit a Donato Arretino Leonardi filio". Like other manuscripts of Coluccio, it was probably bought by Leonardo Bruni directly from the sons of Coluccio. Schmidt gives no evidence for his assertion that Niccoli acquired it from Coluccio's library. His bland assumption that Bruni bought it after Niccoli's death is shattered by the fact that Niccoli willed his books to a committee of executors, who left the matter to Cosimo de' Medici, who in turn founded the library of S. Marco and placed

[45] A. Avena, *Il Bucolicum Carmen e i suoi commenti inediti* (Padua, 1906), p. 6.

[46] A. C. Clark in the preface to his edition of the Philippics (ed. 2, Oxford, 1917), in presenting this suggestion, said that Niccoli made about the same corrections in this manuscript as Poggio made in his (Laur. 48, 22). Poggio's corrections were partly emendations, partly readings from an old manuscript (now Vat. Basil. S. Petri H. 25). Clark seems to mean that Niccoli took his readings from Poggio's manuscript.

[47] O. E. Schmidt in *Abh. phil.-hist. Classe saechs. Gesell. Wiss.*, 1887, pp. 330, 342; H. Sjögren, *Commentationes Tullianae* (Uppsala, 1910), p. 51.

the books there, in which collection (now divided between the Laurenziana and the Nazionale Centrale) most of them still are.

Bandini also advanced the suggestion that Niccoli filled two lacunae in Laur. 73, 1, the tenth-century manuscript of Celsus, by adding several paper leaves. But Sabbadini and Marx credit Battista Pallavicini with these additions, which clearly are not in Niccoli's hand.[48]

In his edition of Cato and Varro (Leipzig, 1884), I, p. XIII, H. Keil indicated his belief that many of the corrections and marginal notes in Laur. 51, 1 were in the hand of Niccoli. This I cannot accept. Keil also says that Laur. 51, 4 is the most accurate copy of the lost S. Marco manuscript known to Poliziano. In spite of this statement Keil strangely did not use it but quoted three other manuscripts descended from the lost manuscript. It would seem that this lost S. Marco manuscript would be a better candidate for the honor of having been Niccoli's.

I have said that Niccoli's humanistic cursive was the kind of script that developed into Aldus' italic type. Until earlier examples are discovered we can give Niccoli credit for inventing this script. In that event we reach the interesting conclusion that the two intimate friends, Poggio and Niccoli, both protégés of Coluccio, originated the two scripts that developed into the two most popular printing fonts of today, roman and italic.

Now that Niccoli's claim to the throne as far as the invention of formal humanistic script is concerned has been shattered and Poggio remains its undisputed inventor, we may proceed to Poggio the master, whose disciples and imitators spread the new gospel not only far and wide but with amazing speed.

[48] *Storia*, p. 294; Marx, *Celsus*, p. XXX.

Chapter IV

DIFFUSION OF THE SCRIPT — THE FIRST DECADE

In Chapter II the attempt was made to show that Poggio was the real inventor of humanistic script and that the earliest known example of his handiwork dates from 1402 or the early part of 1403. His importance does not stop here, for he trained several scribes in his new style and many more imitated his script who were not trained by him.

Just how rapidly the Poggian script spread is a matter for further investigation, which will be greatly facilitated by the lists of dated manuscripts of various libraries which are being assembled at the Institut de Recherche et d'Histoire des Textes in Paris. Some of these lists I have been able to consult, as well as other sources.[1] One naturally looks for manuscripts which are still in Florence or were written there, since the demand for books in the new script seems to have been greatest in that city from the time of Cosimo on. Poggio himself must have produced several manuscripts before 1408, such as Strozzianus 96, for whose copying by Poggio in 1402 or 1403 I hope I made a convincing case in Chapter II, and the Cicero which he was transcribing for Coluccio at Rome in 1403. It is a great pity that this manuscript, presumably written in the new humanistic hand, has not been identified, if indeed it still exists. Perhaps Poggio did not adopt the practice of signing his name until he transcribed Cicero's letters in 1408 (Berlin, Ham. 166). At any rate, the point I want to make here is that several manuscripts copied by him in the new style were probably available

[1] I have examined several hundred manuscripts dated 1400-1420, chiefly in the Vatican, the Florentine libraries, Bologna, Paris, London, and Oxford. I am especially indebted to Mlle J. Vielliard of the Institut, to Prof. A. Campana of the Vatican, to Dr. R. W. Hunt of the Bodleian, and to Mlle M.-T. d'Alverny of the Bibliothèque Nationale.

for Florentine scribes to imitate. After 1408 there was, of course, the Berlin codex of Cicero's letters. The Eusebius now in Florence (Laur. 67, 15), written in 1408-1409, may have been in Niccoli's hands for a time, as many of Poggio's manuscripts were. The same could be true of Vat. lat. 3245 (1410-1414). In fact this is particularly likely, as Poggio went off to the Council of Constance and seems to have left his books with Niccoli until his return to Rome from England in 1423. For in that year he asks Niccoli to send him some of his books, such as his excerpts from various authors and the formularies of the papal chancellery (*Epist.* I, pp. 88, 91), books which Niccoli is not likely to have borrowed of Poggio. But the latter asks for few others except for copying. The fact is that Poggio did not keep many books with him in Rome. On November 27, 1428, he says he wants to keep the copy of Cicero's Orations a while longer, as he has no other (*Epist.* I, p. 265). In repeating this on April 2, 1429, he says that he needs this volume for food to preserve his health, for he has sent almost all his other books home. He would seem to mean Terranuova, where he was born and where he planned to retire. Besides, Niccoli (and other friends) had some of Poggio's books on "indefinite loan". In December of 1429 he writes that Niccoli has held his Lucretius and Asconius for twelve years, his Petronius for seven or more. He wants his Lucretius, which he has never finished reading; in fact, he has very few books (*Epist.* I, p. 295; cf. p. 303).

We can therefore be prepared to find manuscripts in the new style in the first decade of the fifteenth century. However, we discover that most of them are still in various Gothic styles: *rotunda*, notarial, etc. Tedaldo della Casa, an important scribe whose extant work runs from 1357 to 1403, wrote in Gothic. Some forty books of his library, which he gave to Santa Croce in 1406, survive, mostly in Florence. Of these, about one-fourth were copied by him.[2] Coluccio had several trained scribes but all except Poggio used a Gothic hand.

We have Florentine examples dated from 1405 on in the new style or an approximation thereof. Some are actually earlier than any of Poggio's dated transcriptions.

2 R. Sabbadini, *Le scoperte dei codici latini e greci ne' secoli XIV e XV*, II (Florence, 1914), p. 175; Georg Voigt, *Die Wiederbelebung des classischen Alterthums*, ed. 3, I (Berlin, 1893), p. 397.

1. The earliest is Florence, Laur. Conv. Soppr. 111 (formerly Badia 2647) (Fig. 40). It contains Sallust, *Catiline* and *Jugurtha*, and Justinus. On fol. 199: "Postrema tandem manu absolutus est Kalendis Iuniis anno ab incarnato verbo MCCCC quinto". The majuscules include uncial *e* and *m* along with some indifferent capitals. Uncial as well as minuscule *d* is found; final long *s* is regular; ligatured and unligatured *ct* occur, but the dangling ligature is missing; the ligature *et* appears instead of the earlier abbreviation. The mediaeval gathering of eight leaves prevails over the humanistic gathering of ten. The new spellings *mihi, nihil, otium, auctor* are used. The diphthong *ae* is much more common than the monophthong and is written in separate letters, in ligature, and with the cedilla. It occurs even in *caeteri, graegarius, faecerit, honestae* (adv.), *aedoctus, benignae* (adv.), *daecretum*. This peculiarity betrays a lack of experience with the new practice. The chief exceptions are compounds of *pre*, especially at the beginning of the book. An accent is placed over *ádhuc*. I observed unusual word division only in *po-stea* and *po-stquam*. The general appearance of the script is humanistic.

2. Another Laurentian manuscript, Conv. Soppr. 131, is dated 1406 (Fig. 41). It contains Cicero, *De finibus*. On fol. 111r: "Absolvit autem scriptor postrema manu ad IIII Kalendas Iunias verbi anno incarnati MCCCC sexto". The similarity of the subscription to that of the preceding suggests that they were written by the same man, but the writing seems different in general and in detail. The capitals are better in the later codex. In the minuscules, *g* and *ct* are more graceful, as is the script as a whole, ascenders are unusually short, and final round *s* is frequent. It should be said, however, that in the first part ascenders are taller and round final *s* is not used. It may be that one scribe copied both manuscripts and that the differences are to be explained by a growth in the mastery of the script, but indications point rather to three different hands in the two codices. The problem deserves more study than I was able to give it.

3. Another manuscript of the same year is Bologna, Univ. 471. It contains Cicero, *Tusc., N. D., Div.* On fol. 149r we read: "Anno domini MCCCCVI de mense Iunii manu mei Spine Azzolini". The hand is semi-humanistic. It reveals minuscule and uncial *d*, long final *s*, a non-humanistic *g*, both the humanistic

ligature *et* and the Tironian note. *Michi* and *nichil* are the regular spellings. On seven pages not a single diphthong turned up. Then we begin to find cedillas under every single *e*, as in *est*, *ne*, *certe*, *effecerit*, but later they were erased. Unusual word divisions are frequent: *po-sse*, *vid-etur*, *m-agnitudine*, *qu-ibus*, *diff-initur*, etc. Obviously the scribe was just a learner.

4. Somewhat the same can be said of British Museum Eg. 2909, with the subscription: "Per me Odoardum natum Iacobi Bergognini civis Astensis die nono Septembris MCCCCVIIII in Viconovo dyocesis Ferrariensis". It contains Terence. The majuscules still have a mixture of earlier elements, as uncial *e*. The minuscule *d*, long final *s*, *et* ligature are humanistic; the *g*, the unligatured *ct*, and the abbreviation for *et* are Gothic. The script still has a Gothic cast.

5. Oxford, Bodl. Laud. Lat. 70 of the year 1409 is even more Gothic (Fig. 42). It contains Seneca's Epistles. Both minuscule and uncial *d* appear, and the final *s* is sometimes long, sometimes round. The 2-shaped *r* used initially is definitely Gothic.

6. More specifically humanistic is British Museum Harl. 2648, a Juvenal with this date: "1410 Augusti 23". Though humanistic letter forms prevail, the writing does not look fully humanistic because it is somewhat angular and awkward, with a distinct Gothic aspect. It has the spelling *mihi* and the *ae* diphthong.

7. Perhaps the best example of humanistic writing during the first decade of the fifteenth century — except Poggio's — is that seen in a manuscript of Eusebius' Chronicle, translated by Jerome, in St. Gall, Stadtbibliothek (Vadiana) 298 (Fig. 43). It has this subscription: "Liber emendatus Ghuighelmini Francisci Tanaglia viri Florentini quem ipse mea manu scripsi precepto Hieronymi servato IIII kalendas Octobris MCCCCX".[3] The

[3] The allusion to Jerome is to the words with which the work begins in this and other Eusebius manuscripts of the fifteenth century. It is an adjuration to scribes to copy faithfully. It originated with Irenaeus and is found at the beginning of Book V of Eusebius' History translated by Rufinus, where it is attributed to Irenaeus. It appears in Poggio's copy of the Eusebius Chronicle (Laur. 67, 15). I suspect that Niccoli or Poggio was responsible for its introduction into this work. It is also found in a Celsus of the fifteenth century, Vat. lat. 2371, fol. 142r, and probably in other volumes. I know the St. Gall manuscript only from a photograph of fol. 1 and the description by G. Scherer, *Verzeischniss der Manuscripte und Incunabeln der Vadianischen Bibliothek in St. Gallen*

scribe will be discussed below. On fol. 1r the letter forms are uniformly humanistic except for one example of uncial *d*. The ligatured *et* appears nine times, but there are also two instances of the Tironian note. The diphthong *ae* is regular (in the cedilla form) but there are exceptions, chiefly *Grecus*, *sepe*, and the prefix *pre*. The old spelling *autor* turns up twice. Unusual word division appears in *di-fficile* and *rece-ssisse*. The deleted *i* occurs four times at the end of a line, and a lengthened prone round *s* once.

8. Oxford, Bodl. Lat. class. d. 37 is dated 1413 (fol. 34r): "Anno MCCCCXII ydibus Ianuariis Florentie". In Florentine style this would actually be 1413.[4] It contains Cicero, *De or.* II, 343-end, *Or.*, followed by *De opt. gen.* in a different hand. Uncial *e* is found in the majuscules. The minuscules are humanistic throughout, but, like Poggio, the scribe employs Gothic in marginal notes. The text is corrected in Gothic. No diphthongs seem to be used. *Mihi, nihil, auctor* are so spelled in accordance with the new fashion.

9. Bologna, Univ. 2621, containing Catullus, was copied in 1412: "Finivi anno II Pontificatus Iohannis XXIII VIII kalendas Aprilis Rivoalti Hieronymus Donatus patricius", i.e., it was copied on the Rialto of Venice.[5] Other entries show that it passed to Girolamo's uncle Pietro Donato, bishop of Padua and archbishop of Crete, then to Giannino Corradino, who gave it (before 1416, when he died) to the famous Venetian humanist Francesco Barbaro. From him it passed to his nephew Ermolao.

Except for uncial *e* and some other features of the majuscules, we have here a good example of humanistic script. The diphthong

(St. Gall, 1864). In answer to my inquiry the librarian kindly assured me that the date is correct and has not been tampered with.

[4] Fig. 44. A facsimile of the same page in *Annual Report of the Curator of the Bodleian Library* for 1954-55, Plate II. I owe my knowledge of the manuscript to the kindness of Bodley's librarian, Dr. A. S. Hunt, who had the foresight to acquire the volume for the Bodleian.

[5] R. Sabbadini, *Le scoperte dei codici latini e greci ne' secoli XIV e XV* (Florence, 1905), p. 120, n. 26, gives the date as 1411, but John XXIII was elected pope on May 17, 1410. Thus March 24 of the second year of his office (when the Catullus was copied) would fall in 1412. Girolamo copied another manuscript (Trivulzi 661), not seen by me, on July 19 of the third year, which Sabbadini takes to be 1412 but I interpret as 1413 (R. Sabbadini, *Storia e critica di testi latini* [Catania, 1914], p. 165). Reproduction of three pages of the Catullus in I. B. Pighi, *Catulli Codex Bononiensis 2621* (Bologna, 1950). See too Paolo Sambin « La biblioteca di Pietro Donato », *Bollettino del Museo Civico di Padova*, XLVIII (1959), p. 7.

is often indicated (usually with a cedilla), but often not, especially in *letus*, compounds of *pre*, etc. The new spellings *mihi* and *nihil* are used throughout, but the older *ocium* is found in all the five occurrences of the word *otium* in Catullus.

10. I include a manuscript which contains no date but has been assigned to 1413. It is an autograph of Giovanni Aurispa (Laur. Conv. Soppr. 71), written in Chios.[6] The script is only semi-humanistic. It has the minuscule *d*, the long final *s*, ligatured *et*. On the other hand, *s* descends below the line, *g* is Gothic, the abbreviation sign in *-que* is in the shape of the figure 3, not a colon or semicolon, *ct* are not in ligature. By 1422 Aurispa's hand became fully humanistic (Vat. Ottob. lat. 1984; see below), but it has a cursive character in that some of the letters are joined. Where did Aurispa get acquainted with humanistic script? While he was a student at the University of Bologna in 1404–10? Or did he visit Florence immediately after his years in Bologna? We cannot be sure.

Several of these manuscripts are of Florentine origin (presumably Nos. 1, 2, 7, 8) and others may be. No. 9 was copied at Venice, and is one of several instances to be noted of the early spread of humanistic script — and humanistic culture — to that city. No. 4 was written near Ferrara — not far from Florence. Ferrara and Bologna, where No. 3 may have been written, are stepping-stones from Florence to Venice.

At this point it seems wise to anticipate an objection to naming Poggio the inventor of humanistic script. If, it might be said, the script developed at Florence and spread from there, how could Poggio have had any hand in promoting it by training Florentine scribes since he left Florence in 1403 and did not return, except for short visits, for many years? This is a legitimate question and must be answered. One could say, if Poggio was not responsible, who was? There is truth in this parrying defense, but such a defense is negative and insufficient. I have said that copies of Poggio's work were available in Florence from 1402 or 1403. Besides, some scribes may have been sent from Florence to Poggio in Rome for training. But even these are not complete answers. Someone

[6] R. Sabbadini, *Carteggio di Giovanni Aurispa* (Rome, 1931), p. 3, with reproduction.

must have been an active sponsor of the new movement. That sponsor was, I think, Niccoli. Though not the inventor of humanistic script and, so far as we know, no practitioner of it in its Poggian, or formal, style, he recognized its superiority and promoted it. He may even have encouraged the young Poggio in his experiment, just as Coluccio did. There are certain indications that he actively supported the new handwriting, as we may infer from the following observations.

No. 1 is replete with diphthongs, an unusual phenomenon at the early date of 1405. From whom would the scribe have learned about diphthongs if not from the diphthong master Niccoli? No. 3 has no diphthongs at all for many pages, then every *e* blossoms forth into one. The scribe has, it seems, just been told that one should write them but he has not yet learned how to apply his new knowledge. The scribe of No. 7, Guglielmino Tanaglia (or Tenaglia), was one of the sixteen Florentines chosen by Niccoli to be executors of his will, made in 1437; their chief duty was to make suitable arrangements for Niccoli's library. As Tanaglia was a student of law in Padua in 1420, he presumably was quite young when in 1410 he copied the manuscript now in St. Gall.[7] Obviously he was a friend and protégé of Niccoli, who may well have encouraged him to imitate the Poggian script. Finally, Niccoli arranged for Antonio di Mario, an imitator of Poggio's writing, to copy a manuscript for Cosimo de' Medici, as will be noted in the next chapter. All these facts point to Niccoli as the man who encouraged scribes to imitate Poggio's new style, perhaps he even induced Cosimo de' Medici to give preference to books so written.

Scribes either taught themselves by imitating the script of others or wrote under direction. One interesting type of instruction seems to be indicated by Vat. Ottob. lat. 1984.[8] The colophon, written in Greek by Aurispa, states that the manuscript was copied in Constantinople by Iacopo Veneto and Aurispa in 1422. Aurispa and Iacopo alternated in copying the manuscript. For example, Aurispa copied fols. 1-2r, Iacopo, 2v-5r, Aurispa the rest of 5r, Iacopo 5v-7r, Aurispa the rest of 7r, Iacopo 7v-8r, etc. Iacopo did more

[7] Sabbadini, *Storia*, pp. 393-394; G. Zippel, *Niccolò Niccoli* (Florence, 1890), p. 97.

[8] Sabbadini, *Carteggio*, p. 184.

of the writing than Aurispa. My explanation is that Aurispa was showing Iacopo how to write the new script by giving him something to imitate.

While this book deals primarily with the development of the new script in Florence, the capital of the humanistic world, something should be said about its spread to other regions. The many humanists who came to Florence or had contact with its cultural leaders carried the script to their homes. We have already noted the appearance of the script as early as the first decade of the fifteenth century in Bologna, in or near Ferrara, and in Venice. In 1422, as just seen, Aurispa taught Iacopo of Venice how to write like a humanist. In the same year Giovanni Tortelli of Arezzo copied a manuscript at Venice (Vat. lat. 3237).[9] These are just a few examples of activity in Venice. In the same way the script was carried to Milan, Padua, and other centers. When the kings of Aragon, imitating the Medici, began to assemble their library of fine books at Naples, Florentine scribes flocked to that city. Florentine script was dominant in the libraries of the dukes of Urbino, the Malatesta of Cesena, and the king of Hungary, Matthias Corvinus. At Rome Poggio was, of course, the chief source in propagating the new script by training scribes. He has left us a good deal of information on this point but unfortunately none of it antedates 1425.

One June 23, 1425 (*Epist.* I, p. 55), Poggio writes to Niccoli that he is hoping to keep his scribe, who, after hard pushing by Poggio, writes in a script which smacks of antiquity; but, being a Neapolitan, he is not dependable: "Nam et praesto scribit et iis litteris quae sapiunt antiquitatem, ad quod eum trusi summo cum labore; sed Neapolitanus est et ita levis ut ad eum comprimendum esset opus pistrino". The word *antiquitatem* should not, of course, be taken literally; it refers to the *littera antiqua* of the Carolingian period.

Again on August 18, 1425 (*Epist.* I, p. 159), referring to the same scribe, he says: "Hic scriptor meus, quem summo labore litteras antiquas edocui, Neapolitanus est". After violently denouncing this scribe's character, he continues: "Sed tamen omnia ferre

[9] Mancini, *Arch. stor. ital.*, 78 (1920), II, p. 161, gives a reproduction of the colophon. See also Mercati in *Studi e Testi*, 46 (1926), Pl. IV.

proposui quoad hoc opus orationum particularium conficiat; quod etiam dubito an perficiat, ita est levis, inconstans, ac fastidiosus. Sed habeo alium Gallicum qui parum novit; hoc utar". This French scribe is mentioned once more on March 20, 1426 (*Epist.* I, p. 176), by which time Poggio had succeeded in teaching him: "Docui enim quendam Gallicum librarium meum scribere litteris antiquis, qui nunc in manibus habet historiam Helii Spartiani", etc. He evidently has trained him to his satisfaction, for he is in a hurry to have him copy Seneca, if he can obtain an exemplar. Later he speaks of the "librariorum superbia" (*Epist.* I, p. 179).

The most detailed statement about his instruction of scribes is found in a letter of December 6, 1427.[10] For four months he has done nothing else than teach this blockhead, this donkey, to write, but all in vain: "Habeo scriptorem rudis ingenii et moribus rusticanis. Iam quatuor mensibus nil aliud ago quam eum docere ut discat scribere, sed vereor ne litus arem. Scribit modo Valerium, in quo experitur ruditatem suam, sed in diem fit stultior. Itaque clamo, intono, iurgo, increpo. At is habet aures picatas plumbeus, caudex, stipes, asinus, et si quid stolidius ineptiusque dici potest. Dii eum perdant! Obligatus est mecum biennio, forsan corrigetur".

Why did Poggio go to so much trouble in training scribes to write in his new style? Not merely for his own satisfaction but to make legible copies (such at least is my interpretation) available to others, both contemporaries and future generations (*Epist.* I, p. 265; January 7, 1429): "Iamdiu expectavi Iosephi libros... Ego te solicito quia scriptor iam absolvit reliquum opus et difficile est eum tenere sine opera... Non tantum mihi satisfacis quantum communi utilitati et famae illius viri [i.e., Iosephi]. Paro enim libros non mihi soli sed ceteris et etiam posteris, quibus boni viri solent etiam prospicere".

In a letter of July 15, 1429 (*Epist.* I, p. 285), he asks Niccoli's opinion of the work of one of his scribes: "Vide an littera illius qui scripsit Agellium tibi placeat, quia adhuc est mecum. Sed vel novum instituam," etc. In October or November of 1429 (*Epist.* I, p. 293) he again has two scribes. In December of this year

10 A. Wilmanns, "Die Briefsammlungen des Poggio Bracciolini", *Zentralblatt für Bibliothekswesen*, 30 (1913), p. 305.

(*Epist.* I, p. 295) they are gone and he is awaiting two others. On January 6, 1431 (*Epist.* I, p. 340), he tells of dismissing one of his two scribes, "unum qui melius scribit." This is the one who copied three decades of Livy and Cicero's letters to Atticus. In 1443 (*Epist.* II, p. 280) he again has a French scribe — hardly the same that he had in 1426.

The thorough training in *littera antiqua* that Poggio gave to the French and Neapolitan scribes was, it may be presumed, also given to the other copyists that troop across the pages of his letters. When they left him they carried away with them the precious skill that Poggio had taught them and, we may be confident, continued to practice it — even in France and Naples, perhaps, if they returned to their original homes.

Nevertheless good scribes seem to have been scarce, even in Florence, the center of the book trade. For Leonardo Bruni, writing to Poggio in April or May of 1426,[11] approves Poggio's suggestion (in a letter that has not been published, if it exists) that Bruni acquire a scribe. But, says Bruni, there is such a scarcity of them in Florence that he wishes Poggio would find one for him. There were good scribes at Florence, as we shall see, but apparently they were kept busy by Cosimo and others.

Even as late as 1456 good scribes who could write humanistic script were very scarce in Rome, according to Carlo de' Medici, writing to his half brother Giovanni di Cosimo. Most of the scribes were German or French, who still wrote Gothic. Their script would not suit Giovanni, who obviously preferred the humanistic style.[12]

In this chapter I have presented manuscripts dated from 1405 to 1413 as representative of the new humanistic script, though many are far from perfect specimens.[13] No doubt others exist

11 *Epist.*, ed. L. Mehus (Florence, 1741), IV, 23 (I, p. 141).

12 V. Rossi in *Rend. Acc. Lincei*, Ser. V, II (1893), p. 132.

13 Several pretenders to a place in the first decade of the fifteenth century must be disposed of. The British Museum catalogue states that Add. 12007 is dated 1404. It could not possibly have been written that early. The date is actually 1455. The Roman numeral L has so short a bottom stroke that it was taken for I. I later discovered that in the official copy of the catalogue the statement has been corrected with pen and ink. Paris, B. N. lat. 6830A has the date 1409 but this is in erasure. The manuscript was written much later. Vat.

and they should be brought to the attention of scholars. From now on I shall confine myself largely to Florentine scribes who signed and dated their work and who are represented by a number of examples. The first of these is Giovanni Aretino, whose earliest work is dated 1410.

Barb. lat. 57 has the date MCCCCX. Feeling that this date was impossible, I showed the manuscript to Prof. Campana without comment. He at once said it was much later. Perhaps the scribe inadvertently omitted L before or after X. Finally, British Museum Add. 6051 has the date "die Veneris V Decembris MCCCCX", but with an erasure after it. The writing seemed to belong to the end of the century, and so it proved, for December 5 fell on a Friday only in 1404, 1483, and 1494 during this century. The last therefore is the correct date, CIIII being erased. The scribe signed "BSS", which Mr. Alfred Fairbank instantly recognized as "Bartolomeus Sancti Viti scripsit", and compared with Royal 14 C. III, a signed copy by the same well-known scribe of the end of the fifteenth century.

Chapter V

GIOVANNI ARETINO, GIACOMO CURLO, ANTONIO DI MARIO

In the last chapter we noted how quickly the new script caught on during the first decade after its introduction. For the most part the scribes are nameless and are represented by single volumes. The next step is the development of professional scribes who signed their products and left us a number of examples of their workmanship. The first of these is a certain Giovanni Aretino, to whom very little attention has been paid. He is not to be confused, as he often has been, with others of the same name, such as Giovanni Tortelli, the well-known humanist, or Giovanni Corvini. Nothing is known of him except what may be gleaned from the books he copied.

Seven of Giovanni's books are dated from 1410-1417, and one of these (Livy) is in three volumes. In addition I have found six without date. This considerable output is matched by the uniform excellence of the script. This obscure rival of Poggio's was producing volumes in rapid succession at a time when Poggio's output was relatively small, to judge from surviving examples. The quality is better than that of Poggio's Eusebius and vies with his best efforts. Some of Giovanni's books were made for Cosimo de' Medici. All are on parchment. Following are his extant books:

1. Rome, Vat. Pal. lat. 1496. Fig. 45. Cicero, *Fam.* When capitals are used in headings Giovanni, like other scribes, tries to fill out lines, but he carries this practice to extremes in this manuscript, as follows: with *feliciter* (sometimes abbreviated) on fols. 18v, 28v, 36v, 48r, 111v, 145r; with *lege feliciter* on fols. 1r, 11r, 140r, 155r; *feliciter Ioannes* on fol. 58r; *feliciter mi Nicolae* on fol. 68r; [1]

[1] Here the space at the end of the second line proved to be a bit small and the last two letters of *Nicolae* were put at the end of the first line (see Fig. 45).

lege feliciter mi Nicolae on fols. 72v, 102r, 122r; *lege feliciter Nicolae* on fol. 87v. Then at the end (fol. 161v) we read: "Ioannes Arretinus tibi Nicolao Ricio salutes plurimas dicit. Vale. Diu felix mei memor dulcissimas ac suavissimas Romani eloquii epistolas lege feliciter et me ama. Florentiae anno domini MCCCCX Nonis Iuniis indictione tertia. Me ama et vale." [2]

An extension of this practice is to be seen in the last line of a page. Giovanni always wanted the page to end with a full line. So whenever a paragraph ended in a short line at the bottom of a page he filled it out (in minuscules): "Mi dilectissime omnium Nicolae" (fol. 24v), "Vale mi dulcissime ac suavissime Nicolae" (fol. 70v), "Mi Nicolae dulcissime, sapientissime, ac suavis" (fol. 76r), "Mi Nicolae" (fol. 80v), "Lege feliciter, mi Nicolae dulcissime. Vale" (fol. 99v), "Vale mi dulcissime Nicolae" (fol. 112v). I have not seen this practice elsewhere. The avoidance of a short last line resembles the practice of the modern printer, who avoids the "widow", a short line at the top of the page. This is one of many devices, such as justifying the right margin, which scribes (and after them, printers) adopted to improve the appearance of the page.

Who is this Nicolaus Ricius? A man by that name copied Laur. 23, 21; 30, 20; 35, 26; 39, 37; 64, 32; 76, 15; Ashb. 996; Ricc. 492; Vat. Urb. lat. 313; Munich lat. 821; Vienna 2. In one of these (Laur. 30, 20) the father's name Antonius is given. In several an added name is found: "Spenosus vocatus" (Laur. 64, 32) or "Spinosus vocatus" (Laur. Ashb. 996; Ricc. 492; Vat. Urb. lat. 313; Vienna 2). Only one of these manuscripts is dated (Laur. 39, 37): 1458 — a long time after 1410. Another (Laur. 23, 21) contains a work composed in 1456, according to Bandini. So Giovanni's friend may have been another member of the Ricci family.

2. Florence, Laur. 63, 4, 5, 6. Livy (three volumes). In 63, 4 the colophon reads (fol. 215v): "Cosme de Medicis Ioannis filio Ioannes Arretinus Florentiae absolvit." In 63, 5 (fol. 157v): "Ioan-

[2] Ebeling in *Philologus* 42 (1884), p. 403, has a truly extraordinary misreading of the simple colophon. And he is quite wrong in saying that Pal. lat. 1495 (Cicero, *Att.*) was copied by the same scribe in the same year. O. E. Schmidt in *Abh. Phil.-Hist. Cl. saechs. Ges. Wiss.* IV (1887), p. 357, is just as wrong in accepting Ebeling's suggestion and its bearing on the date of Pal. lat. 1495.

nes Arretinus scripsit atque perfecit Florentiae anno domini MCCCCXII IIII Kalendas Maii. Salve atque vale, mi..." The last word, erased, was perhaps *Cosma.*[3] In 63, 6 (fol. 118v): "Lege feliciter. Ioannes Arretinus Idibus Ianuariis anno domini MCCCCXII hunc librum absolvit," then by the same hand but in darker ink: "Cosmo de Medicis Ioannis filio." The dating is in Florentine style and would be 1413. Volume I, being undated, was probably copied at the end of 1411 or the beginning of 1412. Perhaps these volumes are the ones indicated in F. Pintor, *La libreria di Cosimo de' Medici nel 1418* (Florence, 1902), where, apparently through an error, the three decades are said to be in two volumes.

3. Munich, Staatsbibl. lat. 763. Fig. 46. Cicero, *Tusc.*, *Fin.*, *Acad.* At end (fol. 81v): "Ioannes Arretinus IIII Idus Augustas IXV post MIIII[c] annum salvatoris feliciter in urbe Florentina hunc librum absolvit." The date is 1414. Was this the *Tusc.*, *Fin.* in "lettera antica" in Cosimo's library in 1418?

4. Rome, Vat. Basil. S. Petri H. 31. Fig. 47. Two manuscripts bound in one: Pomponius Mela, with which we are not concerned, and Plutarch, Alexander and Caesar. At end (fol. 90r): "Post mille CCCC undequintodecimo salvatoris anno in Florentia urbe Novembribus Idibus hunc librum ego Iohannes origine Florentinus absolvi, qui Arretinus dicor," i.e., 1414 (*undequintodecimo* on the analogy of *undeviginti*; cf. No. 3, where IXV really stands for *undequintodecimo*). Here Giovanni reverts to the Gothic *bastarda* which he presumably used before adopting Poggio's humanistic script. The two manuscripts were illuminated by the same artist and bound together soon after they were copied. The arms of Cardinal Orsini, who wore the red hat from 1405 to 1438, are on fol. 1. Guarino's translation of Plutarch's *Caesar* is supposed to have been finished in 1415, as stated in Chapter III (cf. note 23), but this manuscript indicates a date at least as early as 1414. Cf. A. Campana in an appendix to C. Questa, *De duobus codicibus olim Iordani Ursini Cardinalis Hebraice subscriptis* (Rome, 1957), p. 20, n. 6.

5. Laur. 48, 10. Cicero, Orations. Facsimile in A. Hessel,

[3] Giuseppe Billanovich, with the aid of ultraviolet rays, thought he saw an *s* at the end. He suggested that the last two volumes were originally intended for someone else, and that the first volume was written later (*Italia medioevale e umanistica*, I [1958], p. 254).

Arch. für Urkundenforschung, XIII (1935), Pl. 2a. At end (fol. 305r): "Post mille CCCC quintodecimo salvatoris anno quinto Idus Februarias hoc volumen orationum XXVIII M. T. Ciceronis quod in CCC chartis redactum est Ioannes Arretinus absolvit Cosmae de Medicis Ioannis filio," i.e., 1416, for the dating is Florentine style. Perhaps the book in "lettera antica" of the 1418 catalogue.

6. Laur. 78, 24. Fig. 48; Hessel Pl. 2b. Francesco Barbaro, *De re uxoria*. At end (fol. 58v): "VIIII Kalendas Iunias Florentiae Ioannes Arretinus feliciter absolvit XVI post MCCCC anno salvatoris." Here Giovanni uses a third kind of script, a humanistic cursive, about which more later. This is perhaps one of the two copies in "lettera antica" in Cosimo's library in 1418.

7. Laur. 66, 12. Fig. 49. Justinus. At end (fol. 122v): "Idibus Maiis XVII supra MIIII[c] anno hunc librum feliciter Cosme de Medicis Ioannis filio Ioannes Arretinus absolvit." Perhaps the book in "lettera antica" in the 1418 catalogue.

8. Florence, Naz. Conv. Soppr. I. IX. 35 (Marc. 728). Fig. 50. Juvencus, Proba. At end (fol. 98r): "Cosmae de Medicis Iohannes Arretinus hunc librum Florentiae Idibus Februariis absolvit feliciter." Humanistic cursive. Not in the 1418 catalogue of Cosimo and therefore perhaps written after that date.

9. Laur. 83, 6. Cicero, *N. D.*, *Div.*, *Fat.* Fol. 118r: "Ioannes Arretinus scripsit." Fol. 127r: "Bernardo Portinario Ioannes Arretinus plurimam salutem dicit. Vale diu felixque sis." The first letter and the last four of *Portinario* are in erasure.[4] The same contents in a book in "lettera antica" in the catalogue of 1418.

10. Naz. Conv. Soppr. I. VII. 18 (Marc. 577). John Chrysostom, *Adv. vitup.* At end: "Cosmae de Medicis Iohannes Arretinus hunc librum Florentiae Nonis Februariis feliciter absolvit." Humanistic cursive.[5] Perhaps after 1418, as it is not in the Cosimo catalogue.

11. Florence, Laur. 79, 7. Aristotle, *Eth.*, tr. by L. Bruni. At end (fol. 130r): "Cosme de Medicis Ioannes Arretinus absolvit." Perhaps after 1418, as it is not in the Cosimo catalogue.

[4] Members of the Portinari family of Florence were merchants in Rome in 1402 (Vat. lat. 2664, fol. 147).

[5] F. A. Zacharia, *Iter litterarium per Italiam* (Venice, 1762), pp. 47, 51, mentions this and the preceding manuscript but in the Index wrongly identifies Giovanni as Tortelli.

12. Florence, Ricc. 500. Cicero, *Att.* At end (fol. 309r): "Ioannes Arretinus."

13. Laur. 79, 11. Aristotle, *Eth.*, tr. by L. Bruni. At end (fol. 137r): "Ioannes Arretinus absolvit Venetiis III Kalendas Septembres." The fact that this manuscript is not as well written as No. 11, and that it was copied at Venice, perhaps indicates that it belongs to a later period. Still the manuscript did find its way into the Medici collection.

Since the last dated manuscript signed by Giovanni is of the year 1417, I suspect that he ended his activities as a scribe soon after that date. Attribution of later manuscripts to him probably rests on a confusion with Giovanni Tortelli or someone else.[6]

[6] T. De Marinis, *La biblioteca napoletana dei Re d'Aragona*, I (Milan, 1952), p. 9, mentions three manuscripts owned by Alfonso of Naples "manu Aretini": Ammianus, Statius with Catullus, and Panegyrici. In his Index he says that the reference is to Leonardo Bruni. The Ammianus is now in Paris, B. N. lat. 6120, which was written neither by our Giovanni Aretino nor by Leonardo.

A manuscript of Tacitus in Budapest (Univ. 9) has the words "Io. Ar. legi transcurrendo 1467 sed mansit inemendatus" (A. de Hevesy, *La bibliothèque du roi Matthias Corvin* [Paris, 1923], No. 23; G. Fraknói, *Bibliotheca Corvina* [Budapest, 1927], No. 13; C. W. Mendell in *Yale Classical Studies*, VI (1939], p.69). Hevesy and Fraknói expand Io. Ar. to Iohannes Archiepiscopus, i.e., Janos Vitéz. Mendell would interpret as Iohannes Arretinus and identify as Giovanni the Florentine scribe. But other Corvinus manuscripts have similar notes which can only refer to Vitéz. Note especially Budapest, Univ. 10 (Hevesy No. 24; Fraknói No. 14): "Finivi transcurrendo Nitrie die II Iunii 1468. Emendare bene non potui propter inemendatum exemplar". Cf. Budapest, Nat. Mus. 370 (Hevesy No. 15; Fraknói No. 25) and 344 (Hevesy No. 11; Fraknói No. 22). Nor is the handwriting of the note that of Giovanni Aretino. In his recent *Tacitus* (New Haven, 1957), p. 300, Mendell does not mention the matter at all.

Prof. Campana tells me that he was informed by Father Jadrijević that a Cicero copied by Ioannes Arretinus in 1422 for Francesco Barbaro of Venice is in the library of the monastery of Imotski, Jugoslavia. I feel sure that this Iohannes is Tortelli, for in this very year of 1422, and too at Venice, Tortelli copied Cicero's *De oratore* and *Orator*, now in the Vatican (lat. 3237). For this manuscript see A. Mancini in *Archivio storico italiano*, 78 (1920), II, p. 161 and Fig. 2.

Finally the first and third volumes of a Livy in Besançon (837-839), signed by "Ioannes A. fi.", dated Florence, 1425 and 1427, have been attributed to our Giovanni. In his colophons Giovanni does not mention his father's name, the wording of the Besançon colophons is different, and the script bears not the slightest resemblance to our Giovanni's—nor to Tortelli's for that matter. It is humanistic, but the heavy shading recalls formal Gothic of the *rotunda* style.

Whether he is the man recommended by Traversari in *Epist.* XI, 45 (1432?) and 25 (1438?) cannot be determined.

Giovanni uses three kinds of script, the Gothic *bastarda* (No. 4), the formal humanistic of the Poggio type (Nos. 1-3, 5, 7, 9, 11-13), a humanistic cursive (Nos. 6, 8, 10). The last is particularly interesting as one of the earliest examples, but its particular adaptation of cursive to humanistic did not influence the development of cursive script. Its relation to Giovanni's formal hand is quite obvious, notably in *d* and *g*. From Gothic cursive it took the long *s*, fat in the middle, which is the distinctive characteristic of *bastarda*. From the same source came the round final *s* and the tailed final *m*. The writing is thinner and slopes slightly. The manuscript of 1417 (No. 6) antedates by six years the earliest example of Niccoli's known cursive writing. Its script is more formal than Niccoli's in that it slopes less and preserves the uncial *a* and the rounded *ct* ligature. It shows clearly that humanistic cursive was an admixture of cursive Gothic with formal humanistic script.

Giovanni's spelling is usually new style, but at the beginning of his first manuscript one finds several instances of *michi* and *nichil*. The diphthong is generally written, though the simple vowel is frequent, especially in No. 1. *Caeteri*, *aepistola*, *praecor*, *maetu* are among the spellings noted. Accents are used on *á*, *é*, *ó*, *uná* (adv.), *eó* (adv.).

The dangling ligature in *ct* occurs once only in each of the following: Nos. 1, 2 (Laur. 63, 5), 3, 9, but it is an interesting fact that these are the earliest examples known, as far as I have been able to discover. Did Giovanni invent this fad? Did Poggio and others imitate him? Or did Poggio start the practice in one of his early lost copies? If so, how can one explain why he did not use it again until about 1425? It would seem that, failing further discovery, Giovanni must get the credit — or discredit — for its initiation.

Unusual word division is represented by *qu-aeso*, *prim-is*, *pr-eterea*, *permi-ttat*, *cl-assi*, *q-uarta*, *hu-ic*, *ca-usa*, *q-uenquam*. One noteworthy point is that Giovanni knew enough Greek to copy it himself and did not leave space for another to enter it, as Poggio and Niccoli did. Altogether, he was a man we should like to know more about.

Giacomo Curlo or Curolo (Iacobus Curlus) was born in Liguria and called himself a Genoese, but his first scribal activity, as far as we know, was in Florence. He copied a manuscript for Cosimo de' Medici at Florence in 1423 and another for the same Cosimo at Rome in 1425. That closes his brief Florentine period as a copyist. He engaged in work of a political or diplomatic nature in the service of Genoa and Naples. He also busied himself with literary and humanistic activity. It was not until 1455, to judge from extant manuscripts, that he again took his pen in hand to do professional copying, though he had the title "scriptore" to King Alfonso of Naples from 1446 to 1458. He died about 1459.[7]

We know of the following books that he produced, all on parchment:

1. Florence, Laur. 50, 18. Fig. 51. Cicero, *Brut.*, *Or.* At end (fol. 157v): "Cosmae de Medicis hoc opus absolvi feliciter die prima Octobris MCCCCXXIII ego Iacobus Antonii Curli Ianuensis Florentiae".

2. Laur. 50, 32. Fig. 52. Cicero, *De or.* At end (fol. 216v): "Iacobus Curlus Ianuensis Romae absolvit XVI Kalendas Octobres MCCCCXXV Cosmae de Medicis".

3. Paris, Bibliothèque Nationale lat. 4956. De Marinis, II, Pl. 127. Justinus. At end (fol. 155r): "Divo Alfonso regi Iacobus Curlus ut potuit excripsit". Before 1458 according to De Marinis. D'Ancona [8] II, No. 743.

4. Oxford, Bodl. Canon. Lat. 274. Fig. 53; De Marinis, II, Pl. 17. Vegetius.[9] At end: "Iacobus Curlus mandato serenissimi regis Alfonsi Aragonum et utriusque Siciliae triumphantissimi transcripsit Neapoli XII Kalendas Augusti". Before 1458 according to De Marinis.

5. Syracuse, Bibl. del Seminario. Georgius Trapezuntius, *Rhet.* Fol. 313: "Iacobus Antonius Curlus divi Alphonsi regis iussu excripsit feliciter". Fol. 314: "Divi regis Alphonsi iussu Iacobus Curlus excripsit". Before 1458 according to De Marinis. Not seen by me.

The following have disappeared: 1. Panormita, *De dictis et factis Alfonsi*, written in 1455; 2. Principe di Torella, Naples, Book

[7] The best account of Curlo is in the splendid book of T. De Marinis, *op. cit.*, I, p. 13, etc.

[8] P. D'Ancona, *La miniatura fiorentina* (Florence, 1912).

[9] A description of the manuscript while it was in the Canonici collection in Venice is given by I. Morelli, *Bibliotheca Regia Divi Marci Venetiarum*, I (Bassano, 1802), p. 342; another by H. O. Coxe, *Catalogus Codicum Manuscriptorum Bibliothecae Bodleianae*, III (Oxford, 1854), p. 226.

of Hours, with colophon: "Iacobus Antonius Curlus divi Alphonsi regis iussu exscripsit feliciter"; 3. Curlo, *Epitoma Donati in Terentium*, etc. (De Marinis, *op. cit.*, II, p. 57).

A glance at the two earliest manuscripts of 1423 and 1425 (Laur. 50, 18 and 50, 32) shows quite clearly that Curlo was a disciple of Giovanni Aretino. Particularly striking is the *g*, with the connecting stroke between top and bottom bending toward the left and thus preparing for the type of *g* which was common from about 1440. The *s* and *ſ*, with knobbed centers, also bear much resemblance to Giovanni's. Both scribes write dot *and* accent above *y* (Figs. 49, 52).

One of the most remarkable scribes of the fifteenth century was Antonio di Mario of Florence. His full name is given in one manuscript (No. 42 below) as Antonius Marii Francisci Nini, and so it also appears in the list of notaries of the Signoria of Florence for 1436 and 1446.[10] The last mention of him is in 1461, when he was named "notarius Montiscaroli." [11] He is remarkable for the length of time in which he was active in his profession (his extant work runs from 1417 to 1456) and for the number of manuscripts he copied: forty-one are known to me to exist today, and there are no doubt others not discovered by me.[12] He seems to have signed all his manuscripts and dated them (except No. 42 below) although it is possible that some unsigned ones have not been identified (see note 14). His first dated manuscript is of the same year as the last dated one of Giovanni Aretino. Fifteen of his volumes are in the basic collection of the Laurentian library. Two of these were copied specifically for Cosimo the Elder in 1426 and 1427, as Antonio's subscriptions indicate; a third too was transcribed for Cosimo, in 1426, as we shall see, though the colophon makes no mention of this. We are led to think that others too, especially those finished in these years, were made for Cosimo. The ownership claim of Piero, son of Cosimo, is found in eight. Another was written for Benedetto Strozzi. Five are

10 D. Marzi, *La cancelleria della repubblica fiorentina* (Rocca S. Casciano, 1910), pp. 499-500.

11 De Marinis, *op. cit.*, I, p. 37, n. 150.

12 In his very useful article, "Clues for Dating Florentine Humanistic Manuscripts", *Studies in Philology*, XLIV (1947), p. 127, J. P. Elder lists twenty-five of these.

among later accessions of the Laurentian, coming from collections in or near Florence. Two are in the Nazionale Centrale of Florence. Three, written for William Gray, Bishop of Ely, are in Balliol College, Oxford.

The list, with Antonio's colophons (always in capitals), which sometimes contain allusions to current events, follows:

1. Aug. 24, 1417. Florence, Laur. Conventi Soppressi (Vallombrosa) 287. Figs. 54-55. Lactantius. Fol. 220v: "Hunc librum scripsit Antonius Marius de Florentia MCCCCXVII, XXIIII Augusti peste laborante per Tusciam et maxime Florentiae".

2. Dec. 15, 1419. Rome, Vat. lat. 1865. Fig. 56; Morison, Figs. 13, 18.[13] Curtius Rufus. Fol. 142r: "(H)unc librum scripsit Antonius Marius civis et notarius Florentins [*sic*] XVIII Kl. Ianuarii Florentiae MCCCCXVIIII. Valeas qui legis".

3. Mar. 3, 1420. Laur. 79, 19. Aristotle, *Econ.*, tr. by Leonardo Bruni. Fol. 29r: "Antonius Marius Florentinus scripsit V Nonas Martii MCCCCXVIIII. Valeas qui legis". The dating is presumably Florentine style; therefore 1420. Fol. 39r: "Liber Petri de Medicis Cosme filii".

4. Nov. 11, 1420. Laur. 49, 6. Cicero, *Fam.* Fol. 188r: "Antonius Marius Florentinus transcripsit Florentiae III Idus Novembris anno domini MCCCCXX, XIIII indictione. Tibi Benedicto Strozo salutes plurimas. Lege feliciter meique sis memor. Inceptus dicto anno VIII Idus Septembris".

5. Feb. 8, 1423. Vat. Chig. lat. H. VI. 200. Plautus. Fol. 116v: "Antonius Marius trascripsit VI Idus Februarii MCCCCXXII Florentie. Valeas qui legis". Florentine dating, i.e., 1423.

6. June 12, 1424. Bologna, Università 358. Leonardo Bruni, *Hist. Flor. populi.* Fol. 189v: "Ego Antonius Marii filius notarius et Florentinus civis absolvi Florentiae II Idus Iunii MCCCCXXIIII. Valeant feliciter legentes". "Ex bibliotheca Ioannis Iacobi Canonici Amadei".

7. June 20, 1425. Laur. 54, 12. Apuleius, *Socr.*, *Asclep.*, *Plat.*, *Mund.*, *Met.*, *Mag.* (*Apol.*), *Flor.* Fol. 146r (after *Met.*): "Apulei Platonici Madaurensis Methamorphoseon liber ultimus explicit quem transcripsi cum duobus incorruptissimis exemplaribus me inscio neque cognito. Correptus deinde et emendatus per me ipsum scriptorem cum optimo atque vetustissimo exemplari MCCCCXXV. Valeas feliciter". Fol. 198: "Antonius Marius Florentinus transcripsit Florentiae XII Kalendas Iulii MCCCCXXV". "Liber Petri de Medicis Cosme filii".

[13] Stanley Morison, "Early Humanistic Script and the First Roman Type", *The Library*, XXIV (1943).

8. Sept. 30, 1425. Laur. 54, 30. A. Gellius. Fol. 207r: "Antonius Marii filius Florentinus transcripsit Florentiae I Kalendas Octobris MCCCCXXV quo tempore nostra respublica pro tuenda libertate ardens atque acre bellum cum duce Mediolanensi patiebatur. Valeas qui legis." "Liber Petri de Medicis Cosme filii".

9. May 11, 1426. Edinburgh, National Library 1. 1. 5. Eusebius, *Chron.*, tr. by Jerome. Fol. 76v: "Ego Antonius Marii filius et Florentinus civis absolvi V Idus Mai MCCCCXXVI quo tempore ducalis illustrisque dominatio Venetorum simul cum nostra republica Florentina colligatione facta pro earum libertate tuenda adversus tyrannidem ducem Mediolanensem, qui annis iam elapsis iniquissime et iniuste contra dictam nostram rempublicam Florentinam bellum fecerat, viriliter atque fortiter dimicabant. Valeas qui legis". Not seen by me.

10. May 23, 1426. Laur. 45, 32. Seneca, *Epist.* Fol. 206r: "Ego Antonius Marii filius Florentinus civis absolvi Florentiae X Kalendas Iunii anno domini MCCCCXXVI". Fol. 209r: "Valeas qui legis feliciter". "Liber Petri de Medicis Cosme filii". Written for Cosimo de' Medici, as we know from a letter of Niccoli, to be cited below.

11. May 31, 1426. Laur. 76, 35. Seneca, *Ben.*, *Ira*, *Clem.*, *Prov.*, *Vita Beata*, *Tranq.*, *Brev.*, *Cons. Helv.*, *Cons. Pol.*, *Cons. Mart.*, *Declam.*, *Quaest.* Fol. 198r: "Lege felciter [*sic*] suavissime mi Cosma". Fol. 347r: "Ego Antonius Marii filius Florentinus civis absolvi II Kalendas Iunii MCCCCXXVI. Valeas qui legis". "Liber Petri de Medicis Cosme filii".

12. Jan. 6, 1427. Laur. 65, 24. Plutarch, Lives of Alexander and Caesar, Aristides and Cato, Flaminius [*sic*] and Themistocles, Cimon and Lucullus, Coriolanus, Marcellus, tr. by Francesco Barbaro, Guarino, and Leonardo Giustiniani. Fol. 241r: "Antonius Marii filius Florentinus civis absolvit Florentiae VIII Idus Ianuarii MCCCCXXVI. Valeas qui legis feliciter". Presumably Florentine style dating, i.e., 1427.

13. Mar. 14, 1427. Bologna, Università 656. Emanuel Caleca, *Contra Graecorum errores*, tr. by Ambrogio Traversari. Fol. 210r: "Ego Antonius Marii filius Florentinus civis transcripsi Florentiae II Idus Martias anno domini MCCCCXXVI. Valeas qui legis". Presumably Florentine style dating, i.e., 1427. "Donatus fuit liber iste per reverendum in Christo patrem ac dominum dominum Nicolaum tituli Sancte Crucis cardinalem" (= Card. Albergati).

14. June 25, 1427. Laur. 76, 57. Plato, *Epist.*, tr. by Leonardo Bruni, *Apol.*, *Crito*, *Phaedo*. Fol. 148v: "Antonius Marii filius Florentinus civis absolvit Florentiae VII Kalendas Iulias MCCCCXXVII. Valeas feliciter Cosma mi suavissime".

15. July 8, 1427. Laur. 73, 5. Fig. 57. Celsus. Fol. 203r: "Antonius

Marii Florentinus civis absolvit Florentiae VIII Idus Iulii MCCCCXXVII. Valeas qui legis foeliciter".

16. Aug. 2, 1427. Florence, Naz. Magl. I, 8. V. Federici, *La scrittura delle cancellerie* (Rome, 1934), Pl. LXXXII, 2. Festus. Fol. 101v: "Antonius Marii filius Florentinus civis transcripsit Florentiae IIII Nonas Augusti MCCCCXXVII. Valeas qui legis". "Provenienza Marmi".

17. Sept. 18, 1427. Laur. 51, 5. Varro, *L. L.*, Festus. Fol. 158v: "Antonius Marii filius Florentinus civis absolvit Florentiae XIIII Kalendas Ottobris MCCCCXXVII. Valeas qui legis feliciter". "Liber Petri de Medicis Cosme filii".

18. Nov. 2, 1427. Laur. 76, 11. Cicero, *Acad.* (*Luc.*), *Leg.* Fol. 88v: "Antonius Marii filius Florentinus civis absolvit Florentiae IIII Nonas Novembris MCCCCXXVII. Valeas qui legis feliciter".

19. Oct. 19, 1429. Monte Cassino 529. Reproduction of last leaf in *Paleografia artistica di Montecassino, Latino* (1882), Pl. LXVII. Pliny, *Epist.* "Absolvi ego Antonius Marii filius Florentinus civis Florentiae XIIII Kalendas Novembris MCCCCXXVIIII. Valeas feliciter qui legis". Not seen by me.

20. Nov. 19, 1429. Laur. 39, 35. G. Vitelli and C. Paoli, *Collezione fiorentina di facsimili paleografici* (Florence, 1886), Pl. 48. Valerius Flaccus. Fol. 118r: "Absolvi ego Antonius Marii filius Florentinus civis Florentiae XIII Kalendas Decembris MCCCCXXVIIII. Valeas qui legis". "Liber Petri de Medicis Cosme filii".

21. Feb. 13, 1430. Laur. Strozz. 13. Ephraem Syrus, *Sermones*, Basil, *De vera integritate Virg.*, tr. by Ambrogio Traversari. Fol. 115r (end of Ephraem): "Absolvi ego Antonius Marii filius Florentinus civis Florentiae Idibus Februarii MCCCCXXVIIII". Fol. 176v: "Antonius Marii qui supra transcripsit Florentiae. Valeas qui legis feliciter". Presumably Florentine style dating, i.e., 1430. Fol. 3r: "Lege feliciter".

22. Nov. 19, 1435. Vat. lat. 243. Eusebius, *Chron.*, tr. by Jerome. Fol. 76v: "Antonius Marii Florentinus civis et notarius transcripsit Florentiae anno domini MCCCCXXXV mundi vero ut in volumine hoc manifeste colligitur V̄DCXXXV, XIII Kalendas Decembris. Valeas feliciter qui legis".

23. Sept. 27, 1437. Vienna 344 (Hohendorf f. 4). Reproduction of fol. 1 in H. J. Hermann, *Beschreibendes Verzeichnis der illuminierten Handschriften in Oesterreich*, VIII, VI (Leipzig, 1932), p. 9, Plate II, 1. Eusebius, *Chron.*, tr. by Jerome. Fol. 76v: "Antonius Marii filius Florentinus civis atque notarius transcripsit Florentiae V Kalendas Ottobris MCCCCXXXVII laborante peste per totam Tusciam. Valeas feliciter qui legis". Not seen by me.

24. May 2, 1440. Laur. 89 inf. 5. Eusebius, *Chron.*, tr. by Jerome.

Fol. 76v: "Antonius Marii filius Florentinus civis atque notarius transcripsit Florentiae VI Nonas Maias MCCCCXL. Valeas feliciter qui legis". From the Bibliotheca Gaddiana.

25. May 23, 1440. Vat. Urb. lat. 245. Fig. 58; Morison, *op. cit.*, Figs. 14, 19. Pliny, *N. H.* Fol. 384r: "Antonius Marii filius Florentinus civis atque notarius transcripsit Florentiae X Kalendas Iunii MCCCCXL quo tempore Graecorum aeclesia Romane eclesiae dei ope summoque studio ac labore in dicta civitate unita est virtute atque industria sanctissimorum atque preclarissimorum virorum Eugenii papae IIII summi Romanorum pontificis et Ioseph patriarce Constantinopolitani ad laudem et gloriam Dei et honorem nostrae reipublice Florentine. Valeas feliciter qui legis".

26. Oct. 8, 1440. London, collection of Miss Dorothy Walker, formerly in that of Emery Walker. Ephraem Syrus, *Sermones.* "Antonius Marii filius Florentinus civis atque notarius transcripsit Florentiae VIII Idus Ottobris MCCCCXL. Sis o lector per longeva tempora felix". The L at the end of the date has been erased. Known to me originally from a note by S. C. Cockerell in his copy of J. W. Bradley's *A Dictionary of Miniaturists, Illuminators, Calligraphers and Copyists* (London, 1887-89). I am indebted to Mr. Alfred Fairbank for telling me about this copy, now in the Victoria and Albert Museum, London. Later Mr. J. T. Brown of the British Museum very kindly examined the manuscript for me and had a photograph made of the last page. The manuscript was formerly in the Barrois collection, 321, sold at Sotheby's June 11, 1901, Lot 136.

27. June 13, 1444. Laur. 65, 5. Leonardo Bruni, *Hist. Flor. populi.* Fol. 313v: "Antonius Marii filius Florentinus civis atque notarius transcripsit Florentiae ex originali Ydibus Iunias [*sic*] MCCCCXLIIII quo quidem tempore elegantissimus harum historiarum scriptor feliciter obiit. Nam preter cuncta ornamentorum genera quibus celeberrimum eius funus a populo Florentino egregiae prae caeteris ac mirabiliter ornabatur nos ad peremnem quandam gloriae suae illustrationem publico eiusdem populi nomine a Iannozio Manetto et funebri oratione elegantissime laudatum et laurea coronatum fuisse conspeximus atque ad Crucis templum detulimus lugubre ac prorsus admirandum et omnibus quoque seculis memorandum spectaculum. Valeas feliciter o lector". "Liber Petri de Medicis Cosme filii". Fol. 114r (end Bk. IV): "Bene sit tibi o lector". Fol. 181v (beginning Bk. VII): "Prosequere feliciter". Fol. 264v: "Lege feliciter". D'Ancona II, No. 418.

28. Apr. 9, 1445. Laur. Fies. 190. Virgil. At end: "Antonius Marii filius Florentinus civis atque notarius transcripsit Florentiae V Idus Aprilis MCCCCXLV. Valeas qui legis". Not seen by me.

29. July 2, 1445. Escorial N. II. 3. Leonardo Bruni, *Hist. Flor. populi*. Fol. 332r: "Antonius Marii filius Florentinus civis atque notarius transcripsit Florentiae VI Nonas Iulias MCCCCXLV. Valeant feliciter legentes". From the library of Conde-Duque de Olivares. Not seen by me.

30. Nov. 12, 1445. Oxford, Balliol 248 E. Cicero, *Inv.*, *Her.*, *De Or.*, *Brutus*, *Orator*, *Part.*, *Top.*, *Synonima*. Fol. 251r: "Antonius Marii filius Florentinus civis atque notarius transcripsit Florentiae II Idus Novembris MCCCCXLV. Valeas". This and the other two Balliol manuscripts were copied for William Gray, bishop of Ely, who presented them to Balliol.

31. Feb. 2, 1446. Laur. 65, 25. Plutarch, *Lives* (as in No. 12 above), tr. by Guarino, etc. Fol. 220v: "Antonius Marii filius Florenus [*sic*] civis atque notarius transcripsit Florentiae IIII Nonas Februarii MCCCCXLV. Valeas o lector". Presumably Florentine style dating, i.e., 1446. D'Ancona II, No. 423.

32. Aug. 12, 1447. Balliol 154. John Chrysostom, tr. by Ambrogio Traversari. Fol. 266r: "Antonius Marii filius Florentinus civis atque notarius transcripsit Florentiae I [*sic*] Idus Augusti MCCCCXLVII. Salvus sis o lector". At the end of table of contents (fol. 2v): "Lege feliciter mi suavissime Ghuiglielme". Addressed to William Gray.

33. June 12, 1448. Balliol 78 B. Iohannes Climacus, *Scala spiritualis*, tr. by Ambrogio Traversari. Fol. 190v: "Antonius Marii filius Florentinus civis atque notarius trascripsi Florentiae ab originalibus exemplaribus II Idus Iunii MCCCCXLVIII quo tempore nostra respublica iniquiter et iniuste ab inmanissimo rege Aragonum vexabatur. Valeas mi suavissime Ghuiglielme feliciter". Ghuiglielmus is William Gray.

34. Oct. 30, 1448. Paris, Bibliothèque Nationale lat. 5722. Curtius Rufus. Fol. 180r: "Antonius Marii filius Florentinus civis atque notarius transcripsit Florentiae III Kalendas Novembris MCCCCXLVIII laborante peste quasi per universum orbem. Valeas feliciter o lector". Inside of cover: "Iste liber est mei Simoneti de Campofregoso".

35. Dec. 22, 1448. Florence, Naz. Conv. Soppr. A. 2. 2638. Matteo Palmieri, *De temporibus*. Fol. 95r: "Antonius Marii filius Florentinus civis atque notarius transcripsit Florentiae ab originali XI Kalendas Ianuarii MCCCCXLVIII. Valeas qui legis". From the Badia, i.e., S. Maria Florentina.

36. Sept. 21, 1451. Paris, Bibliothèque Nationale lat. 4927. De Marinis, *op. cit.*, IV, Pl. 186. Matteo Palmieri, *De temporibus*. Fol. 98r: "Antonius Marius Florentinus civis atque notarius transcripsit Florentiae XI Kalendas Ottobris MCCCCLI". From the library of King Alfonso of Aragon, Naples (G. Mazzatinti, *La Biblioteca dei re d'Aragona in Na-*

poli [Rocca S. Casciano, 1897], p. 86; L. Delisle, *Le Cabinet des Manuscrits*, I [Paris, 1868], p. 220). D'Ancona II, No. 742.

37. Nov. 28, 1451. Laur. 67, 25. Nepos. Fol. 135r: "Antonius Marii filius Florentinus civis atque notarius transcripsit Florentiae IIII Kalendas Decembris MCCCCLI. Valeas qui legis". D'Ancona II, No. 448.

38. Feb., 1452. Ferrara, Carmeliti di S. Paolo. Matteo Palmieri, *De temporibus*. "Antonius Marii filius Florentinus civis atque notarius transcripsit Florentiae VIII [*sic*] Nonas Februarii 1451. Sumtum ex originali". From F. A. Zacharia, *Iter Litterarium per Italiam* (Venice, 1762), p. 160, No. 6. The manuscript is now missing.

39. Dec. 26, 1452. Laur. Marc. 362. Eusebius, *Chron.*, tr. by Jerome. Fol. 76v: "Antonius Marii filius Florentinus civis atque notarius transcripsit Florentie VII Kalendas Ianuarias MCCCCLII. Valeas feliciter qui legis".

40. May 8, 1453. Laur. 73, 6. Celsus. Fol. 176r: "Antonius Marii filius Florentinus civis atque notarius transcripsit Florentiae VIII Idus Maias MCCCCLIII. Valeas longeve qui legis". "Liber Petri de Medicis Cosme filii". Arms erased on fol. 1. D'Ancona II, No. 453.

41. Oct. 12, 1456. Vat. lat. 1969. Fig. 59. Sozomenus of Pistoia, *Chronica* (*Hist. univ.*). Fol. 622v: "Antonius Marii filius transcripsit Florentie IIII Idus Octoris [*sic*] MCCCCLVI. Valeas qui legis".

42. Holkham Hall 530. Dante, *Convito*. At end: "Per me Antonium Marii Francisci Nini". Known to me only from S. de Ricci's catalogue (*Transactions Bibliographical Society*, Supplement 7 [1932]) and Edward Moore, *Contributions to the Textual Criticism of the Divina Commedia* (Cambridge, 1889), p. 609.

All these manuscripts are on parchment, with one exception, No. 37. Of several authors there are two or more copies. Plutarch's *Lives* (Nos. 12, 31) of 1427 and 1446 are both in the Laurentian but presumably were made for different members of the Medici family, the former for Cosimo, the latter for Piero or perhaps Giovanni. Festus was written twice in the same year (Nos. 16, 17), but the latter, made for Cosimo, contains Varro too. Celsus was copied in 1427 (No. 15), no doubt for Cosimo, and in 1453 (No. 40) for Piero. Bruni's *History* was copied three times (Nos. 6, 27, 29), in 1424, in 1444 for Piero, and in 1445. The first and third are not in the Laurentian library. Eusebius' *Chronicle* was copied five times (Nos. 9, 22, 23, 24, 39), in 1426, 1435,

1437, 1440, and 1452. None seems to have been written for the Medici.[14]

To judge from known manuscripts, 1427 was one of Antonio's most active years: we have seven manuscripts of that date (Nos. 12-18). The longest interval of apparent inactivity is from February 13, 1430, to November 19, 1435 (Nos. 21-22). Antonio's last year of activity is marked by one volume, and this is the year in which he served as notary of the Signoria.

It is specifically stated in most of the manuscripts that they were written in Florence. Even those that have no such indication were written there. In No. 1 Antonio mentions the plague raging in Florence. No. 3 belonged to Piero de' Medici. In No. 11 Antonio salutes Cosimo with the greeting "happy reading." Further study may show that all his exemplars were in Florence. His products include works and translations by Florentines, some made from the original (author's) copy: Nos. 3, 6, 14, 27, 29 (Leonardo Bruni), 13, 21, 32, 33 (Ambrogio Traversari), 35, 36, 38 (Matteo Palmieri). We know that the transcriptions of at least some of the classical authors were made from Florentine manuscripts (Apuleius, Celsus). Apparently Antonio lived all his life in Florence.

If Antonio spent all his life in Florence and especially spent his youth there, how did he learn Poggio's new writing style? Poggio was in Rome after 1403, in Constance and England from 1414 to 1422, when Antonio was producing his earliest work. The likelihood is that Antonio taught himself from Poggio manuscripts in Cosimo's library and in Niccoli's temporary possession.

14 Several other manuscripts have been proposed for membership in the Antonian group: Vienna 238 (H. J. Hermann, *Beschreibendes Verzeichnis der illuminierten Handschriften in Oesterreich*, VIII, VI [Leipzig, 1932], p. 10 and Plate II, 2) and Vatican Ottob. lat. 1450 (T. de Marinis, *op. cit.*, II, p. 97). Neither is signed but the script of both is thought to resemble Antonio's. This view I must reject. Lachmann in his *Commentarius* to Lucretius, ed. 3 (Berlin, 1866), p. 6, quotes H. Keil as saying that Laur. 35, 31 was copied by Antonio. Munro in his third edition of Lucretius (Cambridge, 1873), p. 24, is quite right in denying this. De Marinis (I, p. 207) suggests that an Aratus in the library of C. W. Dyson Perrins, No. 84 (at Davenham, Malvern, Worcs.) was perhaps copied by Antonio, to judge from the script. I have not seen this manuscript. Someone told me that Oxford, New College 249 was copied by Antonio. The manuscript is unsigned but the script closely resembles Antonio's; it has his distinctive capital A and M.

The other possibility is that he learned from Giovanni Aretino or someone else. That he received encouragement from Niccoli and owed his connection with Cosimo to him is made likely by a letter which Niccoli wrote to Cosimo March 20, 1426.[15] First he reports that a monk who had purchased Cosimo's "Pistole" wished to buy Cosimo's Boethius, a sale which Niccoli recommends, for with the money two manuscripts in "lettera all'antiqua" (i.e., Antonio's style) could be made. Then he informs Cosimo that he has arranged to have Antonio di Mario copy Seneca's "Pistole" in the same script as the other works, but in a smaller volume. The Senecan Epistles agreed on must be No. 10, finished May 23, 1426, two months after the letter was written. The other volume must have been No. 11, Seneca's Dialogues, etc., finished eight days after the Epistles. The subscription says that this manuscript was copied for Cosimo. Niccoli goes on to say that the two volumes will not be bound together, for the other (the Dialogues) is too long — thirty-five *quinterni*. That would be 350 fols. — and No. 11 has 347 in thirty-five numbered gatherings (thirty-four quinternions and one quaternion, with a leaf cut off). So I believe we can say with confidence that No. 11 is the manuscript referred to. No. 10 has 209 fols. (twenty-one quinternions). True, the Epistles (No. 10) were finished eight days earlier, but Antonio may have turned from the other manuscript in order to complete the Epistles.

In thirteen of the manuscripts, beginning with No. 2 (1419) and ending with No. 41 Antonio uses the formula "Valeas qui legis" in the colophon. In twelve others he uses the variations "Valeas feliciter qui legis," "Valeas qui legis feliciter." There are other variants too. The original form was used by Poggio in manuscripts copied in 1408–09 (Laur. 67, 15) and 1425 (Laur. 50, 31). I believe that the first of these (and perhaps other manuscripts now lost that contained the formula) were available in Florence when Antonio began to employ the formula in 1419.

15 Published in *Le Carte Strozziane del R. Archivio di Stato in Firenze, Inventario*, Serie prima, Vol. I (Florence, 1884), p. 590; facsimile in Morison, *op. cit.*, Fig. 5. The signature is merely "N. tuo" but the contents of the letter make clear that the writer was Niccolò Niccoli. The letter is dated March 20, 1425, presumably according to Florentine style dating, which would be 1426.

At the beginning of this chapter we noted Giovanni Aretino's use of the dangling *ct* ligature where the two letters are in separate lines. Antonio follows this practice much more frequently beginning with his first book (No. 1; 1417). Did he imitate Giovanni or someone else? For imitation it must be, since independent excogitation of such a freakish absurdity would scarcely seem possible. Antonio also uses the *ct* ligature in capitals (Figs. 58, 59).

Another Poggian characteristic preserved by Antonio is the use of the Gothic script in long marginal additions. Actually he reverts to a greater extent to the Gothic of Petrarch, Boccaccio, and Salutati than Poggio did.[16]

Antonio's earlier work resembles Poggio's script more than his later products, though even this lacks the graceful firmness of the master. Antonio more and more throws off restraint and indulges in fantastic forms. Fairly long serifs at the ends of descenders distinguish his script from Poggio's.

Antonio's first known manuscript — and perhaps the first he wrote — shows that he was just learning the new script. On fol. 1r we note twenty-five instances of the Gothic 2-shaped *r*, on fol. 220v there are none; on the former, three of round final *s*, on the latter, none. Diphthongs are not often written in the earlier pages. Descenders are too long on fol. 1. Fols. 1 and 199 may be compared in Figs. 54 and 55.

Antonio goes particularly wild on word division at line ends. In his very first manuscript of 1417 we find such things as *pr-ona*, *to-llens*, *sedi-sse*, *rep-udiant*, *asc-endisse*, *mu-ndum* in great numbers — seven on fol. 3r. In later manuscripts we come upon *qui-ppe* (Fig. 56), *gen-us*, *ha-ud* (No. 2); *q-uantum* (No. 3); *a-ut*, *su-mma* (No. 4); *re-dditur* (No. 7); *ferre-ntur* (No. 12); *e-sse*, *m-enbra* (No. 15); *i-dest*, *g-entes* (No. 16); *m-ihi*, *Cecro-ps*, *ur-bs* (No. 22); *eg-redi*, *f-ons*, *m-ugitu*, *gr-andiores*, *b-urirelinus* (No. 25); *po-sset*, *p-otest*, *a-udierint*, *plac-et*, *sc-riptoris*, *o-ccidisti*, *h-anc*, *b-reviter*, *q-uare*, *d-ictum*, *c-ensus* (No. 30); *c-onfingere*, *d-ominus*, *inq-uit*, *sp-iritus*, *perv-ectus* (No. 32); *n-ullum*, *tam-en* (No. 37); *po-stquam* (No. 41). These are just a few samples.

Coupled with this peculiarity is the excessive amount of word division. In No. 34, for example, it is not uncommon for over

16 Morison, *op. cit.*, Fig. 13.

half of the twenty-six lines on a page to end in hyphens. In one case I counted nineteen — and this may not be the maximum.

In spite of the disregard of rules of word division, presumably in the interest of justifying the margin, Antonio occasionally gets reckless about the margin. If the last word is the enclitic *que* he writes a capital Q with an exaggerated tail running into the margin and the abbreviation stroke crawling along it. Similar is the treatment of the abbreviation for *-orum*. Other letters may have long finishing strokes (*s* in Fig. 59). To save space a long capital T is used, a *q* with a long vertical tail. To fill space, the wide round *s* is adopted, an uncial *m*, deleted *i*, etc.

Particularly in capitals Antonio sometimes given rein to his fancy. An uncial M with a cross in the middle is found in No. 2; one with a prolonged center stroke in Nos. 22, 33, etc. *Qui* is sometimes written by putting an I inside the Q (Nos. 12, 13, 16). The A is apt to be an elaborate uncial, especially in his own name.[17] Uncial E occurs. F usually has a flourish at the top (Fig. 59).[18] By and large we can say that Antonio's capitals have lost the epigraphical character of Poggio's.

A character employed by Antonio in several books (Nos. 12, 30, 31, 32, 34, 41, and perhaps others) consists of two overlapping V's, as in *vultis*.

In his first manuscript Antonio usually follows the old spellings *michi* and *nichil*. In No. 2 we find these spellings on fols. 1-7. In the rest of the manuscript and thereafter I think he writes only *mihi* and *nihil*. In the matter of the diphthong *ae* he is as inconsistent as Poggio, though my impression is that he wrote *ae* more often than *e*, whereas Poggio did the opposite. In Nos. 2 and 4 *quaem* frequently appears for *quem*. In No. 16 Antonio became so diphthong-conscious that he wrote *naec* for *nec* five times on fol. 101v! I noticed almost no diphthongs in Nos. 35-41.

Beginning with No. 2 we find accent marks on *á*, *é*, later on *ó*, *illó* and *eó* (adv.), *uná* (adv.), *itáque*, *cedó* (imp.).

From No. 12 on Antonio arranges words in patterns in order

[17] Morison, *op. cit.*, Figs. 13, 14.

[18] Morison's suggestion that the I with a center cross stroke was taken from Greek manuscripts by Antonio is inacceptable, for this form occurs in earlier Latin manuscripts, e.g., Paris. lat. 14080, fol. 1, a manuscript of the tenth or eleventh century.

to fill a page: diamond, sword, pine tree, vase, hour glass, circle, trefoil, tower, triangle, etc.

Antonio wrote to fol. 192v in No. 15 (Fig. 57), then another, very awkward, scribe copied fols. 192v-197v, when Antonio returned to his task to fol. 202r; his substitute continued to the end (fol. 203r). In No. 40 the same thing happened: Antonio copied to fol. 68v, then the same unknown hand of No. 15 went on, Antonio started again on fol. 73r, the other hand did fols. 175-176, as well as adding omitted material covering fols. 77, 167-170. The reader may supply for himself the explanation of this practice.

Antonio's activity ended soon after the mid-century. Next we take up briefly his younger contemporaries and successors during the period which saw the decline of the copyist and the rise of the printer.

Chapter VI

THE LAST HALF CENTURY

When Antonio di Mario ended his career as a copyist in 1456, Gherardo del Ciriagio had been practicing the same art for nine years. His career lasted only twenty-five years in contrast to Antonio's thirty-nine, but in that time his output was relatively greater than that of his older contemporary. Furthermore, it was of better quality. In Florence he was the dominant figure among the scribes of the third quarter of the century.

Gherardo del Ciriagio, or Ciliagio, who Latinized his name as Cerasius, was the son of a Florentine silk dyer. From his earliest or one of his earliest manuscripts on (1447) he called himself a notary. He was notary of the Signoria in Florence in 1457 and 1464.[1] He died in 1472, the year of his last dated manuscripts. Thirteen of his volumes are in the Laurentian, and of these, he tells us in the colophons, nine were made for Giovanni di Cosimo de' Medici and two for Piero di Cosimo. It is practically certain that the other three were written for a member of the same family. Another copied for Giovanni is now in Paris. The last two that he wrote were done in 1472 for Alfonso, Duke of Calabria, and Federico, Duke of Urbino. We may regard it as certain that manuscripts not in the Laurentian which make no mention of the Medici were not executed for members of that family.

The manuscripts copied by Gherardo, all but one on parchment, that are known to me are the following:

1. New York, collection of Adrian Van Sinderen. Petrarch, *Trionfi*. Strozzi arms. "Domini Francisci Petrarche poete clarissimi Floren-

[1] D. Marzi, *La cancelleria della repubblica fiorentina* (Rocca S. Casciano, 1910), pp. 501-502. In Laur, 37, 16, dated 1457, Gherardo called attention to his official position: "dum essem notarius et scriba dominorum civitatis Florentie".

tini Triumphi expliciunt. Lege feliciter. Scripti fuerunt per me Gherardum Florentinum de anno domini MCCCCXLVI indictione decima de mense Martii. Deo gratias". 1447 (Florentine style). I owe a photograph of the colophon (which is in capitals) to the kindness of Mr. Van Sinderen. This example is somewhat doubtful, as the name del Ciriagio is not used and the colophon differs from the others in several respects. A comparison of the capitals strongly favors the identification. Ownership signature of Filippo and Lorenzo Strozzi. Not seen by me.

2. Oxford, Balliol 248 B. Cicero, *Phil.*, *Verr.* "Per me Gherardum Cerasium civem et notarium Florentinum anno domini MCCCCXLVII die trigesimo Septembris". Not seen by me.

3. Goettingen, Univ. Cod. Theol. 136. Poggio, *De varietate fortunae.* "Libri ... scripti per me Gherardum Iohannis Ciriagi civem et notarium Florentinum de anno MCCCCL die XVII Iunii". D'Ancona [2] II, No. 731. Not seen by me.

4. Dresden Dc. 155. Juvenal, Persius. "Scriptus per me Gherardum Iohannis del Ciriagio civem et notarium Florentinum de anno domini MCCCCLII de mense Augusti". F. Schnorr von Carolsfeld, *Katalog der Handschriften der ... Bibliothek zu Dresden* (Leipzig, 1882). Not seen by me.

5. Kew, Surrey, England, collection of B. S. Cron, formerly of Sir Sydney Cockerell. Sotheby sale of library of Samuel Allen of Lisconnan, Co. Antrim, January 20, 1920; B. Quaritch Catalogue 369 (September, 1886), No. 35747; Sotheby sale June 18, 1886, No. 1238. Cicero, *De oratore.* "Scriptus autem fuit per me Gherardum Iohannis del Ciriagio civem et notarium Florentinum MCCCCLIII". One leaf of text and two blanks were missing when Sir Sydney acquired the volume in 1920. Before having the book rebound he gave thirteen damaged or mutilated leaves to various friends. One was given to Graily Hewitt, from whom it passed to Mr. Alfred Fairbank of Hove, Sussex, England. This contains III, 84-91 (*ulla difficilior... maxime in sen-*), as Mr. Fairbank kindly informed me. Another leaf is in the hands of Dr. Eric G. Millar of London, from whom I learn that it contains I, 26-33 (*divinitus a tribus... ad illa summa*). A third, as Mr. Fairbank kindly informed me, is in the library of the Society of Scribes and Illuminators in London, presented to it by Madelyn Walker. It contains I, 7-13 (*qui si... vehementius quam eloquentiae*). The present location of the others is unknown to me nor is it recalled by Sir Sydney. I am indebted to Mr. Cron for his courteous replies to my inquiries. The book originally had thirteen signatures of ten leaves, and one of eight. Lacking today are I, fols, 2, 3, 5, 7, 8; II, fol. 9; IV, fols. 6, 9; VII, fol. 10;

2 P. D'Ancona, *La miniatura fiorentina* (Florence, 1912).

X, fol. 8; XI, fol. 8; XII, fols. 1, 4, 5; XIV, fols. 7, 8 (blanks). Mr. Fairbank's leaf is perhaps XII, fol. 5; the Society of Scribes' leaf is I, fol. 2; Dr. Millar's is I, fol. 5. *Book Handbook*, 2 (1951), p. 16 and Plates 10 and 10a. Not seen by me.

6. Florence, Laur. 39, 8. Fig. 60. Virgil. "Scriptus manu mei Gherardi Iohannis del Ciriagio civis et notarii Florentini de anno domini MCCCCLIII pro magnifico viro Iohanne Cosmi de Medicis". D'Ancona II, No. 325.

7. Rome, Bibl. Corsiniana 44. B. 40. Petrarch, *Trionfi*. "Scriptus per me Gherardum Iohannis Cerasii de Florentia de anno domini MCCCCLIIII". Not seen by me.

8. Florence, Laur. Acquisti e Doni 446, from Libreria L. Gonnelli & Figli, Florence, Boll. 93 (1957), No. 41 (with reproduction). Paper. Plutarch, Basil, Xenophon, tr. by Leonardo Bruni. "Omnia vero opera que suprascripta sunt in presenti volumine ego Gherardus Iohannis del Ciriagio civis et notarius Florentinus quam accuratius potui ex originalibus dicti domini Leonardi sumpsi et exemplavi de anno domini millesimo quattuorcentesimo quinquagesimo quarto indictione tertia et de mense Ianuarii in magnifica civitate Florentina". The date is 1455 (Florentine style). Not seen by me.

9. Dorchester, England, Library of Lady Christian Martin. Virgil. 1455. Not seen by me nor have I been able to secure further information.

10. London, B. M. Harl. 2593. Manetti, *De dignitate hominis*. "Scriptus autem fuit per me Gherardum Iohannis Cerasii civem et notarium Florentinum de anno domini millesimo quadringentesimo quinquagesimo quarto de mense Martii in civitate Florentie post obitum Niccole pape". Florentine dating, i.e., 1455. Nicholas V died March 24, 1455. Facsimile of fol. 25r in E. A. Lowe, "Handwriting", in *The Legacy of the Middle Ages* (Oxford, 1926), Pl. 39; Alfred Fairbank, *A Book of Scripts* (Penguin, 1949, etc.), Pl. 13.

11. Laur. 66, 22. Manetti, *De vita Nicolai V*. "Scriptus autem fuit per me Gherardum Iohannis del Ciriagio civem et notarium Florentinum in civitate Florentie de anno domini millesimo CCCCLV pontificatus Calisti pape anno primo". Therefore after April 8. D'Ancona II, No. 439.

12. Cape Town, South African Public Library Grey 26. Petrarch, *Trionfi*. "Gherardus Cerasius Florentinus scripsit de anno MCCCCLV". H. Bohn, *A Catalogue of Books* (London, 1841), No. 13574; E. Bizzarri in *Rinascita*, IV (1941), p. 861. Not seen by me.

13. Laur. 76, 1. Cicero, *Fin.*, *Tusc.*, *Sen.*, *Am.*, *Par.*, *Off.* "Scriptus per me Gherardum Iohannis del Ciriagio civem et notarium Florentinum de anno domini MCCCCLV de mense Ianuarii pro magnifico

et spectabili viro Piero Cosme de Medicis cive Florentino" Florentine dating, i.e., 1456.

14. Laur. 36, 15. Ovid, *Met.* "Scriptus autem fuit per me Gherardum Iohannis del Ciriagio civem et notarium Florentinum pro Iohanne Cosme de Medicis optimo cive Florentino de anno domini MCCCCLVI de mense Iunii tempore sancti in Christo patris et domini domini Kalisti D. P. pape III". D'Ancona II, No. 311.

15. Laur. 48, 31. Cicero, *Phil.* "Gherardus Cerasius civis Florentinus scripsit pro Iohanne Cosme de Medicis optimo cive Florentino de anno domini MCCCCLVI de mense Iulii".

16. Laur. 33, 12. Catullus, Tibullus. Fol. 49v: "Gherardus Cerasius de Florentia scripsit pro Iohanne Cosmae de Medicis". Fol. 91v: "Gherardus Iohannis del Ciriagio civis Florentinus scripsit pro Iohanne Cosme de Medicis optimo cive Florentino de anno MCCCCLVII de mense Iulii". D'Ancona II, No. 294.

17. Paris, B. N. lat. 6376. Fig. 61. Seneca, *Dial.*, *Decl.* "Scriptus autem fuit hic liber manu mei Gherardi Iohannis del Ciriagio civis et notarii Florentini sub anno domini MCCCCLVII in civitate Florentie pro Iohanne Cosme de Medicis cive optimo Florentino". *The New Palaeographical Society*, Second Series, Vol. II, Pl. 132; D'Ancona II, No. 745.

18. Laur. 37, 16. Silius Italicus. "Scriptus autem fuit [manu *om.*] mei Gherardi Iohannis del Ciriagio civis et notarii Florentini dum essem notarius et scriba dominorum civitatis Florentie dictum librum absolvi. De anno domini MCCCCLVII pro spectabili et generoso viro Iohanne Cosme de Medicis optimo cive et primario Florentino". D'Ancona II, No. 316.

19. Laur. 45, 33. Seneca, *Epist.* Fol. 202: "Scriptus Florentie manu mei Gherardi Iohannis del Ciriagio de anno MCCCCLVIII pro Iohanne Cosme de Medicis optimo et primario cive Florentino". Fol. 207: "Lege eum feliciter. Gherardus Iohannis Ciriagii scripsit pro Iohanne Cosmo de Medicis de Florentia MCCCCLVIII". D'Ancona II, No. 348.

20. Laur. 21, 2. Lactantius. "Scriptus autem fuit manu mea Gerardi Iohannis del Ciriagio civis et notarii Florentini pro Iohanne Cosmi de Medicis optimo et primario cive Florentino de anno domini MCCCCLVIII Florentie". D'Ancona II, No. 281.

21. Escorial V. III. 18. Cicero, *Fin.* "Gherardus Cerasius civis Florentinus hunc librum manu propria scripsit in civitate Florentie anno domini MCCCCLXI de mense Aprilis et Maii". G. Antolín, *Catálogo de los códices latinos de la Real Biblioteca del Escorial* (Madrid, 1910-23). Not seen by me.

22. Rome, Vat. lat. 1811. Fig. 62. Diodorus, tr. by Poggio. "Scrip-

tus autem fuit Dyodorus iste de anno domini MCCCCLXI pontificatus sanctissimi in Christo patris et domini domini Pii divina providentia pape Secundi anno quarto manu propria mei Gherardi del Ciriagio civis Florentini. In civite (*sic*) Florentie".

23. Laur. 65, 18. Bruni, *De temporibus suis*. "Gherardus Cerasius scripsit anno MCCCCLXII".

24. Milan, Ambros. C. 290. Eusebius, *Chron.*, tr. by Jerome. 1463. Prosper, ed. T. Mommsen, *Mon. Germ. Hist.*, *Auct. Ant.*, IX (Berlin, 1892), p. 368. Not seen by me.

25. Paris, B. N. lat. 8233. Catullus, Tibullus, Propertius. Fol. 89: "Scriptus Florentie MCCCCLXV". Fol. 172: "Gherardus Cerasius Florentinus scripsit Florentie".

26. Oxford, Bodl. MS. E. D. Clarke 28 (S. C. 18390). Terence. "Scriptus autem fuit Florentie manu mei Gherardi Iohannis del Ciriagio civis et notarii Florentini de anno domini MCCCCLXVI et mensibus Maii et Iunii". Not seen by me.

27. London, B. M. Add. 16422. Sallust. "Gherardus Cerasius Florentinus scripsit Florentie de mense Novembris anno domini MCCCCLXVI papa Paulo Veneto pontifice existente". *The Palaeographical Society*, Second Series, II, Pl. 59; D'Ancona II, No. 1366.

28. Laur. 63, 2. Livy, I-X. "Scriptus autem fuit per me Gherardum Iohannis del Ciriagio civem et notarium Florentinum in civitate Florentie de anno domini MCCCCLXVI indictione XIIII". D'Ancona II, No. 1511.

29. Genoa, Univ. E V 12. Cicero, rhetorical works. "Gherardus Cerasius Florentinus scripsit Florentie MCCCCLXVII". R. Sabbadini, *Le scoperte dei codici latini e greci ne' secoli XIV e XV* (Florence, 1905), p. 150, n. 44. Not seen by me.

30. Paris, B. N. lat. 6568. Plato, *Phaedo*, tr. by Bruni. Fol. 57: "Gherardus Cerasius scripsit". Fol. 184: "Lege eum feliciter. Gherardus Cerasius Florentinus scripsit MCCCCLXXII". Fol. 200: "Omnia vero opera que supra scripta sunt in presenti volumine ego Gherardus Iohannis del Ciriagio civis et notarius Florentinus quam accuratius potui ex originalibus dicti domini Leonardi sumpsi et exemplavi in magnifica civitate Florentie de anno domini millesimo quattuorcentesimo septuagesimo secundo et de mense Maii".

31. Valencia, Univ. 765 (Gutiérrez 1513). Nepos. "Scriptus autem fuit liber iste in civitate Florentie per me Gherardum Iohannis del Ciriagio civem et notarium Florentinum pro illustrissimo principe duce Calabrie filio regis Ferdinandi de anno domini MCCCCLXXII et de mense Iunii procurante Vespasiano Philippi principe omnium librario-

rum Florentinorum". De Marinis I, pp. 98, 104; II, p. 55; IV, Pl. 306A.[3] Not seen by me.

32. Vat. Urb. lat. 1314. Fig. 63. Plato, *Phaedo*, *Gorgias*, *Phaedrus*, *Apol.*, *Crito*, tr. by Bruni. Fol. 116: "Gherardus del Ciriagio Florentinus scripsit MCCCCLXXII pro magnifico domino Federico Urbini et Montis Feretri comite". Fol. 132v: "Gherardus del Ciriagio Florentinus scripsit". Fol. 165: "Gherardus del Ciriagio Florentinus scripsit anno MCCCCLXXII pro magnifico domino domino Federico Urbini et Montis Feretri domino procurante Vespasiano Filippi principe omnium librariorum Florentinorum". D'Ancona II, No. 1341.

33. Laur. 66, 9. Josephus, *Bell. Iud.* "Scriptus manu mei Gherardi Iohannis del Ciriagio civis Florentini pro Iohanne Cosmae de Medicis cive optimo Florentino". Perhaps copied in the middle 1450's. The formula of the colophon comes closest to Nos. 5 (1453), 15 (1457), 17-18 (1458). D'Ancona II, No. 434; *La miniature italienne* (Paris, 1925), Pl. LXX. G. Biagi, *Cinquanta tavole in fototipia da codici della R. Biblioteca Medicea* (Florence, 1914), p. 14, Pl. XXXV.

34. Laur. 34, 32. Juvenal, Persius. Fol. 74: "Gherardus Cerasius scripsit Piero Cosme de Medicis optimo civi Florentino". Fol. 88: "Gherardus Cerasius Florentinus scripsit". The formula suggests a date in the late 1450's; cf. Nos. 15 (1456), 16 (1457). Furthermore, the other manuscript executed for Piero di Cosimo dates from 1456 (No. 13). D'Ancona II, No. 300.[4]

[3] T. de Marinis, *La biblioteca napoletana dei Re d'Aragona* (Milan, 1947-1952).

[4] D. Pietro Zani, *Enciclopedia metodica critica-ragionata delle belle arti*, VI (Parma, 1820), pp. 216, 337, cites subscriptions from two unidentified manuscripts of Gherardo; the first is No. 28, the second probably No. 12.

A manuscript in Brussels (1608-09) was copied in 1440 and 1442 by a Gherardus Iohannis, but although I had not seen it, I was confident that he is not our Gherardo for these reasons: he does not include the name del Ciriagio; he calls himself a "presbiter", which Gherardo was not; the language of the colophon differs from his; the book contains two mediaeval treatises on vices and virtues, the latter of which is found also in a fourteenth-century manuscript from Gembloux; it is written on paper, in two columns. I suspected that the manuscript was written in Belgium in Gothic script. For a description see J. Van den Gheyn, *Catalogue des manuscrits de la Bibliothèque Royale de Belgique*, III (Brussels, 1903), p. 316, No. 2152. M. F. Masai of the Bibliothèque Royale de Belgique completely confirms my suspicions. V. Rossi (*Rend. Acc. Lincei*, ser. V, II [1893], p. 54, n. 1) is apparently wrong in saying that Laur. 50, 19 was copied by Gherardo. I have not seen the manuscript, but in his catalogue Bandini does not mention Gherardo as the copyist.

The same contents rarely appear more than once in Gherardo's copies, perhaps because he confined his copying to the Medici family to a greater extent than Antonio did. Petrarch's *Trionfi* appears three times (Nos. 1, 7, 12), Juvenal and Persius twice (Nos. 4, 34), Virgil twice (Nos. 6, 9). Tibullus appears twice but in different combinations (Nos. 16, 25). Similarly with Nos. 2 and 15, 5 and 29, 13 and 21, 30 and 32.

If 1427 was Antonio's most active year, 1455 was Gherardo's, as far as we know: he produced five manuscripts in that year. But in his last year (1472) he still executed three. The longest period of apparent inactivity was between 1467 and 1472.

It is to be presumed that all the manuscripts were copied in Florence, though Gherardo did not begin the practice of indicating where the manuscript was written until 1455 (No. 8) nor did he keep it up regularly. But there are other indications — such as the statements that the volumes were executed for Giovanni de' Medici — that point to Florence in almost all cases.

The script of Gherardo presents no striking novelties. It is still fresh and vigorous, of much better quality than that of the often careless as well as exuberant Antonio. He does, like Antonio, use a long-tailed *q* with the abbreviation mark running along it. Other characteristics of the end of a line include the cancellation of *o*, much more often than of *i*, to fill a line. Capital *R* with a tail, minuscule *m*, *n*, etc., with tails are used for the same purpose. The familiar elongated round *s* lying on its side is also in evidence.

One remarkable fact is the apparently almost complete absence of the diphthong *ae*, to judge from the hundreds of pages I examined; some cedillas occur in No. 25. In a word containing *ct*, hyphenation at the end of a line frequently takes place before *ct*, in which case these letters are ligatured. Just as frequently the division may be between *c* and *t*. in which case the ligature is generally omitted. I found the dangling ligature only twice — once in No. 28, once in No. 33. Thus Gherardo parts from his predecessors by avoiding diphthongs and dangling ligatures. Accents appear on *á*, *é*, *ó*, *uná* (adv.), *eó* (adv.), *pené* (adv.), *argentóve*.

Gherardo indulged in unusual word division, though perhaps less so than Antonio: *ling-uarum*, *qu-ot*, *q-uorum*, *titul-us*, *tr-actandam*, *sp-iritu* (No. 10); *qu-as*, *dilig-enter* (No. 11); *deince-ps*, *su-nt*, *ap-ud*, *ca-usas*, *er-ant*, *aq-ua*, *flum-en*, *ed-ucit* (No. 22); *a-ut*, *qu-ando*, *ag-ant*

(No. 30); *ha-nc, op-us, nor-unt, un-us* (No. 32), etc., etc. Excessive hyphenation is as common in his products as in Antonio's. Thus in No. 22 half or more of the lines on a page often end with a hyphen. On fol. 167v eighteen of the thirty lines are so divided. On fol. 168r eight successive lines end in a hyphenated word. In No. 32 on one page seventeen out of twenty-eight lines end in a hyphenated word; on another page eight lines in succession end thus.

One quite unusual feature — I have not seen it elsewhere — appears in No. 6 (Virgil).[5] In order to give the effect of a solid page, i.e., to "justify" the right margin, Gherardo tried the experiment of spacing out and writing in capitals enough letters to fill out the lines — sometimes only a few letters, at other times, entire words (see Fig. 60). He did not repeat this early experiment.

Antonio Sinibaldi's activity overlapped that of Gherardo del Ciriagio by several years, as his first known manuscript is dated 1461, but his chief productivity came later and he dominated the fourth quarter of the fifteenth century in Florence as Gherardo had dominated the third. He was born in 1443, and he nearly always designates himself a Florentine. He gives his father's name as Francesco in Nos. 2 and 24 below, and in the former calls his father a *ritagliatore*, dealer in silk. In No. 1 (1461) he signs himself

[5] A Virgil at Princeton (VGRMS 2945.1470.3, De Ricci 36) has this same characteristic but only in the narrow column to the right of the illuminated initials of the Eclogues and the Aeneid. Thus in the latter only four lines are involved. The capital letters are separated by centered crosses. The illumination is of the Florentine type. The scribe is unknown but wrote a good Florentine hand, as far as can be judged from the poor facsimile of a few lines in Henry B. Van Hoesen, *Bibliography, Practical, Enumerative, Historical* (New York, 1929), p. 320. I think I have seen a similar use of capitals after initials in other manuscripts. Prof. Marvin Colker calls my attention to Einsiedeln MS. 300, a twelfth-century manuscript of Henricus Augustensis, *Planctus Evae*, in which the same practice is followed. This suggests that Gherardo may have found this usage in the Virgil that he was copying. In his copy of Tibullus (Wolfenbüttel 82. 6 Aug.; facsimile in the Leiden *Codices*) Gioviano Pontano often spaced out a word, as in German *gesperrte Schrift*, so that a three-letter word may take the space of five letters, etc. (fol. 23r, 25r, 27v, etc.). Still earlier manuscripts occasionally reveal an attempt to fill out a line in prose. Thus Verona Cap. LV (53) of the eighth century has a wide capital S taking the space of about six letters and an N about eight letters wide (J. Kirchner, *Scriptura Latina Libraria* [Munich, 1955], No. 25). Orléans 162 (ninth century) shows a wide N and *r* (E. Pellegrin in *Bibl. de l'Ecole des chartes*, CXV [1957], p. 26, Plate).

"Sinibaldus C.," which seems to be for Carmignano, where his father came from. Perhaps he had not yet achieved Florentine citizenship. In 1469 he went to the Aragonese court at Naples and worked for the royal family for several years (see Nos. 3-5). He called himself "Ferdinandi regis scriba" or "testudo" (Nos. 3-4), "Ioannis de Aragonia familiaris" (No. 7), and later "quondam regis Ferdinandi regis Siciliae scriptor et librarius" (No. 18). He was back in Florence in 1476 (No. 6) but again in Naples in 1477 (No. 7). He returned to Florence in 1481 or earlier (No. 10) and stayed there the rest of his life. In Florence he continued to work for the Aragon family (Nos. 10, 11, 12, 13, 23). Sinibaldi does not mention the Medici in his colophons, but apparently Nos. 6, 8, 15, 17, 19, 20, 21, 25 were made for them. No. 16 was copied for the Duke of Bavaria; Nos. 18, 20 for King Matthias Corvinus of Hungary.

In making his tax declaration in 1480 Sinibaldi claimed poverty, saying that his work had been so reduced by the invention of printing it hardly kept him in clothes. Yet three-fourths of his extant books were copied after that date. This situation may be explained in part by the loss of some of his earlier work, in part by the not unexpected exaggeration of a claim of poverty in a tax declaration. His last dated work is of the year 1499. The following books of his are known to me.

1. Florence, Laur. Fies. 43. Fig. 64. John Chrysostom, *Adv. vitup.* 1461, presumably at Florence. D'Ancona II, No. 562.

2. Venice, Marc. It. IX, 431 (6206). Petrarch, *Rime e Trionfi*. September 23, 1468. D'Ancona II, No. 701. Not seen by me.

3. Ferrara, Bibl. Comunale Cl. II. 9 N A 1. Ermolao Barbaro, *De coelibatu*. May 31, 1473, Naples, for King Ferdinand. De Marinis II, p. 181.

4. Rome, Vat. Ottob. lat. 36. Fig. 65. Sedulius. March 15, 1474 1473, but Naples presumably followed Florentine style). De Marinis II, p. 149.

5. Besançon, Bibl. Publ. 535. Propertius, Ovid, *Sappho ad Phaonem*. August 30, 1475, Naples. Arms of Sanseverino family, closely associated with kingdom of Naples. De Marinis, I, p. 83, gives the date as 1485. Not seen by me.

6. Paris, B. N. ital. 548. Petrarch, *Canzoniere*, *Trionfi*; Dante, *Canzoni*. September 30, 1476, Florence. D'Ancona II, No. 837.

7. Berlin, Lat. 1019. Suetonius. June 25, 1477, Naples, for Card. John of Aragon. De Marinis II, p. 154. Not seen by me.

8. Florence, Laur. 54, 3. Fig. 66. Bartolomeo Scala, *Apologi centum*. September 20, 1481, Florence, "veloci calamo". Cursive.

9. Rome, Vat. Urb. lat. 666. Fig. 67. Prudentius. November 20, 1481, Florence. D'Ancona II, No. 1328.

10. Oxford, Bodl. MS. Auct. F. 1. 18. Ovid (except *Met.*). May 4, 1483, Florence, for Card. John of Aragon. De Marinis II, p. 183.

11. Valencia, Univ. 818. Seneca, *Trag.* June 5, 1484, Florence, for Card. John of Aragon. De Marinis II, p. 150; IV, Pl. 226. Not seen by me.

12. Naples, Bibl. Oratoriana Pil. X. XXXIX. Propertius, Catullus, Tibullus, Statius. 1484, Florence. The Aragon arms have been erased but are still visible. De Marinis II, p. 321.

13. Escorial T. II. 5. Horace. 1484, Florence, for Card. John of Aragon. De Marinis II, p. 84; III, Pl. 116. Not seen by me.

14. London, B. M. Yates Thompson 23 (formerly Third Series LXXVIII). Book of Hours. 1485, for the Florentine Agostino Biliotti, presumably at Florence. D'Ancona No. 1379. H. Yates Thompson catalogue, Vol. VI, Pl. LXXXIIIB.

15. Florence, Laur. 35, 2. Lucan. 1485, Florence. D'Ancona II, No. 1615. D. Fava in *Accademie e Biblioteche d'Italia*, VI (1932), p. 139, Fig. 42.

16. Munich, lat. 23639. Book of Hours. 1485, presumably at Florence, for the Duke of Bavaria. D'Ancona II, No. 836. Plate in L. von Kobell, *Kunstvolle Miniaturen und Initialen*, ed. 2 (Munich, 1892), p. 92 and Pl. 42.

17. Florence, Laur. Ashb. 1874. Book of Hours. 1485, presumably at Florence, for Lorenzo de' Medici. D'Ancona II, No. 801; G. Biagi, *Cinquanta tavole in fototipia da codici della R. Bibl. Med. Laur.* (Florence, 1914), p. 12, Pl. XXIV-XXVIII; a few lines of text reproduced in S. Vagaggini, *La miniatura fiorentina* (Milan, 1952), Pl. 46, 47; *The Palaeographical Society, Facsimiles*, 2d Series, I, 19. I was unable to see this manuscript.

18. Paris, B. N. lat. 16839; formerly De la Vallière 21 (444). Jerome, Comm. on Psalms. February 28, 1489 (the manuscript has 1488 but this is Florentine style), Florence, for King Matthias Corvinus of Hungary. D'Ancona II, No. 1589; C. Couderc, *Les enluminures des manuscrits du Moyen Age de la Bibliothèque Nationale* (Paris, 1927), Pl. 77 and p. 104; Hevesy No. 82; Fraknói No. 81.[6]

19. Florence, Laur. 21, 17. Lotharius, *De vilitate conditionis humanae*.

[6] A. de Hevesy, *La bibliothèque du roi Matthias Corvin* (Paris, 1923); G. Fraknói, *Bibliotheca Corvina* (Budapest, 1927).

1489, presumably at Florence. "Servitor vestrae magnificentiae Antonius...". D'Ancona II, No. 845.

20. Florence, Laur. 12, 10. Augustine, *Quaest. super Gen.* 1489, Florence, for King Matthias Corvinus of Hungary, but Matthias died April 6, 1490, apparently before delivery was made, for the book passed to the Medici. D'Ancona II, No. 1440; Hevesy No. 35; Fraknói No. 36.

21. Florence, Laur. 12, 8. Fig. 68. Augustine, *Adv. Iulianum.* May 15, 1491, presumably at Florence, D'Ancona II, No. 1438.

22. Rouen, Bibl. de la Ville 366. Book of Hours. 1491, Florence, for Donato Perut(i). Not seen by me.

23. Rome, Vat. Reg. lat. 1816. Psalms, prayer. 1499, Florence. "Infrascripta oratio rex Ferdinandus in quodam libello fecit mihi transcribere... cum apud maiestem [*sic*] suam bibliothecae curam gererem". Known to me only from S. C. Cockerell's manuscript notes in his copy of J. W. Bradley's *A Dictionary of Miniaturists, Illuminators, Calligraphers and Copyists* (London 1887-89), now in the Victoria and Albert Museum, London (which copy Mr. Alfred Fairbank kindly called to my attention) and from details furnished by Prof. A. Campana of the Vatican library.

24. Berlin, Ham. 6. Aesop. No date. Aragon arms. D'Ancona II, No. 703; De Marinis II, p. 5; III, Pl. IA. Not seen by me.

25. Rome, Vat. Urb. lat. 681. Petrarch, *Canzoniere*, *Trionfi*. No date. "Antonius Francisci Sinibaldi filius quam pulcrioribus potuit litteris has chartas scripsit". For Cardinal Francesco Gonzaga of Mantua (1466-83), as shown by his arms on fol. 11.

26. Florence, Laur. 14, 23. Ambrose. No date, Florence. Medici arms. D'Ancona II, No. 1460.

27. Escorial f. II. 17. Cristoforo de' Buondelmonti, *Liber insularum Cycladum*. No date, "veloci manu". "Ioannes M. Cynicus Antonio scrinio transcribi fecit. Ideo manu mea testimonium hic scribere visum est". This is doubtful. Not seen by me.

28. Paris, Baron Edmond de Rothschild. Book of Hours. Present whereabouts unknown. D'Ancona II, No. 1716. Not seen by me.

29. Florence, T. de Marinis. Petition of Tommasa, widow of Bernardo Paganelli, to Pope Innocent VIII. "Antonius Sinibaldus Florentinus scriba gratis scripsit". About 1490. De Marinis, I, p. 55. Not seen by me.

30. Florence, Ricc. 1449. Giovanni Nesi, *Epistola*. The letter is dated September 9, 1476, and the manuscript was probably written soon after, in Florence, "celeri manu"; cursive. Facsimile in De Marinis I, p. 54.

We know of several copies made by Sinibaldi that have now disappeared: a Pliny of 1471 for the King of Aragon (De Marinis, I, p. 253, documents No. 327, 391); a Josephus and a Francesco Barbaro, *De re uxoria*, of 1473 for the King (*ibid.*, document No. 473).

Some other manuscripts, unsigned, have been claimed as Sinibaldi's with more or less probability:

1. Florence, Laur. Acquisti e Doni 152. Petrarch, *Rime*. A modern title page says that Sinibaldi copied the book from a manuscript of 1406. The writing could be his but there is no proof. D'Ancona II, No. 519.
2. Laur. 39, 6. Virgil. Attributed to Sinibaldi by G. Biagi in *Il carattere "umanistico" di Ant. Sinibaldi e il libro bello* (Milan, 1922), p. 12 and Plate. The writing could well be his. At Biagi's suggestion William Dana Orcutt imitated this manuscript in a new font of type; Biagi's book is printed in the "Sinibaldi" type. D'Ancona II, No. 861.
3. Paris, B. N. 6069A. Diogenes Laertius. The writing looks like that of Sinibaldi, to whom De Marinis assigns it. Besides, the volume bears the Aragon arms, and we know that Sinibaldi copied a Diogenes Laertius for that family (De Marinis, I, pp. 53, 261, and Pl. 11; II, pp. 66, 322).
4. Paris, B. N. 2082. Augustine, *Contra Faustum*. Attributed to Sinibaldi by De Marinis I, p. 55; II, p. 20, III, Pl. 23. Not seen by me.
5. Oxford, Bodl. MS. Canon. Class. Lat. 31. Propertius. Mr. Alfred Fairbank, a connoisseur in such matters, identified it to me as Sinibaldi's, though it is unsigned. I have a photograph of one page, enough to show that the identification is plausible. Favoring it is the dot over capital I and the mixture of dots and strokes over small *i*. Made for a member of the Medici family.

Other attributions of unsigned manuscripts to Sinibaldi must be rejected. Jean Duchesne in *Voyage d'un Iconophile* (Paris, 1834), p. 19, wrote that a fine Virgil in Munich seemed to be in the same hand as Sinibaldi's Book of Hours in the same library (lat. 23639). The only Virgil in Munich that fits Duchesne's description is lat. 829. In answer to my letter of inquiry Dr. Kaltwasser of the Munich library courteously assured me that 829 was not copied by Sinibaldi.

Bandini, who had a genius for wrong identifications, assigned Laur. 12, 9 to Sinibaldi on the basis of script. This manuscript contains the motto "Omnium rerum vicissitudo est" (Terence, *Eun.* 276). Ir was this motto and the identification that apparently led P. Durrieu (*Bibl. Ecole des Chartes*, 50 [1889], p. 381) to attribute to Sinibaldi Phillipps 2163 (Scriptores Historiae Augustae), now in the Public Library of Victoria, Melbourne, Australia (obtained at a Sotheby sale July, 1946, lot 26). I have not seen the manuscript and so cannot pass judgment on Durrieu's claim. But this book has the following colophon: "Anno ab incarnatione domini MCCCCLXXVIII et XXI Ianuarii opus hoc celeberrimum ruri apud Florentiam consumatum est, die autem Iovis, hora vero diei XXI. Laus, honor, imperium, et gloria sit omnipotenti Ihesu Christo per infinita seculorum amen. Omnium rerum vicissitudo est". Nothing like any part of this formula is found in any of the thirty manuscripts signed by Sinibaldi — and that is a strong argument against identification. Sinibaldi does not refer to the incarnation, to a place in the country, to the day and time of day, he uses neither of the two expressions that follow (*Laus*, etc., *Omnium*, etc.).

De Marinis too was at first misled by Bandini into thinking that Paris, B. N. lat. 1890, 1891, 5081 were copied by Sinibaldi because they had similar colophons (II [1947], p. 184; cf. p. 69). Later he partially abandoned the idea: in I (1952), p. 55, he rejects Sinibaldi as the one who quoted Terence and "with great caution" proposes Verrazano. But on pp. 95 and 126 he suggests that perhaps Sinibaldi and Verrazano between them copied the volumes containing this quotation. In I, p. 94, he lists sixteen unsigned manuscripts with the Terentian motto. I do not believe that Sinibaldi wrote any of them and I doubt very much that Verrazano did. More likely is another scrbe, Neri Rinuccini, whe in Paris, B. N. N. a. l. 2455 signs his name and quotes the motto. He is a much more likely candidate, but De Marinis objects (I, p. 87) on the ground that the difference in writing between a Cicero in Florence (Laur. 90 sup. 76) and a Josephus in Paris (N. a. l. 2455) is too great. I have not looked into this matter but would point out that the former is an early and unpretentious manuscript of 1458 written on paper, the latter a de luxe illuminated book, copied in 1492 for Card. Giovanni de' Medici. It is hard to believe with De Marinis that Rinuccini was really a bookseller, and that he told Verrazano to copy the Josephus and to substitute his (Rinuccini's) name as the scribe.

Pietro Cennini, born in 1444, was a contemporary of Sinibaldi, though his career was much shorter. His first known work (1462) is only one year later than Sinibaldi's. He was the son of the well-known goldsmith Bernardo Cennini, who helped Ghiberti with one of the famous gilded doors of the Baptistery in Florence. Later Bernardo got interested in the printed books which were beginning to appear. He built himself a press, cut type, and printed the first book to appear in Florence, a Servius (1471-72), with Pietro's editorial assistance. The latter calls himself Bernardides in No. 1 below and several times refers to his father as a famous goldsmith. Pietro was a notary, in the employ of Florence in 1473 and 1481.[7] As a copyist he is not in the class of his predecessors. Though he employed a formal humanistic script at times, he more frequently used a cursive script typical of his period, the kind that led to italic type, and for that reason he is considered here as a representative of that script. He wrote chiefly on paper, apparently in part for his own use.

1. Paris, B. N. N. a. l. 1705. Fig. 69. Servius. July 1, 1462. Paper, cursive.

2. Cesena S. I. 6. Martial. August 24, 1463. Cursive. Fava, *op. cit.*, p. 137, Fig. 40. Not seen by me.

3. Lisbon, Bibliotheca Nacional 476. Leonardo Bruni, *De bello adversus Gothos*. 1465. Paper. *Neues Archiv Gesell. ält. deut. Gesch.*, VI (1880), p. 397. Not seen by me.

4. Budapest, National Museum 160. Curtius Rufus. April 7, 1467. Parchment. Hevesy No. 8; Fraknói No. 17; D'Ancona II, No. 713. Not seen by me.

5. Kraków, Czartoryski Library. Frontinus, *Strat.* June 13, 1467. Parchment. Fraknói No. 32. Not seen by me.

6. Milan, Hoepli (bookdealer). Suetonius. 1467. De Marinis I, p. 26, n. 21 (1941). Not seen by me.

7. Rome, Vatican (?). Benedictus Crispus. October 20, 1469. A. Mai, *Classicorum auctorum e Vaticanis codicibus editorum*, V (Rome, 1883), p. XLIII. I could not find this manuscript.

8. Florence, Marucelliana C. 376. Miscellaneous grammatical and other works collected by Cennini. July 27, 1468 to October 20, 1469, Naples. Paper, cursive. *Ioannis Ioviani Pontani Carmina*, ed. B. Soldati, I (Florence, 1902), p. XCVI.

9. Florence, Laur. 38, 38. Tibullus, etc. February 2, 1470 (dated 1469 but in Florentine style). Paper, cursive.

10. Venice, Marc. 4708. Antonio Panormita, *Alphonsi regis dicta ac facta*, etc. Written at Naples for Antonio Ridolfi in August, 1469.

[7] Marzi, *op. cit.*, pp. 504-505.

Paper. Iac. Morelli, *Codices manuscripti Bibliothecae Nanianae* (Venice, 1776), p. 80.

11. Paris, B. N. lat. 4865. Eusebius, *Chron.*, tr. by Jerome. November 6, 1472. Paper, cursive.

12. Florence, Laur, 53, 28. Fig. 70. Landino, *Quest. Camald.* 1474, "declinante vere". Parchment, cursive. D'Ancona II, No. 873.

13. Florence, Naz. II. IX. 14. Miscellany obviously put together by Cennini, including letters of his dated 1475, but without his name in the colophon. Paper, cursive. It contains a work of Galeotto, which, according to the subscription, was printed at Bologna in 1476 (Hain 7436).

14. Cambridge, Mass., Harvard 43. Plautus. No date, but since it contains the same verses as Nos. 1 (1462), 2 (1463), 5 (1467), and in part 15 (after 1464), we may surmise that it was written about 1462-67. Paper, cursive.

15. Lucca 1444. Maffeo Vegio, *De verborum significatione*; Pier Candido Decembrio, *De proprietate verborum.* Apparently copied in 1464. Not seen by me.

16. Vat. lat. 11459. Ovid, *Tristia.* No date. Paper, cursive.

17. Laur. 33, 21. Acro, *Comm. in Horatium.* No date. Paper. Not seen by me.

Actually Cennini was more of an editor than a mere copyist. As early as his first manuscript he disclaims responsibility for errors and has something more to say about his exemplar (later partly erased). In Nos. 1, 2, 5, 14 he identifies himself and absolves himself from criticism in these verses:

> Hoc opus, o lector, transcripsit Petrus, avorum
> Cuius Cennina est nomine dicta domus.
> Error si quis inest, exemplar semina sevit.
> Si secus esse putas, invidiosus abi.

The second verse occurs also in No. 15. In No. 2 he rejects certain epigrams that purport to be Martial's. In No. 7 he says that he corrected a work of Pontano's with the author's own original and that the reader may therefore be assured that the copy is a faithful one and can be safely quoted. He was in Naples at the time as secretary of Antonio Ridolfi. Again he states in No. 10 that it was corrected from the copy that the author (Panormita) gave to Pontano. Another work in this manuscript (Bartolomeo Fazio) he copied from the author's exemplar. He also transcribed in this manuscript a work of Pontano's. On his return to Florence he came upon a copy corrected by the author and so, he tells us, he emended his own copy in 1471. No. 12 was corrected from the archetype. Of greatest interest is the colophon to the Servius printed by his father. Pietro says that he emended the text and collated with the oldest manuscripts, taking care that nothing be added to or subtracted from Servius' text. He explains too why he omits the Greek, leaving space for it. Did Pietro suggest to his father to use some of the fine examples of Florentine penmanship then current or even his (Pietro's) own cursive as the basis for his type? We do not know; in any event, Bernardo imitated earlier printed books.

There were other Florentine copyists in this period who have left us signed and dated copies of their work. Apart from the aforementioned Alessandro da Verrazano, whose dozen signed works date from 1487-1506, there is Pietro Strozzi, born in 1416, but we have only four of his manuscripts, written in an excellent humanistic script. The earliest dates from 1453, his last from 1486. In the colophon of a manuscript copied when he was sixty-seven he states that he wrote in "manu tremula", but the script belies his statement. Two scribes in their colophons mention him as their teacher: Giovanni Maria Veloce of Parma and Giovanni Marco Cinico, both excellent scribes who worked at Naples. Another copyist at Florence was Giovanni Francesco Marzi of S. Gemignano, who has left us at least seven undated manuscripts, most of them in Florence. Other scribes could be listed, not to mention the numerous books of anonymous workers.

The introduction of printing into Italy brought to an end the great period of copying in the humanistic hand. Some scribes became proofreaders for the printers.[8] Cennini took to editing his father's printed edition of Servius in 1471-72. In 1480 Sinibaldi complained that the invention of printing had so reduced his work that he hardly earned his clothing. The copying of books did not end, but there was a difference. Earlier there had been *copyists*, who produced books primarily to be read; now there were *calligraphers*, whose labor resulted in volumes intended chiefly for display and artistic enjoyment. Of course this generalization

[8] Hevesy, *op. cit.*, p. 23. Cf. R. A. B. Mynors in *Transactions of the Cambridge Bibliographical Society*, I (1949-53), p. 97.

is a half-truth, perhaps only a quarter-truth. Even before the invention of printing princes bought books that were not read; after the introduction of the printed book some manuscript books were read. Many of the volumes of Sinibaldi and others were copied after printed books made their appearance. Thus Sinibaldi might be called a calligrapher, by my definition. Be that as it may, we use the term calligraphy, not palaeography, for the later but uninterrupted development of handwriting. This is an interesting field in itself but outside the scope of the present book.

Not only is the history of writing continuous and unbroken in the last part of the fifteenth century and thereafter, but writing itself develops almost imperceptibly into the printer's art. It is well known that the lay person sometimes has difficulty in distinguishing an incunable from a contemporary manuscript. Type fonts were based on the script of the time, identical parchment and paper were employed, printed books were often illuminated by hand like the manuscripts they imitated. But in addition to these familiar practices there were others less well known that deserve attention. For example, it is not merely the shapes of the letters and the manner of making them that require study but also their size, the spacing between lines, the size and proportion ot the printed page, the nature of the signatures, the ruling, and other matters that I cannot go into here. But it is worth pointing out that Poggio generally spaces his horizontal rules seven millimeters apart, two of which were occupied by the main body of the writing, not including the ascenders and descenders. Occasionally he will drop to about five millimeters, with the letters a little over one millimeter high. That is true of Strozz. 96, a small manuscript, and Laur. 67, 15, a large volume but one in which, as already noted, he was trying to save space. The early dated manuscripts run about the same way, except that Bodl. Lat. class. d. 37 (1413) is only 5-1, like Poggio's smaller script. Giovanni Aretino generally adopted the 7-2 ratio for his formal script, though his first book (Vat. Pal. lat. 1496) has an eight - millimeter space. The same is true cf his second book (Laur. 63, 4). This is the first of the three volumes of Livy; the other two have a 7-1 $^1/_2$ ratio, as do a few others. His next manuscript (Munich 763) is reduced to 6-1 $^1/_2$, but that is exceptional. The three books in cursive script have a 6-1+ ratio. Curlo extended the space to 8-9 mm., with a 2 mm. letter. Antonio di Mario started with 6-1; in the next two manuscripts he used 7-1 1/2; after that he shifted back and forth between 7-2 and 8-2, except that in one case he went up to nine (Paris. lat. 4927). Gherardo del Ciriagio generally followed the Poggian norm of 7-2, but individual examples of 5-1, 5-1 1/2, 6-1, 6-1 1/2, 6-2 are found with no apparent reason for the smaller size. Antonio Sinibaldi also favors 7-2, but we find 5-1 in an Italian manuscript (Vat. Urb. lat. 681) and in cursive (Ricc. 1449), 5-1 1/2 in a Book of Hours (B. M. Yates Thomposn 23), and 6-1 in an Italian manuscript (B. N. ital. 548).

The two-millimeter height of the letters so common in these manuscripts is also frequent in incunabula, though the space between lines is generally less.[9]

The Renaissance book abandoned the favorite two-column arrangement of the Gothic period, as if determined to change everything Gothic. Four vertical rules divided the page, the first two and the last two about six millimeters apart. The narrow column formed by the first two might be occupied by a capital letter at the beginning of a paragraph and in verse by the initial capital of each line. Of course the second rule served to guide the scribe in producing a straight, or "justified," left margin. At the right, the usual practice in the fifteenth century seems to have been to reach the third rule even if one had to resort to "fillers" (to be discussed in a moment). The space of some 6-7 mm. between the third and fourth rule could be used but the careful scribe avoided writing beyond the fourth rule. Thus complete justification at the right was not generally achieved. Poggio was not particularly careful about this.

The matters to be presented now were discussed under the several scribes, but it seems worth while to bring them together here because some of them left a permanent mark on the printed page. From the earliest times lines were kept from running long by the use of abbreviations and ligatures. So it is that in the oldest manuscripts abbreviations are generally at or near the end of the line. This practice was continued, and even extended, throughout the manuscript period. Final letters could also be written above the line, especially a narrow lengthened form of the round *s*. Hyphen-

[9] Cf. David Thomas, *Type for Print*, ed. 2 (London, 1947), p. 52.

ation was, of course, introduced for the same reason. We have noted the excessive hyphenation of Gherardo, who often divided more than half of the words on a page. Unusual word division occurs occasionally in Poggio but becomes very frequent in his successors. This device did not persist. One wonders whether the advantages of syllabic word division over "literal" division, if we may so call it, are sufficient to give it the preference. Awkward as *qu-as* may seem to us, it appears to be more logical than the current English *req-uisite* (the result of using syllabication to indicate pronunciation) or even the European division of *o-mnis*, etc. Our problems of justification would be solved if we could divide words after any letter.

When the line was short, fillers were resorted to. One method was to use a long form of the last letter: *m*, *n*, etc., could have long tails. Since *r* had no tail, a capital tailed R was employed. A fat round *s*, varying in corpulence according to need, was a favorite; the *s* might be placed on its side and greatly stretched where a large space had to be filled. A wide NT ligature also occurs. This phenomenon is indeed curious, for this ligature originated in antiquity to save space, not to fill it.

When a scribe started a word only to discover that he had reached the end of the line he might delete a letter or part of a letter he had written and start over again on the next line. Out of this arose the practice of deliberately writing a stroke which might be called an *i* or the first stroke of *m*, *n*, *r*, *u*, and then cancelling it. This began earlier and was kept up and developed in the humanistic period. In his first manuscript (Strozz. 96) Poggio so used *o* five times, though he employed the cancelled *i* more frequently. This cancelled *o* persisted in the practice of some scribes.

Gherardo tried a remarkable experiment in a copy of Virgil (Laur. 39, 8) in using spaced capitals to fill out the line (Fig. 60). It shows how anxious he was to have a full line. He did not try this scheme again. The printer has achieved perfect justification in prose but does not attempt it in verse.

Pontano used a somewhat different system to justify the margin in a Tibullus copied by him, probably in 1460. In the first part of the volume he usually resorts to abnormally wide letters at or near the end of the line. The connecting strokes of *a*, *c*, *e*, *g*, *r* may fill a space of three to five letters. The tail of *l* fills from two to seven letter spaces. Capital letters are used instead of minuscule: T with a long cross stroke, N with a long middle stroke, etc. This method is more common in the first part of the book; spacing out is favored in the latter part. Sometimes the two are combined.

Antonio di Mario's interesting system of filling a page at the end of a book by arranging words in patterns, such as a diamond or a triangle, persisted in part in the printed book. Thus Aldus, for one, tapered off the text at the end of a book to form an inverted triangle. This may be seen, e.g., in his Pliny's Letters of 1508. He did it also with capitals in a title (Statius of 1502). Other printers did the same thing.

Some copyists were not satisfied with avoiding the printer's "widow", a short line (as at the end of a paragraph) at the top of the page. Giovanni Aretino did not like a short line at the bottom of a page. So in his copy of Cicero's Letters (Vat. Pal. lat. 1496) he filled out the last line, when it came at the end of an epistle, with remarks addressed to his friend Nicolaus Ricius, as we saw. This experiment appears to be unique; at least I have come upon no other examples. A sort of combination of Gherardo's and Antonio's practice occurs at least as early as the thirteenth century; on a leaf in the Poole collection of Indiana University (No. 98-44) the scribe filled out the last line (of prose) by writing the last three letters in spaced capitals.

In another respect some of our fifteenth-century Florentine scribes were more sensitive about the last line of a page than we are: they sometimes avoided dividing the last word, especially on the recto page. Poggio's usage varies. In Vat. lat. 3245, written between 1410 and 1414, no word runs over to the next page, but in one case the word was so long that Poggio had to put the last syllable below the rest of the word.[10] Similarly in Laur. 48, 22 (1425?), except that, to avoid dividing a word, he here extends it into the margin, beyond the last vertical rule. In another manuscript of the same year 1425 (Laur, 50, 31) the last word is divided in two instances on a verso page, but not at all on a recto. None

10 This practice occasionally occurs in earlier manuscripts. In British Museum, Add. 31031, fol. 79r ends with *expectet*, with the last syllable just below the second. This is an eighth-century manuscript in Laon az script.

of the scribes we have discussed in detail imitate this practice, but we have an interesting variation of it in four manuscripts copied at Florence in 1471, 1472, and 1473 by Petrus de Traiecto (Vat. Urb. lat. 305, 196, 383, 30). When a syllable of two to four letters was left over at the end of a page he wrote these letters in capitals in column form below the last letter of the line. In other manuscripts Petrus carries over the last syllable to the next page (Urb. lat. 386, 488).

The celebrated Vespasiano da Bisticci is not infrequently referred to as a scribe, and it may therefore be wondered why no mention of him has been made in this book. A publisher and bookdealer, not a scribe, he made his influence felt by helping the spread of humanistic script. He was a stationer, *cartolaio*, as he was frequently called. The stationer sold not only parchment, paper, and other writing materials but books as well. In 1425 Poggio asked Niccoli to buy for a friend some books that he (Poggio) had left for sale at "Petrum tuum chartularium" (*Epist.* I, p. 152). Quite a number of manuscripts sold by Vespasiano are known to us. Vat. Urb. lat. 833 is a fourteenth-century manuscript which Tommaso di Sarzana (later Pope Nicholas V) bought from the heirs of Coluccio "per manum Vespasiani". A twelfth-century manuscript (Laur. Marc. 762) has a note indicating that Vespasiano, "librorum diligentissimus investigator", gave it to a monk in 1490. In other words, Vespasiano, like dealers today, knew where to find rare books. But when the humanistic movement spread throughout Italy and all Western Europe, when kings and princes, popes and cardinals, bishops and leading men hastened to build up libraries, Vespasiano expanded his business enormously by furnishing copies of books made to order. There are, however, two misapprehensions about him. One is that he copied manuscripts. So far as I know, not a single manuscript exists that he himself transcribed.[11] In the fifteen or more manuscripts in which his name appears, either the purchaser states that he bought the book of Vespasiano or such formulas are used as "scriptus et compositus opera Vespasiani", "Vespasianus fecit fieri", "Vespasianus transcribere fecit", "Vespasiano... procurante Ugonis... manu descripta est",

11 We may expect further light on Vespasiano from Miss Albinia C. de la Mare's studies (The Warburg Institute, Annual Report 1955-1956, pp. 3-4).

"Scriptus... per me Gherardum... procurante Vespasiano", "Vespasianus transcribendum curavit", "Scriptum per Petrum de Traiecto... sub Vespasiano". The meaning of all these is clear enough, that Vespasiano had the copying done by others, whose names are sometimes given, usually not. But it is said that one such manuscript was "written" by him[12] or "produced" by him.

The other, even more common, misapprehension about Vespasiano (at least at present writing I think it is a misapprehension) is that all the scribes who worked for Vespasiano did their copying in his shop. He himself is responsible in a way for this interpretation, for he says that he hired forty-five scribes and got out two hundred volumes in twenty-two months.[13] That he crowded so many copyists into his *bottega* seems to me unlikely — perhaps I should say absurd. Besides, large as the number of books produced appears to be at first sight, forty-five scribes might well have copied a thousand or more manuscripts in a period of nearly two years. I interpret the facts as showing that Vespasiano hired scribes to do one or more manuscripts — in their own homes or shops. Evidently most of them worked for others as well during this period. In the third place, only two of Gherardo del Ciriagio's thirty-four manuscripts known to us (Valencia, Univ. 765; Vat. Urb. lat. 1314) have the note "procurante Vespasiano". This probably indicates that he copied his others without the agency of Vespasiano. Incidentally, Gherardo quite rightly calls this bookdealer "principe omnium librariorum Florentinorum". Similarly a scribe not discussed by me in detail, Petrus de Traiecto, of whose work I have seen eight examples, all but one among the Urbinates of the Vatican, mentions Vespasiano in only one of them (Urb. lat. 383): "sub Vespasiano librario". I can see no justification whatever for such a statement as that of Fraknói about a manuscript copied by Cennini: "Il carattere della scrittura e della decorazione ci dice

[12] F. Madan, etc., *A Summary Catalogue of Western Manuscripts in the Bodleian Library*, II, 1 (Oxford, 1922), No. 2497. J. M. Bradley, *A Dictionary of Miniaturists*, III (London, 1889), p. 377, calls Vespasiano a "copyist and agent"; the latter term is correct, the former is not. M. Meiss, *Andrea Mantegna as Illuminator* (New York, 1957), p. 60, speaks of the many manuscripts "produced" by Vespasiano. Does he mean "written" or "caused to be written"?

[13] Vespasiano da Bisticci, *Vite di uomini illustri del secolo XV* (Milano, 1951), p. 414 (in the life of Cosimo de' Medici).

che il copista lavorava nella bottega fiorentina del Bisticci" [14] There was no specific style to the manuscripts which Vespasiano sold. I doubt whether he instructed scribes how to write; at most, he may have asked for books in humanistic script. As a matter of fact, most of those that I have seen are rather indifferent specimens of humanistic writing, not on a par with the two copies that Gherardo made for him. In other words, Vespasiano was neither a copyist nor a supervisor of copyists nor a publisher but a dealer and broker.

Scribes too seem to have turned brokers occasionally. The well-known copyist Giovanni Marco Cinico, whom we have mentioned as a pupil of Pietro Strozzi, says in a manuscript now in Dresden (R. 28) that he "fieri curavit" (Hevesy, *op. cit.*, No. 30; cf. Escorial f. II. 17, above under Sinibaldi No. 27).

Most of the scribes that we have discussed were notaries. This points up the fact that humanistic writing was a member of the corpus of humanistic activity, for most of the humanists were notaries, from Coluccio Salutati and Poggio down. Poggio, the inventor of humanistic script, was a leading humanist. His successors in the scribal fraternity were not prominent in the humanistic movement, contenting themselves with being merely copyists. The explanation is that the demand for fine books became so strong that copying was no longer a substitute for a siesta, as in Poggio's case, but a profession which took all of a man's time. A profession, not an occupation, for the scribes experimented with methods of improving their products for the sake of greater legibility and handsomer appearance. Some of their experiments failed but others have persisted to this day in the shops of their successors the typographers.

The scribes were not the only ones responsible for the spread of humanistic script. If the buyers of books, or rather those who commissioned their copying, had not eagerly preferred the new style, it could not have succeeded. Chief credit is due to Cosimo de' Medici. The catalogue of his library made in 1418 indicates that most of his Latin books were written in *lettera antica*, i.e., human-

[14] G. Fraknói, *op. cit.*, p. 14. Similarly the claim of a modern Vespasiano that a certain manuscript is "probably from the workshop of Vespasiano" is merely good advertising, without a factual basis.

istic script. One was probably Poggio's copy of Cicero's Letters to Atticus (Berlin, Ham. 166). Another perhaps was the Eusebius he copied (Laur. 67, 15). Several extant manuscripts were copied by Giovanni Aretino for Cosimo and may be identified among the manuscripts in *lettera antica* in the catalogue of 1418: Livy (Laur. 63, 4, 5, 6), Cicero, Orations (Laur. 48, 10), Francesco Barbaro (Laur. 78, 24), and Justinus (Laur. 66, 12); perhaps the *Tusculans* and *De finibus* (Munich lat. 763). A Sallust and a Cicero, *Verrines*, in *lettera àntica* may be Laur. 64, 22 and 48, 27 (*s*. XV), both of which belonged to Cosimo, Cosimo's preference for humanistic script can be inferred from Niccoli's letter to him in which he advises Cosimo to sell his Boethius, since for the money received from its sale two books "di lettera all'antiqua" could be copied. The Boethius is presumably the one listed in the 1418 catalogue without indication that it was in *lettera antica;* therefore it was in Gothic.[15] As we saw, Curlo copied two manuscripts for Cosimo. Antonio di Mario copied at least three for him and eight for his son Piero. Gherardo del Ciriagio made two for Piero and nine for his brother Giovanni. The Medici established the vogue and all the other great families of Italy followed their lead.

Humanistic script was, then, inspired by Coluccio Salutati, invented by Poggio Bracciolini, encouraged by Niccolò Niccoli, preferred by the Medici and their imitators among the book collectors, even in far-off Britain, sold and promoted by canny book dealers such as Vespasiano da Bisticci. It was inevitable that it should be preferred by the early Italian printers.

Humanistic, in its printed form, may be said to be the most important of all the past forms of the Latin alphabet, partly because it is so much more widely used, partly because it is destined to have a longer life than any of its predecessors. True, it was based on Carolingian writing, but that in turn grew out of earlier styles.

[15] It is a fair assumption that the volumes not in *lettera antica* were older manuscripts not specially made for Cosimo. A Valerius Maximus belonged to the sons of «messer Colui» (i.e., Coluccio) and no doubt to Coluccio himself. A Justinus in *lettera logonbarda* is to be identified as Laur. 66, 21, in Beneventan script from Monte Cassino. A Horace, Juvenal, and Persius is probably Laur. 34, 6, dated 1379. An Ovid *Epistole* is presumably Laur. 36, 28, a *Heroides* of the fourteenth century which Cosimo used as a schoolboy.

INDICES

I. INDEX OF NAMES

II. INDEX OF MANUSCRIPTS

III. LIST OF ILLUSTRATIONS

1. Bloomington, Indiana University, Poole 186, fol. 1v. S. XII. Cf. p. 12.

2. Rome, Vat. Urb. lat. 165, fol. 4r. S. XIV, Bologna. Cf. p. 12.

3. Florence, Laur. Strozz. 95, fol. 1r. S. XIV, Florence. Cf. p. 12.

4. Rome, Vat. lat. 3358, fol. 46r. Petrarch's script. Cf. p. 12.

5. Florence, Laur. 54, 32, fol. 3r. Boccaccio's script. Cf. p. 12.

6. London, British Museum Add. 11987, fol. 12r. Salutati's script. Cf. p. 12.

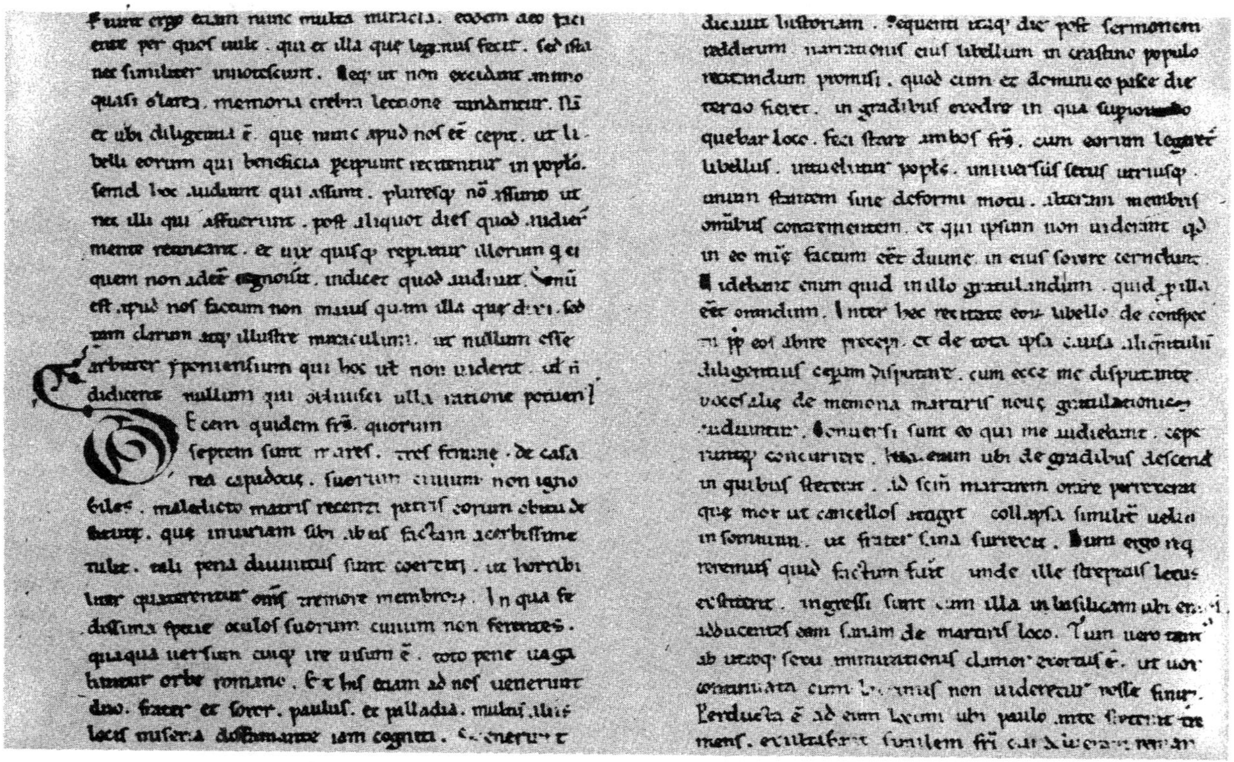

7. Rome, Vat. Ottob. lat. 349, fol. 161r. S. XIV. Cf. p. 14.

8. Florence, Laur. Marc. 284, fol. 77v. Salutati. Cf. p. 17 ff.

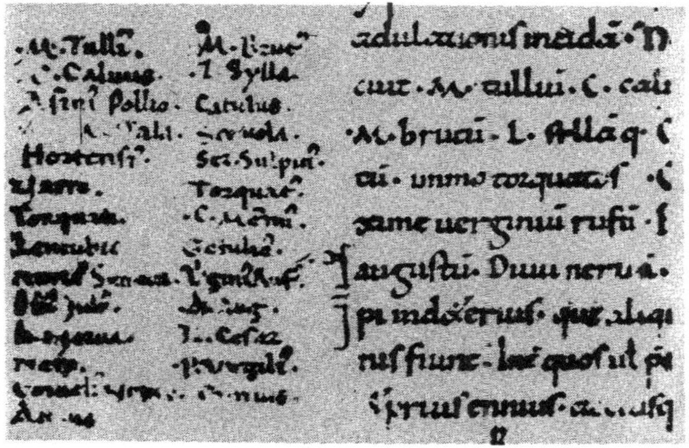

9. Florence, Laur. Marc. 284, fol. 74v. Salutati (margin). Cf. p. 17.

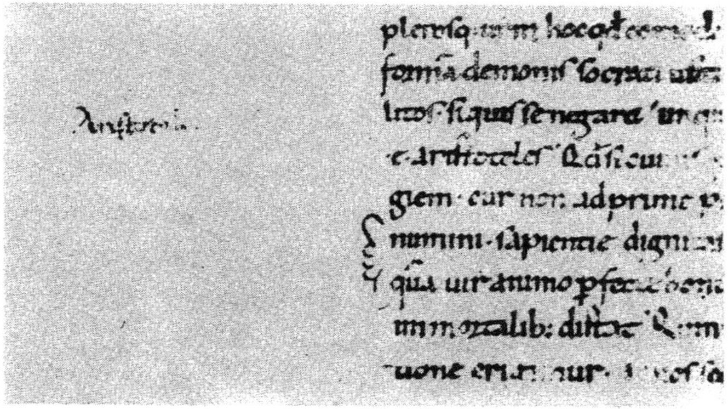

11. Florence, Laur. Marc. 284, fol. 6v. Salutati (margin). Cf. p. 17.

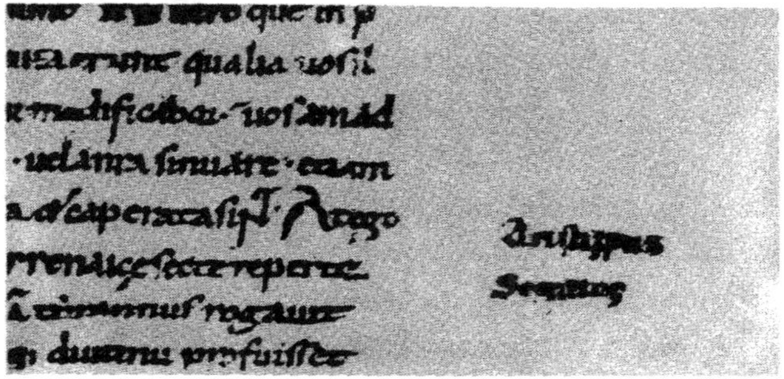

10. Florence, Laur. Marc. 284, fol. 1r. Salutati (margin). Cf. p. 17.

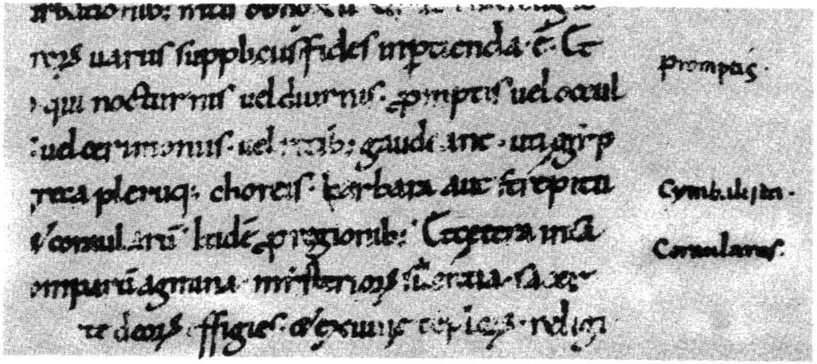

12. Florence, Laur. Marc. 284, fol. 5r. Salutati (margin). Cf. p. 17.

13. Florence, Laur. Strozz. 96, fol. 22v. Poggio, 1402-03. Cf. p. 21.

14. Florence, Laur. Strozz. 96, fol. 2r. Poggio, 1402-03. Cf. p. 21.

15. Berlin, Ham. 166. Poggio, 1408. Cf. p. 27.

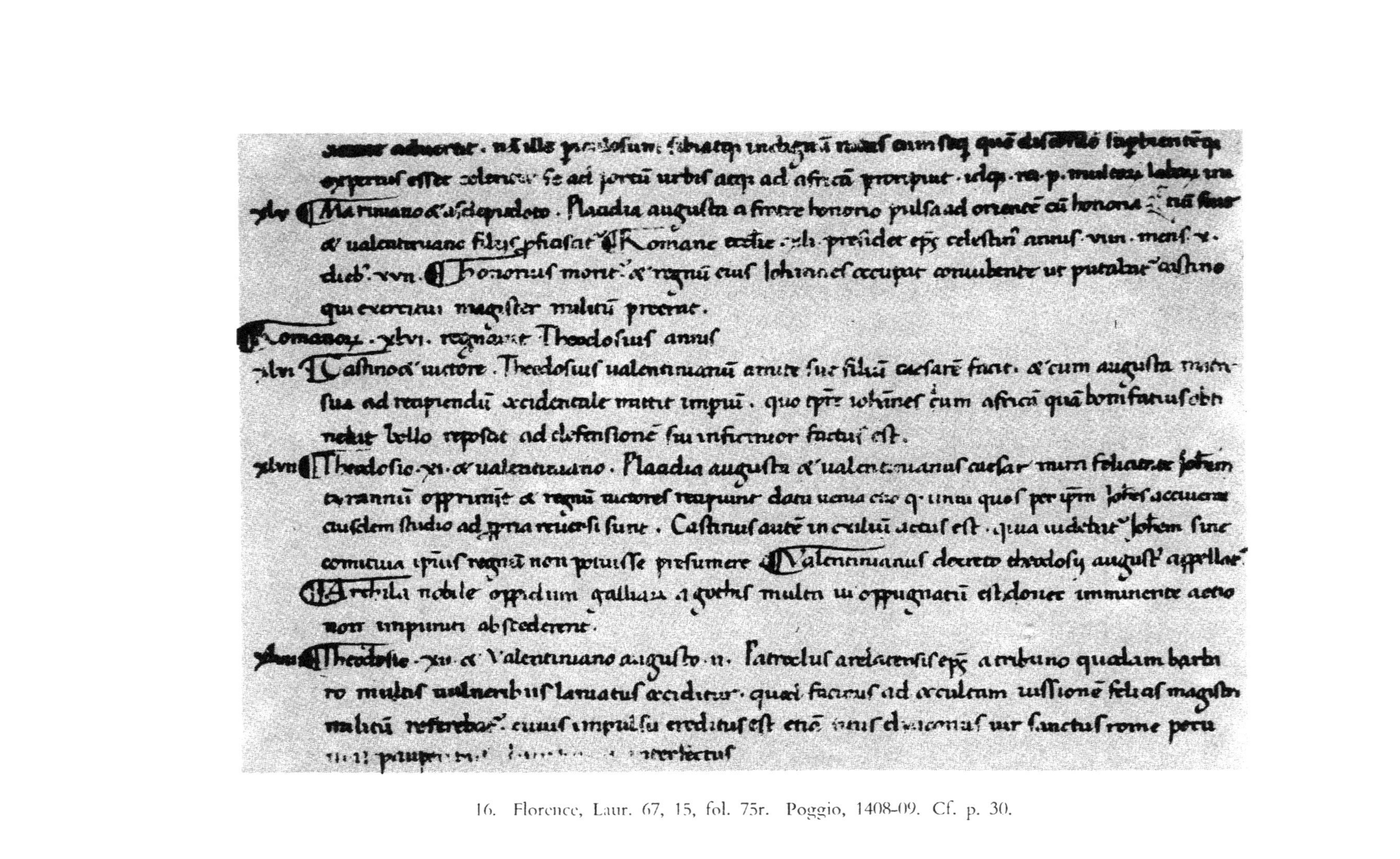

16. Florence, Laur. 67, 15, fol. 75r. Poggio, 1408-09. Cf. p. 30.

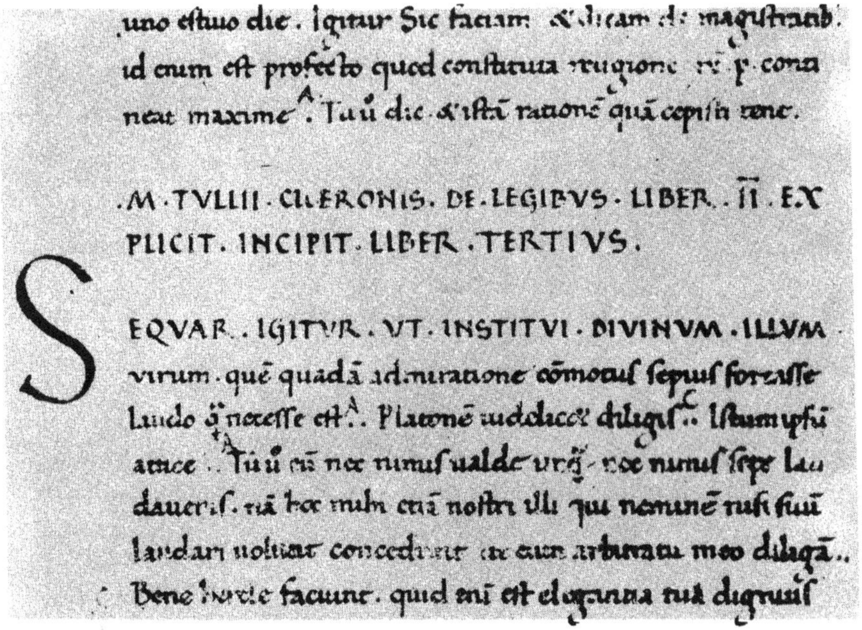

17. Rome, Vat. lat. 3245, fol. 61v. Poggio, 1410-14. Cf. p. 31.

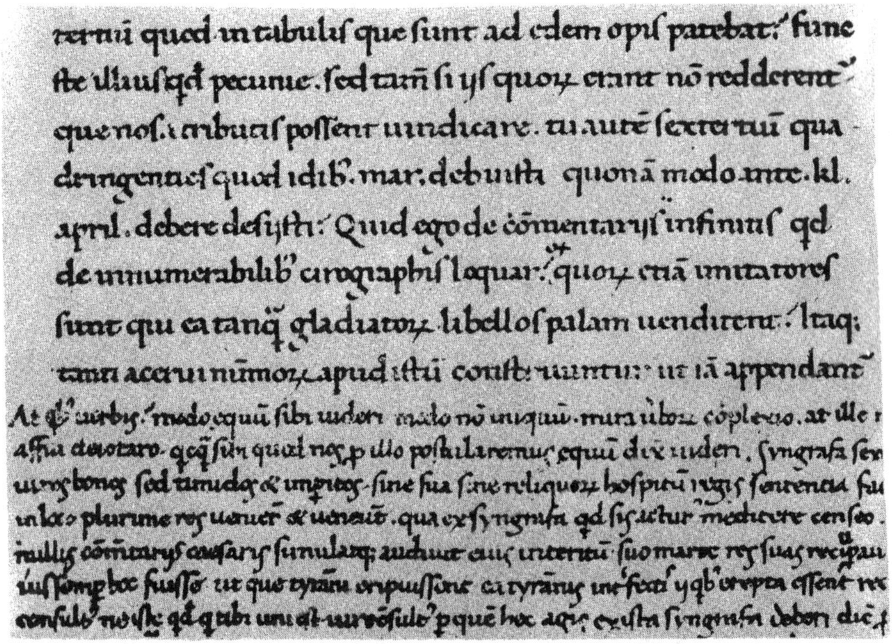

18. Florence, Laur. 48, 22, fol. 22r. Poggio, 1425. Cf. p. 33.

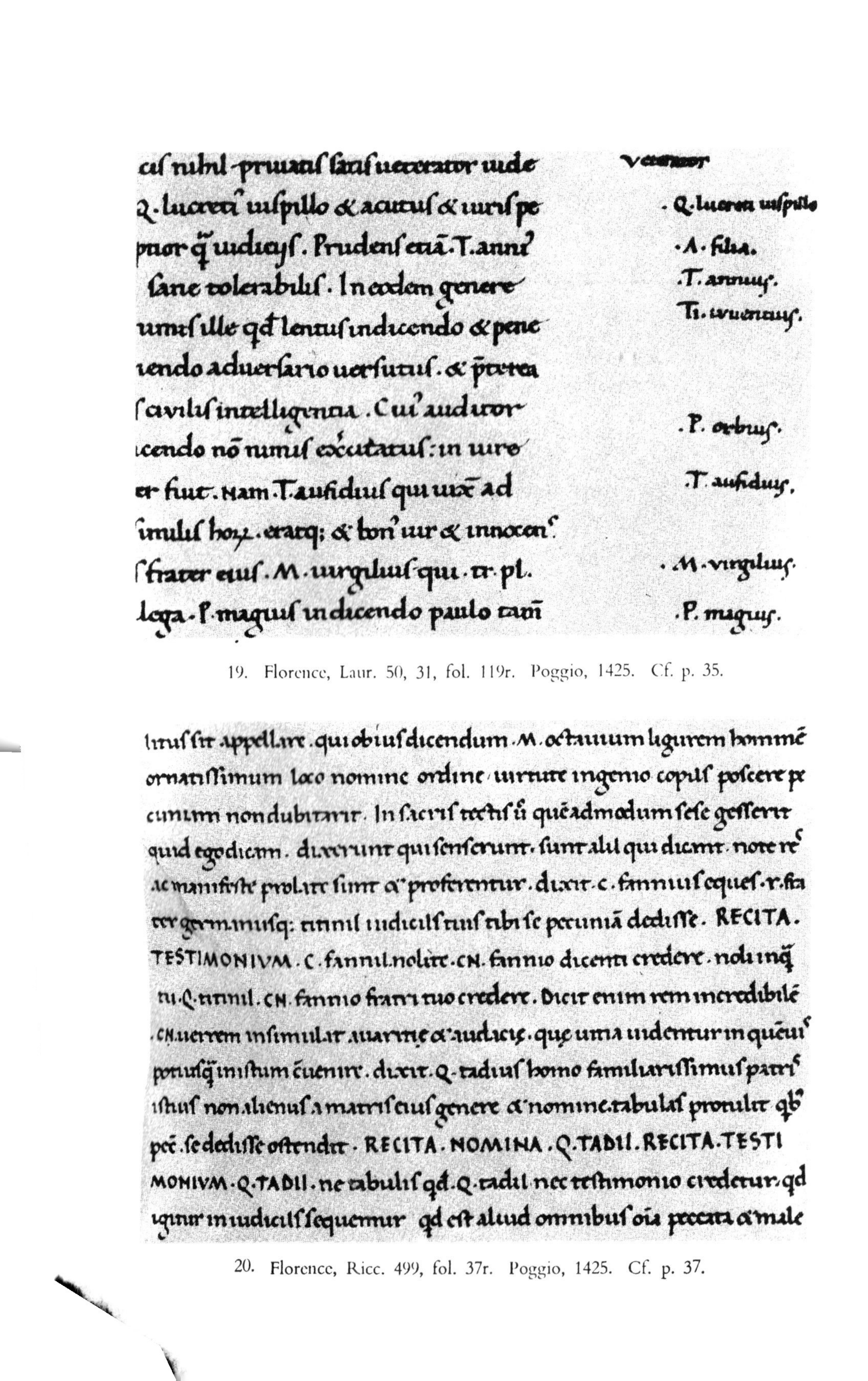

19. Florence, Laur. 50, 31, fol. 119r. Poggio, 1425. Cf. p. 35.

20. Florence, Ricc. 499, fol. 37r. Poggio, 1425. Cf. p. 37.

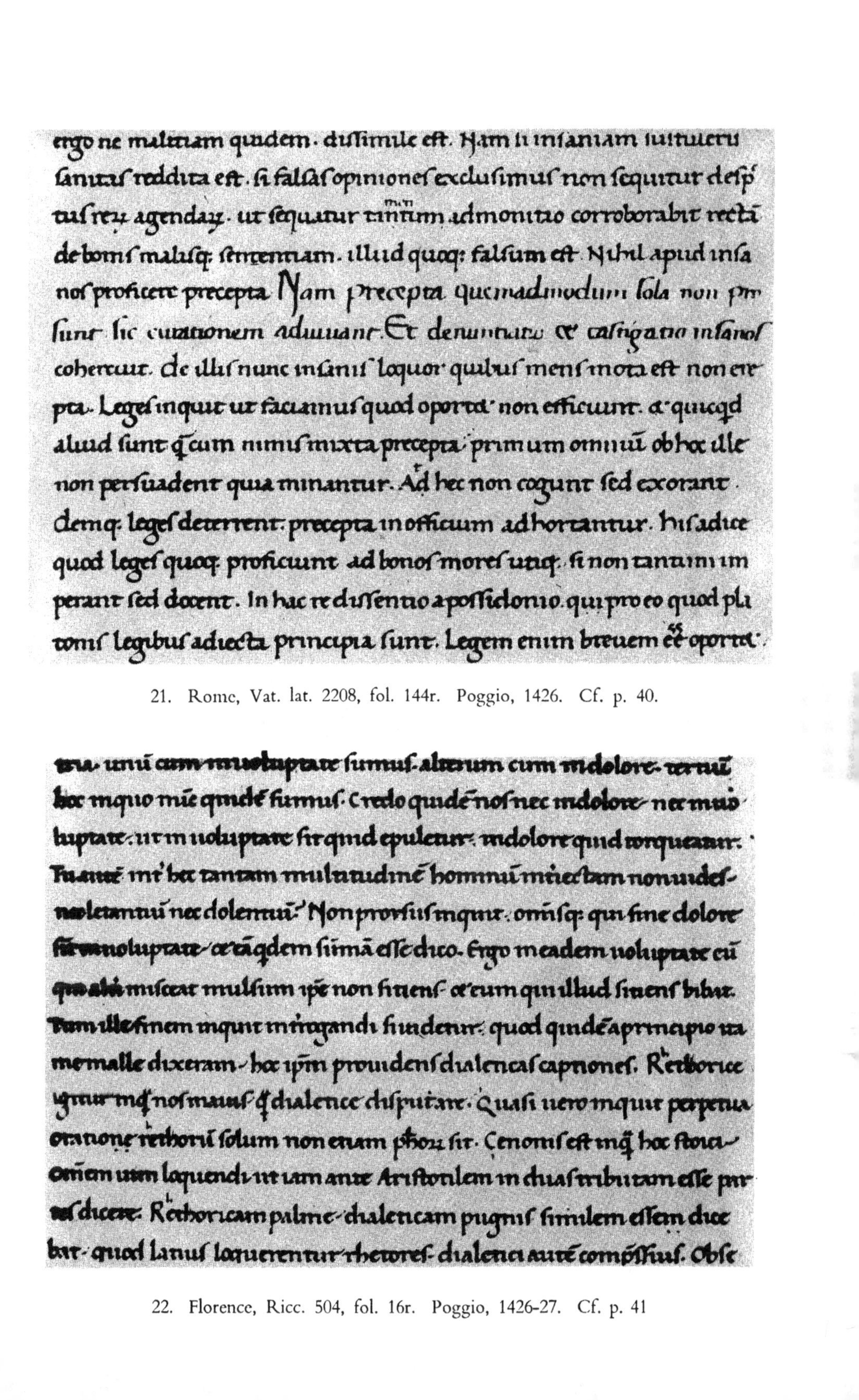

21. Rome, Vat. lat. 2208, fol. 144r. Poggio, 1426. Cf. p. 40.

22. Florence, Ricc. 504, fol. 16r. Poggio, 1426–27. Cf. p. 41

ti esse debebunt pompeium hortari ut malit mihi esse amicus quam his qui et illi et
mihi semper fuerunt inimicissimi. quorum artificiis effectum est ut res. pu. in hunc
BALBVS. ciceroni imp. sal. Subpostea quam litteras statum peruenirete.
comunes cum oppio ad te dedi ab cesare epistolam accepi cuius exemplum
ad te misi ex quibus perspicere poteris quam cupiat concordiam et pompeium
reconciliare. et quam remotus sit ab omni crudelitate. quod eum sentire ut debeo
ualde gaudeo. de te et tua fide et pietate idem me hercule mi cicero sentio.
quod tu non posse tuam famam et officium sustinere ut contra eum arma feras
a quo tantum beneficium te accepisse predices. Cesarem hoc idem probaturum ex
ploratum pro eius singulari humanitate habeo. eique cumulatissime satisfactu
rum te certo scio. cum nullam partem belli contra eum suscipias. neque socius eius
aduersariis fueris. atque hoc non solum in te tali et tanto uiro satis habebit sed
etiam mihi sua concessit uoluntate ne in his castris essem que contra lentulum
aut pompeium futura essent. quorum beneficia maxima haberem. sibique satis esse dix.
si togatus urbana negotia officia sibi prestitissem. que etiam illis si uellem prestare
possem. Itaque nunc rome omnia negotia lentuli procuro. sustineo. meumque officium

23. Florence, Laur. 49, 24, fol. 125r. Poggio, 1425. Cf. p. 43.

coriolano matres coniugesq; crinibus sparsis obuię ab urbe uenerant. Tumultus cor
legiones quia romanum habebant ducem quieuer̄. Vos romanus exercitus ne de
stiteritis impio bello. te T. quincti quocunq; illic loco seu uolens seu inuictus con
stitisti. si dimicandum erit in nouissimos te recipito. fugeris etiam honestius tergum
q; cum dederis quam pugnaueris contra patriam. Nunc ad pacificandum bene atq; ho
neste inter primos stabis. et colloquii huius salutaris interpres fueris. postulate
equa et ferte: quanquam uel iniquis standum est potius quam impias inter nos conseramus
manus. T. quinctius plenus lacrimarum ad suos uersus. Me quoq; inquit milites. si
quis mei usus est. meliorem pacis quam belli habetis ducem. Non enim illa modo uulscus
aut samnis sed romanus uerba fecit. Vester consul uester imperator milites cuius
auspitia pro uobis experti. nolite aduersus uos experiri uelle. qui pugnarent uo
biscum infestius et alios duces senatus habuit. qui maxime uobis suis militibus
parceret. cum plurimum uos imperatori uestro crederetis elegit eum. Pacem enim qui uince
re possunt uolunt. quam nos uelle oportet. quin omissis ira et spe fallacibus auc
ctoribus nos ipsos mãq; omnia cognite permittamus fidei. Approbantibus clamo
re cunctis. T. quinctius ante signa progressus in potestate dictatoris milites fore

24. Rome, Vat. lat. 1843, fol. 140v. Poggio, 1425–26. Cf. p. 45.

dragenos eris duxit. Morte subtractus spectaculo magis hominū q̄ triūphantis
glorie syphax est tibur[e] audita. multo ante mortuus q̄ ab alba traductus fuerat.
Conspecta tamen mors eius fuerit. quia publico funere est elatus. hunc regem in
triūpho ductum polibius haud quaq̄ spernendus auctor tradit. Secutus scipionem
triūphantem est pilleo capiti imposito. Q. terentius culleo. omniq: deinde uita ut
dignū erat libertatis auctorem coluit. Africani cognomen militaris primū fauor
an popularis aura celebrauerit. an sicuti sylle magniq: pompei patrū memoria
ceptum ab assen[ta]tione familiari sit parum compertum habeo. Primus certe hic
imperator nomine uicte a se gentis est nobilitatus. exemplo deinde huius nequaq̄
uictoria pares. insignes imaginū titulos claraq: cognomina familie fecere.

.T. LIVII. PATAVINI. HISTORICI. PRECLARISSIMI. LIBER. XXX.
EXPLICIT. BELLI. PVNICI. SECVNDI. LEGE. FELICITER.

LIBER. POGGII.

25. Rome, Vat. lat. 1849, fol. 182r. Poggio, 1425–26. Cf. p. 45.

26. Florence, Laur. Fies. 13, fol. 65v. Poggio (? margin). Cf. p. 48.

27. Madrid, Bibl. Nac. X, 81. Poggio, 1416. Cf. p. 48.

uis in ea loca ubi nc roma ē deuenisse p tyberī. Deīn sua
dente Rome nobilissima captiuarum que his comes erat. incen
sis nauibus posuisse sedes. instruxisse menia. et opidū ab ea
Romen uocauisse. Agathocles scribit. Romen ñ captiuā ut
supradictū ē fuisse. sed ascanio natā. enee neptē. appella
tionis istius causā fuisse. Tradit̄ etiā pprium. Rome nomē.
uerū tam uetitū publicari. qnquidē quo minus inclare
scerēt. cerimoniaꝝ archana sanxerī. ut hoc pacto notitiā
aboleret fides placite taciturnitatis. Valerius deniq;
Sorani. qđ contra interdictū id eloqui ausus foret. ob me
ritū pro fane uocis. neci datus. Int̄ antiquissimas sane
religiones. sacellū colitur angerone. cui sacrificatur añ
diē. xii. kł. ianuarii. Que diua psul. silentii ipsiu
prenexo obsignatoq; ore simulacrū habet. De tpribus
urbis condite ambiguitati questiones excitauit. qđ que
dam ibi multo ante Romulū condita sint. Quippe arā
hercules. quā uouerat si amissas boues repperisset. punito
caco. patri inuentori dicauit. Qui cacus habitauit locū
cui saline nomē ē. ubi trigemina nc porta. Hic ut celius
tradidit. cū a tarchone tyrreno ad quē legat̄ uenerat
missus marsie regis. socio megale. frigie custodie foret
datus. frustratꝰ uincula. et unde uenerat redux. psidiis am
plioribus occupato circa uulturnū et capaniā regno. dū
attrectare etiā ea audet que cesserant in archadū iura.
duce hercule qui tunc forte aderat. oppssus ē. Mega
len sabini receper̄. disciplinā augurandi ab eo docti.
Suo qq numini idē hercules instituit arā. que maxima
apud pontifices habetur. cū se ex nycostrata euandri ma
tre. que a uaticinio carmētis dicta ē. immortalē copisset.
Conseptū etiā. intra qđ ritus sacroꝝ factis bouicidiis do
cuit poticios. Sacellū herculis in bouario foro ē. inquo
argumta et conuiuii et maiestatis ipsius remanent. Na
diuinit̄ neq; muscis illo. neq; canibus ingressus ē. Et enim
cū uisceratione sacricolis daret. myagrū deum dr̄ inpcat.
Clauā uō in aditu reliquisse. cui olfactu refuger̄ canes. Id
usq; nunc durat. Edem etiā q sacrariū eius fertur

28. London, British Museum Eg. 818, fol. 3r. S. XII. Cf. p. 54.

tatem · quae duo sunt ad iudicandum notissima . sed ne in maximis
quidem rebus quicquam adhuc inueni firmius quod tenerem . aut quo
iudicium meum dirigerem · quam id quodcumq; mihi quã simillimi
ueri uideretur . cum ipsum illud uerum tam in occulto lateret . Tu au
tem uelim si tibi ea quae disputata sunt minus probabuntur . ut aut
maius opus institutũ putes quam effici potuerit : aut dum tibi rogãti
uoluerim obsequi : uerecundia negandi scribendi me imprudentiã
suscepisse :-

M · TULLI · CICERONIS · ORATOR · EXPLICIT · FELICITER

M · TULLI · CICERONIS · BRUTUS · INCIP · LEGE FELIC

Cum ẽ cilicia decedens rhodum uenissem · et eo mihi de · q · hortensii
morte esset allatum : opinione omnium maiorem animo coepi dolorẽ

29. Florence, Naz. Conv. Soppr. I. I. 14, fol. 32r. Niccoli, 1423. Cf. p. 61.

tionibus iratorum militum impetuq; cum conuictus pene confossus ẽ
obicientium · ideo tripolitanos non potuisse defendi quod ipsi ad ex-
peditionales usos praebere necessaria detrectarunt · & ob haec tru-
sus in carcerem diu consultus super eo quid conueniret agi decer-
nere & imperator sollicitatis ut dabatur propinari custodibus in
urbem romam abierat profugus : ibiq; delitescens fatali lege discess-
sit · hoc memorando fine externis domesticisq; cladibus uexa-
ta conticuit tripolis non indefensa quia uigilauit iustitiae oculus
sempiternus ultimaeq; legatorum & praesidis dirae · Diu enim
postea huiusmodi casus emersit · solutus sacramento palladius destitutus quae fastu quo tumebat discessit ad otium · & cum theo-
dosius ductor exercituum ille magnificus oppressurus firmum per-
niciosa coeptantem uenisset in africam praescripti romani remmo-

30. Florence, Naz. Conv. Soppr. I. V. 43, fol. 199r. Niccoli, 1423. Cf. p. 63.

Q. SEPTIMI . FLORENTIS . TERTULLIANI . CAR
THAGINIENSIS . DE . VIRGINIBUS . VELANDIS .
. LIBER . INCIPIT . FELICITER .

ROPRIUM . iam negotium passus meae opinionis . Latine q(ue)
ostendam . uirgines uestras uelari oportere . Ex quo transitum
aetatis suae fecerint . hoc exigere ueritatem . cui nemo praescribere po
test . non spatium tempor(um) . non patrociniu personar(um) . non priuilegium
regionum . Ex his enim fere consuetudo initium ab aliqua ignoran
tia uel simplicitate sortita in usum per successionem corroboratur . &
ita aduersus ueritatem uindicatur . Sed d(omi)n(u)s noster christus ueritate

31. Florence, Naz. Conv. Soppr. I. VI. 11, fol. 84r. Niccoli, 1426–27. Cf. p. 63.

Eius aute(m) quae uictu morbos curat longe clarissimi auctores etiam
altius quaedam agitare conati rerum quoq(ue) naturae sibi cognitione(m)
uindicauerunt tanq(uam) sine ea trunca & debilis medicina esset . Post
quos Serapion primus omnium nihil hanc rationalem disciplinam
pertinere ad medicinam professus in usu tantu(m) & experimentis eam
posuit . Quem Apollonius & Glaucias & aliquanto post Heraclides Ta -
rantinus aliiq(ue) non mediocres uiri secuti ex ipsa professione se
ΕΜΠΕΙΡΗΥΟϹ appellauerunt . Sic in duas partes ea quoq(ue) quae ui -
ctu curat medicina diuisa est . Aliis rationalem artem aliis usum ta(n) -
tum sibi uindicantibus . Nullo uero quicqua(m) post eos qui supra co(m) -
prehensi sunt agitante nisi quod acceperat donec Asclepiades me -

32. Florence, Laur. 73, 7, fol. 3r. Niccoli, 1427. Cf. p. 64.

· CAPITVLA ·

Plus hominibus profuisse qui sapientiam inuene-
rit. quam cererem. liberum. herculem. Animam natiuam esse. De mundo. De lunae lu-
mine. De solis et lunae cursu. De anni temporibus. Mare. caelum. terra. interitura. De e-
clipsi. Animam animum non posse esse sine cor-
pore. De solis et lunae offectione. De natiui-
tate mundi et dies. Mundum non esse ab disco-
positione rerumque statutum in eo sunt. Cui
pars natiua sit totum natiuum esse. De centa-
uris. De scylla. De terra. De aqua. De aere.
sine anima. De chimera. De igni et sole non po

33. Florence, Laur. 35, 30, fol. 102r. Niccoli, 1418-29 (?). Cf. p. 64.

[illegible] platonem scripsere quod potum dixit defluere ad pulmonem ..
[illegible] siccis umectatio dimanare per eum quia sit rimosior. & confluere
inde in uesicam. erroris q; istius fuisse alceum ducem qui in poemate suo
scriberet. ΤΕΓΓΕ ΠΝΕΥΜΟΝΑ ΟΙΝΩ ΤΟ ΓΑΡ ΑΣΤΡΟΝ ΠΕΡΙΤΕΛ
[illegible] · ipsum autem erasistratum dicere duas esse quasi canaliculas quas
dam uel fistulas. easq; ab oris faucibus proficisci deorsum per [illegible]
[illegible] deduci delabiq; in stomachum esculenta omnia & poculenta
ex eoq; ferri in uentriculum qui graece appellatur · Η ΚΑΤΩ ΚΟΙΛ[illegible]
atq; ibi subigi degeriq;. Ac deinde aridiora ex his recrementa in al
[illegible] uenire quod graece · ΚΟΛΟΝ · dicitur · umidiora per renes
[illegible] per alteram autem fistulam quae graece nominatur thra

34. Florence, Naz. Conv. Soppr. I. IV. 26, fol. 92v. Niccoli, 1431 (?). Cf. p. 66.

Nobis non magis potis est quam tingo umber
Intro hinc abeamus nuntiam saltatum satis prouinost
Vosq: spectatores plaudite atq: ite ad nos cōmissatum ·

· PLAVTI · STICHVS · EXPLICIT · FELICITER ·

· PLAVTI · TRINVMMVS · INCIPIT · FELICITER

Thensaurum abstrusum abiens peregre charmides
Remq: omnem amico callicli mandat suo
Isthoc absente male rem perdit filius
Nam & aedis uendit has mercatur callicles

35. Florence, Naz. Conv. Soppr. I. I. 12, fol. 196v. Niccoli, 1431-32. Cf. p. 66.

36. Florence, Naz. Conv. Soppr. I. VI. 6, fol. 65v. Niccoli, 1432. Cf. p. 67.

37. Florence, Naz. Conv. Soppr. I. X. 44, fol. 1v. Niccoli. Cf. p. 68.

38. Florence, Laur. Marc. 268, fol. 7r. Niccoli (margin). Cf. p. 76.

39. Florence, Laur. 49, 7, fol. 9v. Niccoli (margin). Cf. p. 76.

uniuersam hispaniam domuit. Inde romanis illato bello italiam
per annos sedecim uariis cladibus fatigauit. Dum interea ro
mani missis in hispaniam scipionibus primo poenos prouincia
expulerunt. postea cum ipsis hispanis grauia bella gesserunt.
nec prius perdomitae prouinciae iugum hispaniae capere potu
erūt. quam caesar augustus perdomito orbe uictricia ad
eos arma transtulit. Populumque barbarū ac ferum legibus ad
cultiorem uitae usum traductū in formam prouinciae re
degit.
POMPEII TROGI LIBER .xliiii. FELICITER EXPLICIT.
Postrema tandē manu absolutus est. Kal. Iuniis anno ab incar
nato uerbo. Mccccquinto.

40. Florence, Laur. Conv. Soppr. 111, fol. 199v. 1405. Cf. p. 81.

nostram quidem inquit pomponius iocans. Sed mehercule pergrata mihi oratio tua. Que enim dici Latine
posse non arbitrabar: ea dicta sunt a te: nec minus pla
ne q̄ dicuntur a graecis: uerbis aptis. Sed tempus est si
uidetur: & recta quidem ad me. Quod cum ille dixis
set: & satis disputatum uideretur: in oppidum ad pom
ponium perreximus omnes.
M.T. CICERONIS DE FINIBVS BONORVM ET MALORVM
LIBER QVINTVS FELICITER EXPLICIT.
Absoluit autem scriptor postrema manu. ad.iiii.kal.iunias:
uerbi anno incarnati .m.cccc sexto.

41. Florence, Laur. Conv. Soppr. 131, fol. 111r. 1406. Cf. p. 81.

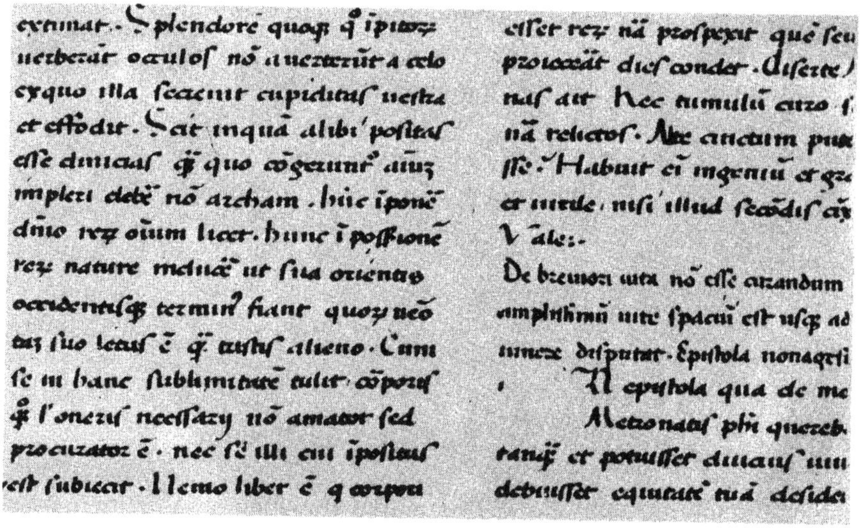

42. Oxford, Bodl. Laud. Lat. 70, fol. 97r. 1409. Cf. p. 82.

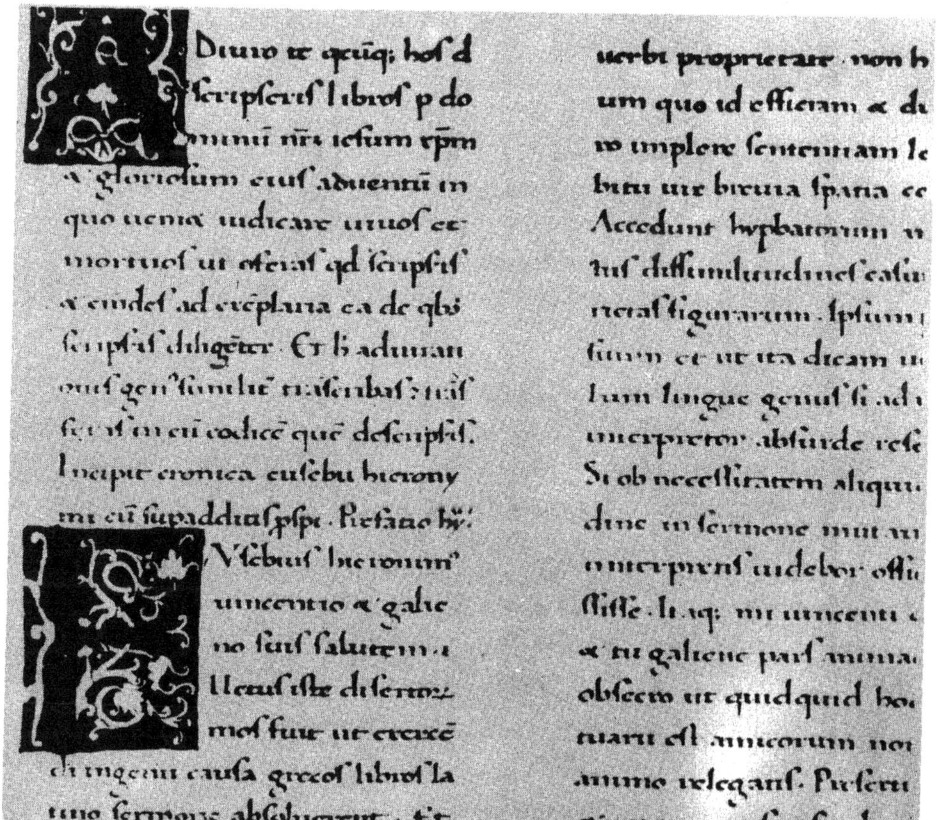

43. St. Gall, Stadtbibl. 298, fol. 1r. 1410. Cf. p. 82.

teo more. uel quo eschynes aut demosthenes utitur
tunc illos existimabo non desperatione reformida
uisse genus hoc sed iudicio refugisse. aut reperiat
ipse eadem conditione qui uti uelit ut aut dicat
aut scribat utra uolet lingua eo genere quo illi uo
lunt. facilius est enim apta dissoluere quam dissipa
ta conectere. Res autem sic se habet ut breuissi
me dicam quod sentio. apte sine sententiis dicere
insania est sententiose autem sine uerborum & ordine & modo
infantia: sed huiusmodi infantia ut ea qui uta
tur non stulti homines haberi possint & iam plerum
que prudentes quo qui est contentus utatur. Elo — Eloquens
quens uero qui non approbationes solum: sed admi
rationes clamores. plausus si liceat mouere debet
omnibus oportet ita rebus excellat ut ei turpe sit
quicquam aut aspectari aut audiri libentius. Ha
bes meum de oratore brute iudicium. quod aut se
quere si probaueris. aut tuo stabis si aliud quoddam
est tuum. in quo neque pugnabo tecum. neque hoc meum
de quo tantopere hoc libro asseueraui umquam affirma
bo esse uerius quam tuum. Potest enim non solum aliud
mihi ac tibi sed mihi met ipsi aliud alias uideri.
Nec in hac modo re: que uulgi ad sensum spectat
& ad aurium uoluptatem: que duo sunt ad iudicandum
leuissima. sed ne in maximis quidem rebus quicquam in
ueni adhuc firmius quod tenerem: aut quo iudici
um meum dirigerem: quam id quodcumque mihi quam simil
limum ueri uideretur: cum illud ipsum uerum tamen
in occulto lateret. Tu autem uelim si tibi ea que di
sputata sunt minus probabuntur ut aut maius opus
institutum putes quam effici potuerit: aut dum tibi
roganti uoluerim obsequi uerecundia negandi
scribendi me impudentiam suscepisse.

MARCI TULLII CICERONIS VIRI DOCTISSIMI
AC ELOQUENTISSIMI DE ORATORE LIBER EX
PLICIT. Anno M.cccc.xiii. ydibus ianuarii. Florentie.

44. Oxford, Bodl. Lat. class. d. 37, fol. 34r. 1413. Cf. p. 83.

tuas mihi litteras longissimas quasq; gratissimas fore.

M.T.C. EPISTOLARUM AD M. MARIUM LIBER EXPLICIT. AE
INCIPIT EIUSDEM AD M. CAELIUM FELICITER MI NICOL

CAELIUS ciceroni salutem. Quod tibi decedens pollicitus sũ
me omnes res urbanas diligentissime tibi perscripturum.
data opera paraui qui sic omnia psequeretur. ut uerear ne
tibi nimium arguta haec sedulitas uideatur. tam & si tu scio
quam sis curiosus & q̃ omnibus peregrinantibus gratum sit minimaꝝ
quoq; reꝝ quae domi gerantur fieri certiores. Tamen in hoc te depre
cor ne meum hoc officium arrogantiae condemnes quod hunc laborem
alteri delegaui. Non quin mihi suauissimum sit et occupato & ad litte
ras rescribendas ut tu nosti pigerrimo tuae memoriae dare operam

45. Rome, Vat. Pal. lat. 1496, fol. 68r. Giovanni Aretino, 1410. Cf. p. 91.

tiori. nos consuetudine prohibemur. Poeta ius suum tenuit & di
xit audacius. Cadit igitur in eundē & misereri & inuidere.
Nam qui dolet rebus alicuius aduersis: idem etiam alicuius secun
dis dolet: ut theophrastus interitum deplorans callisthenis soda
lis sui rebus alexandri prosperis angitur. Itaq; dicit callisthenē
incidisse in hominē sūma potentia sūmaq; fortunā: sed ignarū
queādmodū rebus secundis uti conueniret. Atqui queādmo
dum misericordia egritudo est: ex alterius rebus aduersis:
sic inuidentia egritudo est ex alterius rebus secundis. In
quem igitur cadit misereri: in eundem etiam inuidere. Nō
cadit autē inuidere in sapientem: ergo ne misereri quidem.
Quod si hoc egre ferre sapiens soleret: misereri etiam soleret:
abest ergo a sapiente egritudo. Hec sic dicuntur a stoicis con
cluduntur q; contortius. Sed latius aliquando dicenda sunt

46. Munich, Staatsbibl. lat. 763, fol. 37r. Giovanni Aretino, 1414. Cf. p. 93.

Ea propter declamatum est omnino: id alicuius numinis opus extitisse. eo rem
peragendam ducenti conuocantibusq;. Cassius igitur antequam facinus adoriret
ad pompeii statuam aspiciens. eam tacitus inuocasse dicitur. quamquam haud multum
ab epicuri opinione foret alienus. Verum enim vero cum terribilia iam ingrui
erent. consternatione tempus incusserat. et priorem subinde sententiam
mentis egritudo mutarat. Antonium fidum usquequaque cesari et precipua
pollentem robustate brutus albinus extrorsus detinebat. longum de industria
sermonem innectens. Ingredienti deinde cesari honorifice senatus assurgit.
Bruti vero complices partim post eius sellam constiterunt. partim ei ob
uiam processere. ut vinacii metillio cimbro pro fratre exule supplicanti
intercederent. Sicque magnis cum obsecrationibus ad sellam usque sunt co
secuti. Cum vero sedens rogantes submouisset. in violentius innectit.
Quod grauiter ferente cesare. metillius comprehensam utraque manu
togam deduxit ex collo. Id enim aggrediendi signum erat. Primus cas
[illegible]

47. Rome, Vat. Basil. S. Petri H. 31, fol. 89r. Giovanni Aretino, 1414. Cf. p. 93.

siue principari cogitent: & de se commune iudicari
sibi psuadeant. Ne domestice rei cura studio &
& diligentia desint. Ad eam rem magnopere
conducet. si quod ad ipsas maxime pertinet.
domi manere & cuncta inuisere consueuerint.
quo in loco uenit in mentem prudentis illius
stabularii: qui cum interrogaret quidnā potis
sime pinguem equū redderet. herilis inquit ocu
lus. Quod officium ut posteritati cōmendaret.
apud gaię cecilię tarquinii filię statuā ęreā
calceum domesticum & colum & fusum refixe
runt: ut assiduam assiduitatē uenturis imi
tandam quodāmodo significarent. Quis negli

48. Florence, Laur. 78, 24, fol. 49r. Giovanni Aretino, 1416. Cf. p. 94.

Diuiduntur prouincie.

Ptholomeus.

Cleomenes.

Laumedon.

Philotas.

Accoporatus.

Scinus. Antigonus.

Nearchus. Cassander.

Menander. Leonatus.

Lisimachus.

sit de singulis manipu
Reuersus inde prouincia
mouere & munus u
meo ęgyptus & afric
gario milite alexan
dendam prouinciam
datus. Confinem hu
liciam philotas cum
coporatus: minori soc
no. Phrygia minor a
& pamphiliam nearc
der sortiuntur. Le
niones ... maris ...

49. Florence, Laur. 66, 12, fol. 52v. Giovanni Aretino, 1417. Cf. p. 94.

D esine conspectu mentem turbare uerendo
N am tua concipient celesti uiscera iussu
N atum quem regnare deus p secula cuncta.
E t propriam credi sobolem gaudeq; iubeq;
h unc ubi sub lucem dederis sit nomine iesus
A d quem uirgo dehinc pauido sic inchoat ore
N ullos conceptus seri sine coniuge dicunt
V nde igitur mihimet sobolem sperabo uenire
N untius haec contra celeri sermone profatur
V irtus celsa dei circu͂uolitabit obumbrans
S piritus et purus uenie(t) lectissima uirgo
At tibi mox pueru͂ casto sermone iubebit.

50. Florence, Naz. Conv. Soppr. I. IX. 35, fol. 2v. Giovanni Aretino, after 1448 (?). Cf. p. 94.

et Lentuli duo. Primas in causis agebat hor
tensius magis magisq; quotidie probabatur.
antistius piso saepe dicebat. minus saepe po
ponius. raro carbo semel aut iterum phi
lippus. At uero ego hoc tempore omni.
noctes et dies. in omnium doctrinarum me
ditatione uersabar. Eram cum stoico dio
doto. qui cum habitauisset apud me cumq;
uixisset. nuper est domi meae mortuus.
a quo cum in aliis rebus tum studiosissime
in dialectica exercebar. qua quasi contract'
ta et astricta eloquentia. putanda est. sine

51. Florence, Laur. 50, 18, fol. 82v. Giacomo Curlo, 1423. Cf. p. 97.

plato atq; eum idem ille: non linguę solum +
uerumetiam animi ac uirtutis magister ad libe
randam patriam impulit: instruxit armauit.
Alius ne igitur artibus hunc dionem instituit
plato? alius isocrates clarissimum uirum thi
moteum cononis prestantissimi imperatoris
filium. summum ipsum imperatorem homi
nemq; doctissimum? aut alius pytagoreus ille
lysias thebanum epaminondam: haud scio an
summum uirum unum omnis grecię? Aut

52. Florence, Laur. 50, 32, fol. 193v. Giacomo Curlo, 1425. Cf. p. 97.

et uexillum suum in tantis permixtionibus
in ipsa prolusione comitentur ne inter doc
tos aliquis error existat quod multitudini
sit tanta confusio. Ad palum quoque uel
sudes exerceri percommodum est. cum latera
uel pedes aut caput petere punctum cesimq;
condiscant. Saltus quoque et ictus facere
pariter assuescant. insurgere tripudianter
in clipeum. rursusque subsidere. & nunc ge
stiendo prouolare cum saltu. nunc cedentes

53. Oxford, Bodl. Canon. Lat. 274, fol. 42r. Giacomo Curlo, after 1446 (?). Cf. p. 97.

Nimis perverse se ipm amat q et alios vult errare. Item Augustinus:
ut suus error lateat. Illius quippe scripta summa sunt autoritate di
gnissima qui nullum verbum non quod revocare nollet sed quod re
vocare deberet emisit. Hoc quisquis non dum est assecutus Secundas
partes habeat modestie quia primas non potuit habere sapientie. Qui
non valuit oia non penitenda dixisse peniteat que cognoverit dicen
da non fuisse. Ex verbis Jeronimi.
Lactantius quasi quidam fluvius eloquentie tullyane Crispum fi
lium constantini latinis litteris erudivit Vir oium suo tpre erudi
tissimus sed adeo in hac vita pauper ut plerumque etiam necessariis indi
geret Utinam tam nostra affirmare potuisset quam facile aliena
Lactantium propter eruditionem. Idem Jeronimus. destruxit.
sic interdum legendum arbitror quomodo origenem arnobium
et non nullos ecclesiasticos scriptores grecos pariter et latinos ut bona

54. Florence, Laur. Conv. Soppr. 287, fol. 1r. Antonio di Mario, 1417. Cf. p. 99.

Quisquis ergo anime vitam maluerit. vitam corporis cōtepnat ne
cesse est. nec aliter vita ad summum poterit nisi que sunt ima
despexerit. Qui autem corporis vitam fuerit amplexus et cupi
ditates suas in terram deiecerit illam superiorem vitā consequi
non potest. Sed qui mavult bene vivere in eternū male vivet
ad tempus. et efficietur omnibus molestiis et laboribus quādiu
fuerit in terra. ut habeat divinū et celeste solatiū. et q malue
rit bene vivere ad tempus. male vivet in eternū. Damnabitur
enim sententia dei ad eternam penam. quia celestibus bonis
terrena preposuit. Propterea igitur coli se deus expetit. et ho
norari ab homie tanquā pater. ut virtutem ac sapientiā te
neat. que sola immortalitatem parit. Nam quia nullus alius
preter ipm donare eam potest. quia solus possidet pietatem

55. Florence, Laur. Conv. Soppr. 287, fol. 199r. Antonio di Mario, 1417. Cf. p. 99.

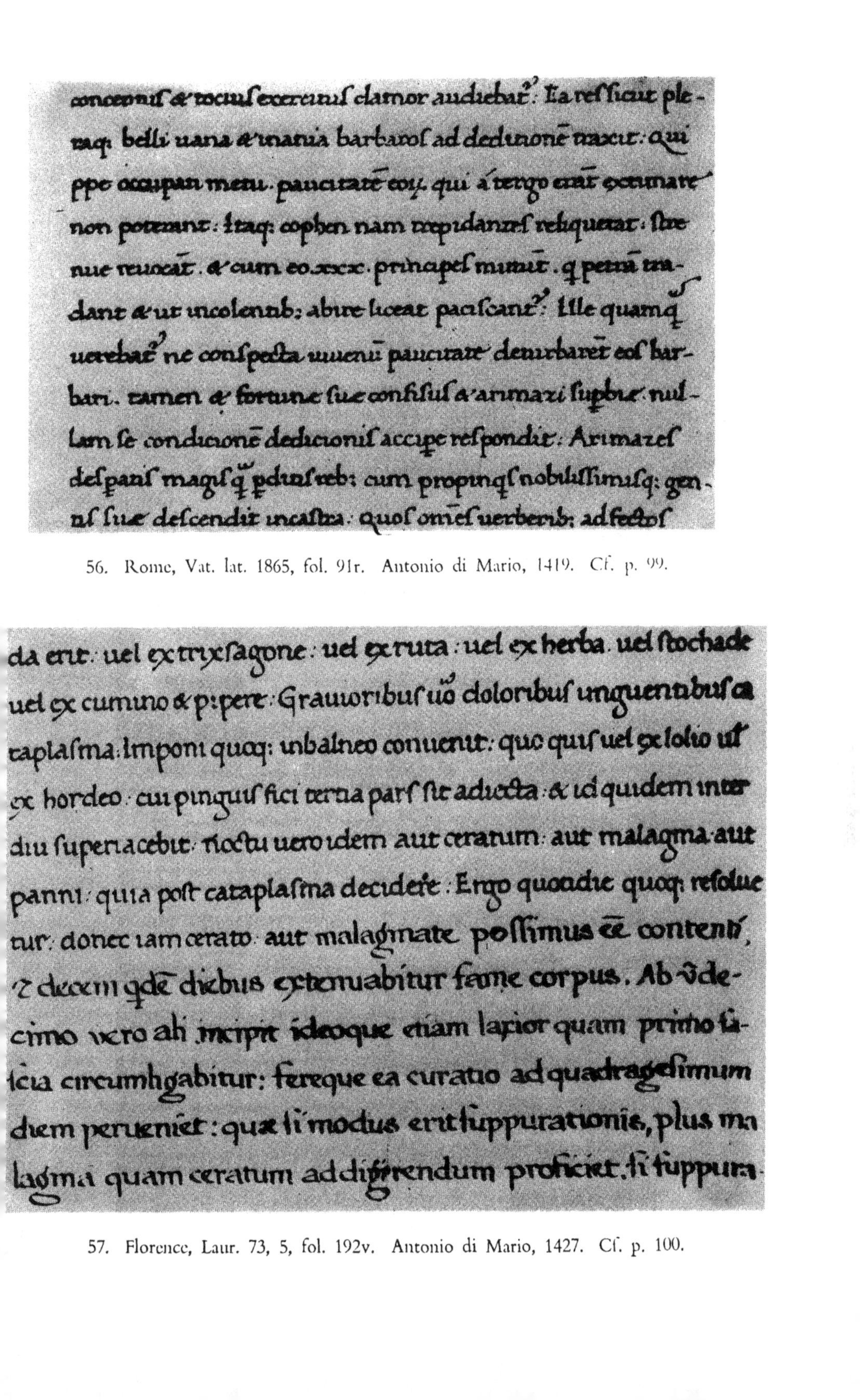

56. Rome, Vat. lat. 1865, fol. 91r. Antonio di Mario, 1419. Cf. p. 99.

57. Florence, Laur. 73, 5, fol. 192v. Antonio di Mario, 1427. Cf. p. 100.

ACTENVS DE SITV ET MIRACVLIS TERRAE
aquarumq: & syderum ac ratione uniuersitatis atq: mẽsura. Nuc
de partibus. quanq̃ in infinitum id quoq: existimet: nec temere sine
ulla reprehensione tractandum. haud ullo in genere uenia iustiore
si modo minime est mirum hominem genitum non omnia humana
nouisse. Quapropter auctorem neminem unum sequar: sed ut quenq̃
uerissimum inquaq: parte arbitror: quoniam comune ferme omnibus fuit: ut eos qsq: di
ligentissime situs disceret: ex quibus ipse prodibat. Idoq: nec culpabo: nec coarguam quenq̃ locorum
nuda nomina: & quantum dabitur breui ponentur claritate: clausisq: dilatis in suas partes.
Nunc enim sermo de toto est. quare sic accipi uelim: ut si diuidua fama sua nomina qualia
qualia fuere primordio ante illas res gestas nuncupentur: & sit quedam in hiis nomẽ datura q
dem: sed mundi reruq: nature. Terrarum orbis uniuersus in tres diuidit ptes. Europam. Asi
am. Africam. origo ab occasu solis: & gaditano freto: qua irrumpens occeanus athalanticus in
maria interiora diffunditur. hic intranti affrica dextra est. Leua europa. Inter has asia term

58. Rome, Vat. Urb. lat. 245, fol. 22v. Antonio di Mario, 1440. Cf. p. 102.

Quamobrem ad te utiq: omnes romane: atq; aliarum ecclesi
arum pontifices: reges principes: aliiq: trium linguarum
eruditi. si humanitatis cognitionem cupiunt. gressus suos diri
gunt. Ego autem ipse ut pro veritate loquar: auxilio tuo in
doctorum virorum documentis ab eis relictis potissimum usus sum:
quorum multa mihi à te demostrata: ac deinde diligenter per
quisita. in hoc primo nostro volumine conservi. Esto ergo in
mortalis ut ita dixerim: dummodo hec mea scripta satis in
cepte pro ingenioli mei facultate prolata. tu etiam permanebis

· F I N I S

ANTONIUS · MARII · FILIUS · TRĀSCRIPSIT · FLOREN
TIE · IIII · IDUS · OCTOBRIS · M · CCCCLVI ·
VALEAS QUI LEGIS.

59. Rome, Vat. lat. 1969, fol. 622v. Antonio di Mario, 1456. Cf. p. 104.

L uctantes uentos: tempestatesq; SONORAS
I mperio premit ac uinclis & carcere FRENAT.
I lli indignantes magno cum murmure montis
C ircum claustra fremunt: celsa sedet eolus arce
S ceptra tenens: mollitq; animos: & temperat iras.
N i faciat: maria ac terras celumq; profundum
Q uippe ferant rapidi secum uertantq; per auras:
S ed pater omnipotens speluncis abdidit atris
H oc metuens: molemq; montes insuper ALTOS
I mposuit: regemq; dedit: qui federe CERTO
E t premere & laxas sciret dare iussus habenas:
A d quem tum iuno suplex his uocibus usa est.
E ole namq; tibi diuum pater atq; hominum rex

60. Florence, Laur. 39, 8, fol. 52r. Gherardo del Ciriagio, 1453. Cf. p. 113.

tem possit. Non pudet uos iouem debere sacrilego? Super
io: sed artifex periit. Penam nobis fidie non fidiam reddi-
amus que solebant deos facere: nunc ne homines quidem ro-
ssunt. Talem fecit iouem at hoc eius opus elii esse ultimum
: Manus commendauimus: manus reposcimus. Elius est te
ius est accusator. Elius iudex. Atheniensis tantum reus.
leos: & illos quos fecit fidias: & illos quos facere potuit. Re
s fidiam. Confiteor si possumus commendare. Pars altera.
uimus aurum olim sacrum. Habuimus ebur. Sacre mate
artificem quesiuimus. Disposueramus quidam ut alius quo
nplis simulacra fidias faceret. Sed non erat tam necesse or
os q̄ iudicare. INFAMIS IN NURUM.
rum iuuenum pater: uni uxorem dedit. Quo peregre pro

61. Paris, B. N. lat. 6376, fol. 240r. Gherardo del Ciriagio, 1457. Cf. p. 114.

in egyptum nauigassemus. Videntur hec forsan indig
na fide nonnullis: & fabulis quam uero similia. Sed indignio
ra multo audiri debent que sequuntur. premente aliquan
do egyptios fame adeo ut plures ab humana carne ob inopi
am cibi non abstinerent: animalia sacra omnino intacta
reliquere. Sicubi uero canis domi mortuus repertus esset
singuli eius domus totum corpus acta lamentatione radunt.
oc quoque est mirabilius. Sicubi uinum frumentum ue a
ut aliud quid uictui accomodatum ubi simile animal expi
rauit inuentum esset, non amplius illis utebantur. Eodem
que luctu etiam ad alia loca profecti elures & accipitres mor
tuos ad egyptum deficiente persepe uiatico deferebant. Q
uanuis etiam facile sit quomodo apud memphim apis: ap
ud eliopolim Mneuis. Apud midetam hircus. Crocodillus
apud myridem paludem. Leo apud leontem ciuitatem: &

62. Rome, Vat. lat. 1811, fol. 42r. Gherardo del Ciriagio, 1461. Cf. p. 114.

quo singula contendunt: mare: portus: am
nes: fontesque efficiunt. Hinc uero rursus sub
terram euntia: partim per longiores anfrac
tus: partim per breuiores ac tardiores in tar
tara redeunt: alia multo profundius quam antea
fuerint: alia parum omnia tamen infra efflu
xionem irrumpunt & quedam aduersum quam
effluunt: quedam uero circum euntia semel
aut pluries: spirasque circa orbem terrarum
uelut angues facientia: & quantum fieri po
test descendentia: rursus immiscentur. Potest
autem utrinque usque ad medium fieri de
scensus: ultra uero nequaquam: nam deince
ps ascensus foret ad utranque partem. Sunt
igitur & alia multa ac uaria fluenta: sed pre

63. Rome, Vat. Urb. lat. 1314, fol. 49r. Gherardo del Ciriagio, 1472. Cf. p. 116.

claro fine claudebatur. cum illi interim didicerunt ac
per illos universi, quos non homines profecto oppugnare
pertexerant. neq; mitridates modo tunc aut alius quis
piam: sed quisquis omnino eis hominibus adversus
atq; infestus ee maluerit: qui boni aliquid agere insti
tuunt, ipsum potissimum qui per illos honoratur deu,
oppugnare contendunt. Is autem qui adversus deum
bellare instituit: clementiore fine desinere nunquam
penitus valebit. At is qui eiusmodi est initio qdem
facinoris nihil fortasse patietur mali: deo illum
ad penitentiam vocante atq; admonente: velut ex
quadam ebrietate resipiscere. Sin vero in hac amen
tie sue temeritate persistit: nihil q: ex tanta cleme
tia divine patientie fuerit lucratus: certe vel aliis
summa conferret emolumenta: pena sua erudiens atq;

64. Florence, Laur. Fies. 43, fol. 3r. Antonio Sinibaldi, 1461. Cf. p. 119.

F ixa magi sidusq; micans regale secuti
O ptatam tenuere viam: quae lege futura
D uxit adorantes sacra adcunabula reges
T hesaurisq; simul pro religione solutis
I pse etiam ut possent species ostendere christi
A urea nascenti fuderunt munera regi
T ura dedere deo myrram tribuere sepulchro.
C ur tria dona tamen? quin spes maxima vitae est:
H unc numerum confessa fides: et tempora summus
C ernens cuncta deus: presentia: prisca: futura
S emper adest: semperq; fuit: semperq; manebit
I n triplici virtute sui: tunc celitus illi

65. Rome, Vat. Ottob. lat. 36, fol. 15r. Antonio Sinibaldi, 1474. Cf. p. 119.

et Sexcenta huiusmodi sequebantur. Agmen Laruę clau
debant multiplices atq; omnigena monstra referentes. Quo
cunq; aduenisset: effuse pene populariter obuiam: nati
ones adorabant: Ac certatim collatis Donariys templa
extruebant. Necnon ex solido Argento atq; Auro
constituebant simulacra. Ad Heliopolim autem ea
est Solis ciuitas cum uenisset: Heliopolitani portas
clauserunt. Quod quidem portento necessitatem fecit
experiundarum uirium. Et quod erant per pauci
intra muros defensores haud magno negotio expugna
turum ratum, Tormentis primum machinisq; admo
tis: ut urbem dederent postulabat. Cum nihilominus
repugnarent fortes: Maiores hostis multo conatus
parat. Terraemotib; ergo et lapidibus quibus super ur
bem pluebat & carnibus aggressus: & ardenti cęlo
infestior comparebat. Nec Laruę minus terribiles
inferebant signa. Quę nescio quo pacto maiorem
etiam: q̄ ueri metus consternationem solent afferre:
His in difficultatibus oraculum obsessi adierunt.

66. Florence, Laur. 54, 3, fol. 11r. Antonio Sinibaldi, 1481. Cf. p. 120.

Fugerat inuerso mutabilis ore: reuisit.
Atq; inter patrias perstat durata fauillas
En tibi signatum libertatis documentum
Quod uoluit nos scire deus quodcunq; sequendum est.
Sub nostra ditione situm: passimq; remissum.
Alterutram calcare uiam: duo cedere iussi
De sodomis alter se proripit: altera mussat.
Ille gradum celerat fugiens. contra illa retutat.
Liber utriq; animus: sed dispar utriq; uoluntas
Duxit huc illuc rapiens sua quemq; libido
Talem multa sacris speciem notat orbita libris.
Aspice ruth gentis moabitidis: & simul orpham.
Illa socrum noemi fido comitatur amore.
Deserit haec: atquin thalamis & lege iugali
Exutae: hebreisq; toris: sacrisq; uacantes:
Iure fruebantur proprio: sed pristinus orfae
Fanorum ritus praeputia barbara suasit.
Malle: & semiferi stirpem nutrire Goliae.
Ruth dum per stipulas agresti excurritur aestu:
Pulchra booz meruit. castoq; ascita cubili
Christigenam fecunda domum: dauitica regna
Edidit. atq; adeo mortales miscuit ortus.
Saepe egomet memini fratres geminos adhuulcū
Peruenisse simul biuium: nutante iuuenta.

67. Rome, Vat. Urb. lat. 666, fol. 150r. Antonio Sinibaldi, 1481. Cf. p. 120.

ipse in eodem opere. Non enim uirilis coytus inquit uulue uirgi-
nalis secreta reserauit, sed immaculatum semen inuiolabili utero sanc-
tus spiritus infudit. Solus enim per omnia ex natis de femina sanc-
tus dominus Ihesus qui terrene contagia corruptele immaculati
partus nouitate non senserit, et celesti maiestate depulerit. Itemque
in eodem ipso. omnes inquit in Adam morimur: quia per unum
hominem peccatum intrauit in mundum, et per peccatum mors. et
in omnes homines pertransiit. in quo omnes peccauerunt. Illius igitur
culpa mors omnium est. Item loco alio in eodem Euangelio. Caue
ergo inquit ne ante nuderis. sicut Adam nudatus est. mandati
celestis custodia destitutus, et exutus fidei uestimento: et sic letale
uulnus accepit, in quo omne genus occidisset humanum nisi Sama-
ritanus ille descendens uulnera eius acerba curasset. Rursus in
opere ipso alio loco. Fuit inquit Adam: et in illo fuimus omnes.
Periit Adam. et in illo omnes perierunt. Rursus idem ipse in Apo-
logia prophete Dauid. Antequam nascamur inquit maculamur con-

68. Florence, Laur. 12, 8, fol. 3r. Antonio Sinibaldi, 1491. Cf. p. 121.

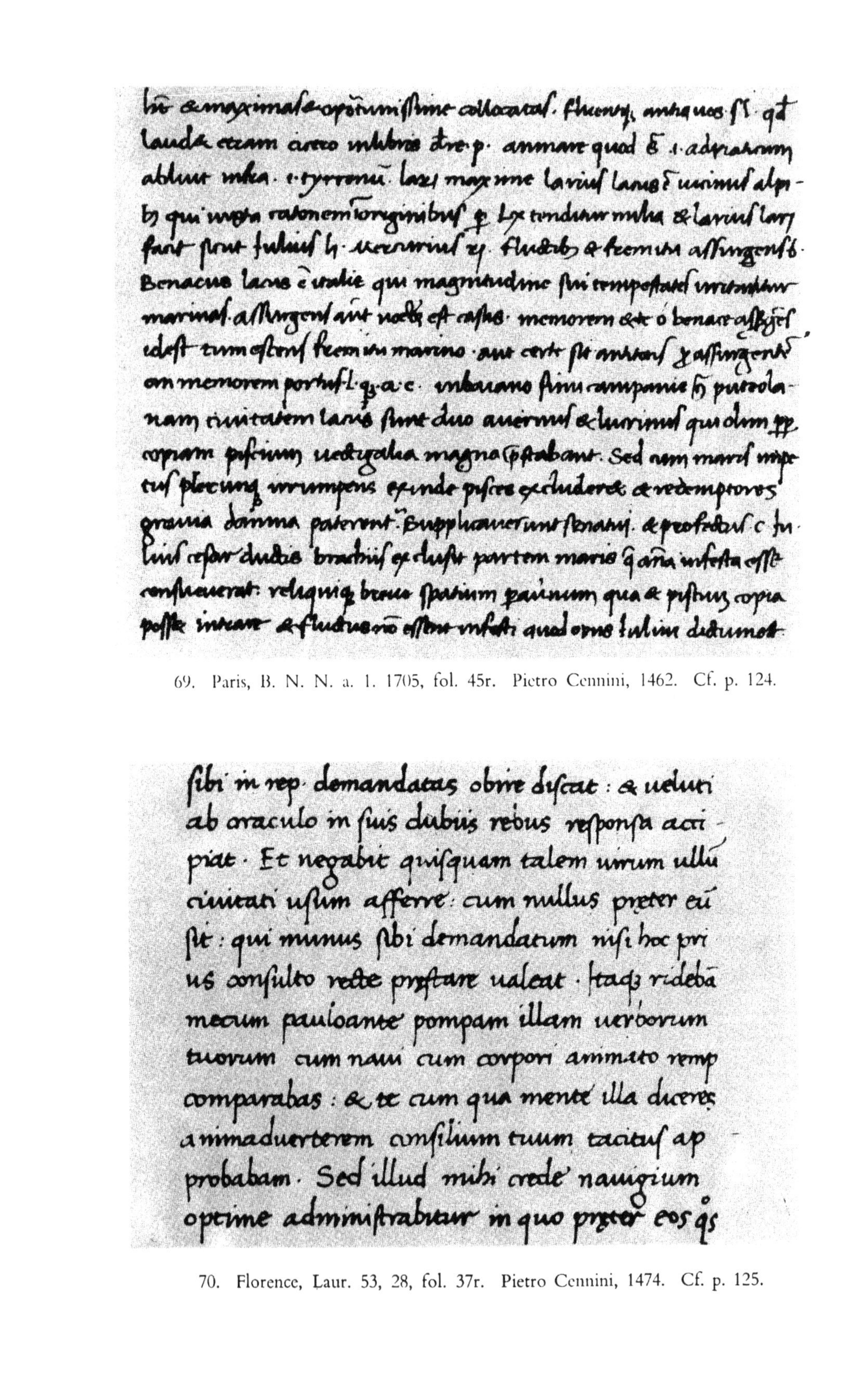

69. Paris, B. N. N. a. l. 1705, fol. 45r. Pietro Cennini, 1462. Cf. p. 124.

70. Florence, Laur. 53, 28, fol. 37r. Pietro Cennini, 1474. Cf. p. 125.

TABLE OF CONTENTS

www.ingramcontent.com/pod-product-compliance
Lightning Source LLC
LaVergne TN
LVHW050639100826
845148LV00011B/1913

9781597405133